William Dexter Wilson

The Church Identified

By a Reference to the History of Its Origin, Perpetuation and Extension into the

United States

William Dexter Wilson

The Church Identified
By a Reference to the History of Its Origin, Perpetuation and Extension into the United States

ISBN/EAN: 9783337812829

Printed in Europe, USA, Canada, Australia, Japan

Cover: Foto ©Lupo / pixelio.de

More available books at **www.hansebooks.com**

THE CHURCH IDENTIFIED,

BY A REFERENCE TO

THE HISTORY

OF ITS

ORIGIN, PERPETUATION, AND EXTENSION,

INTO

THE UNITED STATES.

BY THE REV. W. D. Dexter WILSON, D. D.,

PROFESSOR OF MORAL AND INTELLECTUAL PHILOSOPHY AND OF HISTORY
IN GENEVA COLLEGE.

NEW-YORK:
H. B. DURAND, No. 11 BIBLE HOUSE.
1866.

Entered according to Act of Congress, in the year 1850,
BY W. D. WILSON, D. D.
In the Clerk's Office of the District Court of the United States,
for the Northern District of New York.

TO

WILLIAM C. PIERREPONT, ESQ

OF

PIERREPONT MANOR,

THIS VOLUME

IS,

BY HIS PERMISSION,

MOST RESPECTFULLY

DEDICATED

BY THE

AUTHOR.

PREFACE TO THE STEREOTYPE EDITION.

In sending forth this Edition of THE CHURCH IDENTIFIED, I hardly know whether to call it the *second* or the *third*. The Work consists of a series of Articles, which appeared in "the Churchman" during the Autumn and Winter of 1848–9. This was the first "*Edition*," or "*giving forth*" of the Work to the public. The Articles were so kindly received that a proposal was soon made to issue an edition in a book form, with a specific reference to its circulation in the Diocese of Western New York. That edition consisted of only one thousand copies, and was exhausted almost at once. I now send forth the Work a third time in a form, and under circumstances, as I trust, calculated to give it a much wider circulation, and to supply it in larger quantities. Hence this is really the third "*editio*" or "*edition*'."

In preparing this edition I have carefully considered all the criticisms and suggestions concerning it which have come to my knowledge.

In some cases I have rewritten a paragraph or statement, and expanded it without adding anything more than what seemed necessary to guard against the misapprehension into which readers had fallen concerning my meaning and design. In other cases I have noticed that an important point, did not make the impression which it ought to make in order that the force of the argument might be duly appreciated. This defect I have also endeavored to remedy so far as I could; either by resorting to a new arrangement of the matter, or a new form of the statement.

PREFACE.

Besides this I have added some new matter. For the sake of comparing this edition with the previous, and to show at once what has been added, I give the following list of the Sections in which the new matter will be chiefly found.

Chapter	§
I.	§ 7 and 12.
II.	§ 10
III.	§ 10 and 21—24.
IV.	§ 1—5
V.	§ 65.
VII.	§ 3 and 7.
VIII.	§ 4, 5, 7 and 8.
X.	§ 1—37 inclusive.

The first part of Chap. IV. in the last edition, has been transferred to the beginning of Chap. III. in this.

The defence of the PROTESTANT EPISCOPAL CHURCH in the *United States* has hitherto, for the most part, been made to depend upon the successful vindication of the several points of its Polity, and the Apostolical Succession of its Bishops.

Perhaps a proper regard to what is due under the circumstances, would require me to enter, somewhat at length, into the reasons for resorting to a new mode of doing what has been so successfully done heretofore, in the old. . I shall not, however, enter upon a detail of the reasons and motives for this work. Many of them will occur to the reader as he passes over the pages : some of them are stated in the body of the work itself : and perhaps the fact that the novelty of the plan will attract and interest readers in what can never be too well understoood, may be regarded as all the apology that my course demands.

The position of those who defend, and those who oppose the Episcopal Polity of the Church, is now greatly changed from what it was when the controversies on this subject first commenced in England ; and we seem to have followed the line of argument then marked out and pursued by the great minds of the mother Church without sufficiently considering the change that has taken place in the nature of the issue itself, and in the relative position of the parties to the controversy.

The question then, was not whether a Church could be instituted without Episcopacy and the Apostolic Succession —or whether such a Church could be acknowledged as a part of the Church of Christ, in case it should be instituted— but it was whether Episcopacy and the Succession should be retained or not in a Branch of the Church already established and identified with the Church of Christ. The early opposers of Episcopacy seem not to have designed to leave the English Church and found one on another basis, but rather to remodel that Church upon a Presbyterian platform.

But, with us, the question has been treated as if it were whether there could be a Branch of the Church of Christ, without Bishops in the direct line of Apostolic Succession.

The following pages present to the consideration of the reader an entirely different question; and enter into no discussion of points of external order and organization, either as it regards their nature or their importance.

This distinction can be seen and appreciated by any one who will devote to it a few moments of attention. The former was simply a question of reformation in what already existed by divine right, which men had a right, indeed, to reform, if reformation were needed, but which they could not abolish, and were most sacredly bound to preserve and perpetuate. The latter was a question of instituting anew that which had had no existence before. Hence it may follow that even if Episcopacy and the Apostolic Succession are not essential to the Church, the modern sects are none the more to be regarded as branches of Christ's visible Church on this account; for it will at once be seen that it may appear on investigation that something more than any particular form of organization or Ministry is necessary to constitute a Branch of the Church of Christ.

The main conclusions of my work are so coincident with what has been generally held and taught by Episcopalians in this country, that I shall hardly need to say any thing more about them.

I suppose that most persons have felt that there is something of the acrimony of sectarian zeal inseparable from all the discussions and controversies between those who advocate and those who oppose the claims of the Protestant Episcopal Church. And indeed, so long as we make the peculiarities of its Constitution, Polity, and Worship the ground of our preference for it, I do not well see how the subject can be treated without exciting some of those unholy and carnal feelings which are most directly opposed to the spirit of Christianity and most repugnant to the feelings of humble and devout piety.

I hope that the mode of presenting the subject, pursued in the following pages, will avoid, to a very great extent, if not altogether, this evil, which has already led the great mass of the people to shrink with dread from every thing that has the appearance of a controversial design, or of treating a controverted subject.

In pursuing my plan, I have carefully abstained from every statement and expression that could seem to proceed from unkind feelings, and, as far as possible, from all that could give pain to the reader. I have wished and designed, that even if he could not agree with me in my conclusions, he might feel that I have done him no wrong and intended none. I have had no motive for writing but love for Christ and for the souls for which He died: I hope my reader will allow himself to be influenced by no other, while he reads what I have written.

My method of treating the subject has necessarily involved a great deal of historic discussion and narrative. But it is the history of the Church itself that has been called into requisition. Of this we cannot know too much. I trust that this feature of my book will not only make it more interesting than it could otherwise be, but also more instructive and profitable, by producing a greater familiarity with those great cardinal facts in the history of the Church with which every Christian ought to be acquainted. The attentive reader will hardly fail to get a pretty good idea of the outline of the Church's History from the following pages. Thus while pursuing the main object, an incidental one of scarcely less importance will be accomplished also, without additional labor or effort.

With the PRAYER that " all who profess and call themselves Christians, may be led into the way of truth, and hold the Faith in unity of spirit, in the bond of peace, and in righteousness of life," I commend the work to the serious and prayerful attention of all those who, in sincerity and truth, desire a knowledge of the LORD's ways.

W. D. WILSON.

GENEVA, NEW-YORK, *September*, 1850.

CONTENTS.

		PAGE
CHAPTER I.—THE IMPORTANCE OF THE IDENTITY OF THE CHURCH CONSIDERED INDEPENDENTLY OF THE PECULIARITIES OF ITS CONSTIUTION.		13
" " II.—THE MODE OF HISTORIC IDENTIFICATION STATED AND ILLUSTRATED.		31
" " III.—THE CHURCH BEFORE THE REFORMATION, AND ITS CONDITION AT THE TIME.		64
" " IV.—THE REFORMATION IN ENGLAND, AND ITS EFFECTS UPON THE CONDITION OF THE CHURCH.		112
" " V.—THE ORIGIN OF MODERN SECTS AND THEIR RELATION TO THE CHURCH.		160
" " VI.—THE CHURCH OF ENGLAND SINCE THE REFORMATION.		260
" " VII.—THE INTRODUCTION OF THE CHURCH INTO THE UNITED STATES.		278
" " VIII.—THE ROMISH CLAIM TO JURISDICTION IN THE UNITED STATES CONSIDERED.		318
" " IX.—THE IDENTITY OF SPIRIT.		343
" " X.—THE MORAL DESIGN OF THE CHURCH AND THE EFFECTS OF SECTARIANISM.		365

THE CHURCH IDENTIFIED.

CHAPTER I.

THE IMPORTANCE OF THE IDENTITY OF THE CHURCH CONSIDERED INDEPENDENTLY OF THE PECULIARITIES OF ITS CONSTITUTION.

There is hardly any fact more certain, with regard to Christianity, than that our Blessed Saviour founded a Church, or caused one to be founded, by His Apostles, in His name. It is also admitted that this institution was, and is, most intimately connected with His Religion. The proposition seems self-evident, and is almost universally held. Yet in this age but little seems to be known about that Church, its nature, object, and designs, and the great mass are ready to acknowledge that there is no small difficulty in identifying it, among so many claimant sects.

In the midst of this difficulty, some have thought that the identity of the Church is a matter of no importance—that if we can find a church that is evangelical in its character, encourages sincere piety, and good morals, all is accomplished that can be necessary.

Still, however, people are not satisfied with this.

They have some idea of a church established by Christ and his Apostles, as a visible and distinct thing; and even when they affirm that it is of no material consequence what church we belong to, if it is only sound in its doctrines, they do nevertheless betray no little uneasiness when it is said, or intimated, that the church to which they belong is not the same identical Church as that which our Saviour founded.

This uneasiness occasioned by the intimation that any particular organization of people, professing to be Christians, is not a branch of the Church which was once established by divine authority, is proof that there is in every heart a feeling, or consciousness, of the importance of the identity of that Church.

§ 2. To get rid of this feeling, or to avoid the difficulties that arise from its admission, there has arisen, of late years, a theory which holds that this importance attaches only to an *invisible* Church, and not to the outward and visible society which we call by that name. This *invisible Church* is supposed to consist of the number of persons—secret to us, and known only to God—who have been elected from eternity to eternal life—or of those who have been the subjects of an inward change or renewal; and it is also held that this number is independent on, and regardless of, outward signs and visible organization.

The theory of an invisible Church.

Without discussing this theory at all, it is sufficient for the present to note the fact that it is unsatisfactory. If the theory of the invisible Church were satisfactory to their own minds, those that adopt it would be entirely indifferent to the identity of the visible Church. But they are none the less unwilling to admit that the *visible society to which they belong* is not, or by any possibility may not be, a branch of that visible Church which has existed from the Apostles' days, than they would have been if they had resorted to no such theory.

§ 3. The common impression, with regard to the Church, is, that all protestant denominations stand before him who is in search of the truth and the true fellowship of Christ's Disciples, on an equal footing—that there is one Church, called the *Catholic*, or sometimes the *Roman Catholic*, which has existed ever since the Apostles, and that all the others, being alike the result of voluntary association and combination among men since the Reformation, it is absurd and wicked for any one of them to claim any superiority over the other—to be exclusive, or judge another unworthy of its fellowship. *Another theory stated.*

§ 4. If the hypothesis here assumed be correct, the conclusion is inevitable. For, if any number of men, taking the Scriptures for their guide, have originated a church in one form, another similar body of men, differing from them in their views of the meaning of the Scripture, may originate another church in another form, and so on; each being obliged, by the condition of its existence, to concede to the other the validity which it claims for itself. *This impression inadequate.*

And such is the opinion, or rather, perhaps I should say, the feeling, of the vast majority of the people of our land, in regard to the relation that ought to exist between the various religious bodies of which it is composed.

And yet there is not a denomination that acts upon

this principle, unless it be some of those whose claims are generally considered to be the least worthy of regard. Thus, the Episcopalians will not allow ministers of other denominations to minister at their altars. The Baptists will not receive to their communions any who have not been immersed on profession of faith. The Presbyterians—that is, the old Scotch Presbyterians—will not fellowship with Congregational denominations. The Methodists and Congregationalists have also certain views of the nature of Christ, and of the duration of the future punishment of the wicked, which exclude large classes of persons who profess to be guided by the same rule, aiming at the same result, and equally as sincere as themselves.

§. 5. This practical exclusiveness has been found indispensable, not only to the exercise of discipline, but also, and still more, to the preservation of the distinct existence of the bodies themselves. If no test were proposed, no profession required, and no rule adopted, it would be impossible to tell what the Church is, where it is, or of whom it is composed. Accordingly each sect has singled out what it regards as its leading feature, or distinctive point, and makes that its test; as Episcopacy, Presbytery, Immersion, or agreement in some articles of faith which it has decided to consider fundamental; and excludes, more or less stringently, all who do not agree with it on these points.

This exclusiveness necessary in practice.

§. 6. There seems to be a precept in the Scriptures for this exclusiveness: "Have no fellowship with the unfruitful works of darkness, but rather reprove them."[1] "Now we command you, brethren, in the name of our Lord Jesus Christ, that ye withdraw yourselves from every brother that walketh *disorderly*, and not *after the tradition* which ye received from us."[2] "A man that is an heretic after the first and second admonition, reject."[3] "If there come any unto you and bring not this doctrine, receive him not into your house, neither bid him God speed."[4] "If he neglect to hear the Church let him be unto thee as an heathen man and a publican."[5]

^{This exclusiveness seems warranted by the Scriptures.}

§ 7. The passages just cited, imply a rule or *tradition* after which men are to walk, and the departure from which is called *walking disorderly*.

^{This implies the identity of the Church.}

We must, however, be able to identify our church, as a visible society, with the Church of which the Scriptures were then speaking, or we have no right to exercise its discipline, and exclude those who do not walk orderly, according to its rules and traditions. Otherwise we are taking to ourselves an authority which was never given us, and are intruding ourselves into the office of others.

Authority may be conferred upon an individual personally, and then it dies with him. Such were the Prophets under the old dispensation. But, again; authority may be conferred upon a class or order of men—as with the Priesthood—and then it belongs alike to each one that belongs to that class, and as a consequence of his regular admission to it. And as

---

[1] Ephes. v. 11.   [2] 2 Thess. iii. 6.   [3] Tit. iii. 10.
[4] 2 John 10.   [5] Matt. xviii. 17.

authority of the first kind may not be assumed by any one on whom it has not been conferred individually— so authority of the second kind may not be assumed or exercised by any one until he has been admitted to the class or order to which it belongs.

Now, exclusiveness implies authority to exclude. In its exercise we exclude those whom we judge to be unworthy, according to the Scriptures, from certain religious privileges, from what we regard as the Sacraments and fellowship of the Church. It is no trifling matter to say to one that he shall not come to the Lord's table. And yet that is what we say when we refuse communion with any one, unless we will admit that our table, the one from which we exclude him, is not the Lord's.

If then, we are of the class of persons to whom these precepts of exclusiveness were addressed, we have a right to exercise the authority to be exclusive If not, the claim is something worse than an empty mockery.

But as the authority was not conferred upon the persons addressed in the Scriptures individually—for then it would have died with them and may now be exercised by no one—but as a class, as the Church of Christ—we must identify ourselves with them before we can have even the shadow of a right to exclude any one who chooses to come to our communion, from doing so. For it is not merely communion with us— but it is, in our view at least, communion with the Lord in His Sacraments which we refuse to those who profess to be His children.

THE IDENTITY CONSIDERED.

§ 8. Again. There are but few, if any, who will not acknowledge, that the Christian has duties to perform, and that the performance of them, if he have opportunity, is necessary to his salvation. We fully admit the doctrine of justification by faith alone. Yet we affirm, and we expect all Christians to assent to our affirmation, that the Christian must keep the commandments, and bring forth the fruit of such good works as God has ordained for us to walk in. I shall not now stop to inquire into the grounds of this necessity of obligation. All persons will agree in acknowledging its existence.

We have duties to perform which imply the Identity of the Church.

1. I say, then, that we, as Christians, have the duty of obedience, to them that are over us in the Lord,[1] which can be performed only in connexion with the true Church. The command itself implies that there are some persons whom Christ hath set over us to be our governors. And the commandment is, that we obey *them*, and not others whom we may put in their stead, or who may claim to be in their place. In human affairs, to obey the rightful officers of the government under which we live is patriotism, and a high virtue. But to obey others, who have no such authority—and who set themselves up as claiming authority—is not patriotism, but treason or rebellion. So in religion, Christ has appointed some to have authority over us, and He requires that we obey them. Obedience to them, therefore, is a duty. But obedience to others, *in the same matter*, is a rejection of their authority, and therefore a sin.

[1] Heb. xiii. 17.

2. Again, the Lord has ordained that they who preach the Gospel shall live of the Gospel.[1] And consequently He has commanded that he that is taught in the Word—minister unto him that teacheth.[2] Here the duty of doing something for the support of the Ministry is expressly taught. He that gives for the support of the true Ministry in the true Church performs this duty. And the declaration is made, "he that soweth little shall reap little: and he that soweth plenteously shall reap plenteously."[3] But he that is not in the true Church, and gives to the support of another ministry than that which Christ hath appointed, is not performing this duty. He is rather doing its opposite.

3. Once more—there are in the Scriptures a variety of commands to preserve the unity of the Church,[4] and for this purpose to avoid all those that cause divisions and all false teachers.[5] Now it is perfectly obvious that unless we are in the true Church, we cannot be performing this duty. But on the contrary we are continually committing the sin against which the commandments were directed.

It is obvious therefore, that one cannot keep these commandments of God, and perform the duties which are required of him, unless he is in the Church. So far as these commandments and duties are concerned, it is no matter what is its name, organization, or form of government, whether it be Papal, or Episcopal, Presbyterian, Methodist or Baptist. Like circumcision or uncircumcision, these things in themselves are nothing, but only the keeping the commandments.

---

[1] 1 Cor. ix. 13, 14. Luke xxii. 29.   [2] Gal. vi. 6.   [3] 2 Cor. ix. 6, 7.
[4] Eph. vi. 3.   [5] Rom. xvi. 17.

But these commandments and the duties growing out of them, do imply a distinction and a difference between the true Church and the false ones. The importance depends not upon *the form* of the Church, but upon its Identity.

§ 9. Let us pass now to another topic. At the close of St. Matthew's Gospel, we find a promise of Christ's perpetual presence "always, even unto the end of the world."[1] *Christ's Perpetual Presence promised to His Church.*

Now so far as our present purpose is concerned, it is no matter whether this promise was made to a particular order in the ministry or not. Suppose that it was made to the Church at large, to all of Christ's people—it is the same; for whether, by the terms of the promise, He is to be with the ministry or with the people, they must be together, and so in effect He will be with both. But the promise that He will be with them, in which way soever we understand it, implies that He will not be elsewhere—that there may be gatherings, and assemblies, and associations with which He will not be. The promise is of a special blessing to His Church. If we are in that Church, we shall have that blessing, if we are worthy. But if we form another organization—a false church—we forfeit that blessing, we forsake His presence. He certainly cannot be with two or more different and opposing bodies. He cannot be contending and divided against Himself.

Here, then, again we see the inestimable importance of the identity of the Church. Be its name, or organization what it may, the importance is the same. It depends not upon outward form, or local name,

[1] Matt. xxviii. 20.

but upon the identity of that Church to which the blessed promise of Christ's perpetual presence was made—to be with it always, every day, even unto the end of the world.

The Church the Temple in which is the true Worship. § 10. In 1 Cor. iii. 16, St. Paul calls the Church the Temple of God. He had just alluded to the divisions and contentions in the Corinthian Church—some preferring Paul, some Apollos, and some Peter. He assures them that these men were but the Ministers by whom they had believed in Christ; they were not founders of distinct sects, each for himself; they were laborers together in building the Temple of God; Christ was the only foundation, and no man could lay another. They were not baptized into the name of Paul. Paul was not crucified for them—therefore he could not be a foundation. There could be no other foundation than Christ, and as He was not divided, there could be only one Church with Him for its chief corner-stone and foundation. "Do ye not know," asks the Apostle, "that ye are the Temple of God, and that the Spirit of God dwelleth in you?"[1] And again, the Apostle writing to the Ephesians, uses the same figure. He says, "Ye are built upon the foundation of the Apostles and Prophets, Jesus Christ Himself being the chief corner-stone, in Whom all the building, fitly framed together, groweth unto an holy Temple in the Lord."[2]

Undoubtedly, this language is figurative. But the figure must have been designed to mean something. The Temple is that in which dwells the Holy Ghost. It is also the place in which God is worshipped. Wor-

---

[1] 1 Cor. vi. 19. [2] Eph. ii. 20, 21.

ship is the leading idea for which Temples are built. This must therefore have been St. Paul's meaning. And yet he says that the Church—the true Church—consisting of those who are "built upon the foundation of the Apostles and Prophets, Jesus Christ Himself being the chief corner-stone," is the Temple of God, and the Spirit of God dwelleth in it.

Now this fact suggests rather than explains, the immense advantage that the Church of which St. Paul was then speaking, has over all other societies and associations of men. Herein is the Holy Ghost, and the true worship of God; and they who are within it, have "fellowship with the Father, and with His Son Jesus Christ."

§ 11. One more thought on this subject: The Church is in several places compared to a living body. In Romans[1] it is compared to an Olive tree, and we Gentiles are said to be grafted in and to have our life only as scions that are grafted in, from the tree and stalk into which we are grafted. In 1 Cor. xii. the Church is compared to a Human Body, and the individuals belonging to it to the members of the human body, as hands and feet, head, ears, and eyes—each of which has life in the body, and only in connection with it. Take them away and they are dead. Again, in Ephesians iv. 16, Christ is called the Head, and the Church His Body, and we each and severally the members—"fitly joined together and compacted by that which every joint supplieth"—and, it is said, thus to grow, "to make increase of the body unto the edifying of itself in love." And hence we

The Church a mystical Body.

---

[1] xi. 17.

are said to be "members of His body, of His flesh, and of His bones."¹

These, again, are figurative expressions, confessedly so. But, as figures, they must have been used to mean something. They may point to a mystery, as, indeed, St. Paul calls it.² But it is something of great importance—some great advantage, that depends upon membership in the Body—the Identity of the Church. Christ is not divided. His Body is not divided. St. Paul says, "There is one BODY," and the advantage signified by these obscure but frequent figures, must, therefore, depend upon union with the true Church—which of course implies its identity.

<small>The common definition of the Church considered in relation to the foregoing topics.</small> § 12. The definition of the Church that is most commonly adopted, says that "*a Church* is a community voluntarily associated on the foundation of revealed truth for religious purposes."

Now I shall not at present go into a consideration of all the points involved in this definition. Two only shall I notice in passing:

1. It changes the Scripture phraseology, and is a total departure from it. The expression "*the Church*," is used in the Scriptures somewhere from seventy-five to an hundred times. But the expression "*a Church*" is used once, and then only in the last member of a sentence which makes the expression as definite as though the definite article "the" itself had been used. The expression occurs in Eph. v. 25, 26, 27.

2. This change of expressions from "*the Church*" to *a* Church," implies that there are, or may be, many

---

¹ Eph. v. 30. ² Eph. v. 32.

answering to all the conditions of the definition. And so it is intended. The design is, so to define the Church as to include all the voluntary associations which may have been devised and called by that name, and which are nevertheless regarded and spoken of as distinct churches.

Be it so. Then each one of them is regarded as "*a* Church," and not as "*the* Church." The question then arises, to which of them may we apply what the Scriptures say of "*the* Church?" They say nothing about "*a* church," which may be only one out of many. Which one of those many churches may exercise the authority of exclusiveness which our Lord has conferred upon His Church? In which may we perform the duties we owe to the Church of which the Scriptures speak? In which is the perpetual presence of Christ promised to His followers and people? Which is the Temple where the true and acceptable worship of God may be offered? Which is the mystical Body in which, as members of His body, we may have the life of Christ flowing through our souls, and we become partakers of Him?

These are grave and momentous questions, and yet they are all involved in the identity of the Church.

To illustrate this point by a comparison which will exhibit its force more fully, let us suppose a writer to be setting forth our duty to God. He begins by a definition, and says that "*a* god is that which is acknowledged to be the proper object of religious worship."

Now this definition is such an one as the experience and practices of men have made true. It defines "*a* god;" and does it in such a way as to include the true and only God; but so also as to include with Him any idol, which the fancy of man may devise or his hands may make. But may he therefore apply what the Scriptures say of the only true God, to any being or object which men may choose to acknowledge to be "*a* god?" If so, then we can justify any system of idolatry that has ever existed, or that man may choose to invent; and the command "thou shalt worship the Lord thy God," may be applied to Jupiter, Baal, or Vishnu, just according as we may choose to have the one or the other for the "Lord *our* god." As there are "gods many, and lords many," so there are "churches many." And as the Scriptures speak of the ETERNAL JEHOVAH as "*the* God" whom we ought to worship, so do they speak of that Church which our Lord and His Apostles founded, as "*the* Church," that is, the *only* one in which we can perform our duties and obligations to the Church, and enjoy the blessings and privileges promised to it.

Conclusion. § 13. Now we have seen that, as Christians, we are commanded to obey those that Christ has appointed to have the rule over us.[1] We are to esteem them very highly in love for their work's sake, the Lord has ordained that they shall live of the Gospel,[3] and we that are taught are commanded to minister to their support in all good things;[4] we are to mark and avoid all those that cause divisions,[5] and strive to preserve the unity of the Spirit in the bond of peace.[6]

We may place a very different estimate upon these

---

[1] Heb. xiii. 17.   [2] 1 Thess. v. 12.   [3] 1 Cor. ix. 14.
[4] Gal. vi. 6.   [5] Rom. xvi. 17.   [6] Eph. iv. 3.

duties. Some may deny that they are duties at all. It is true that many act as though they did not consider them so. But surely such persons cannot have taken their views from the Word of God. Duties at any rate they are, if the Bible is to be our standard and rule, whether we consider them of a greater or of a lesser magnitude.

We must admit, then, that there are duties which we, as Christians, are required to perform, that can be performed only in the Church, and which do, therefore, imply its Identity. Grant that elsewhere we may have the rule of life and duty truly explained to us; grant that elsewhere we may enjoy the presence and influence of the Holy Spirit; grant that elsewhere we may have all the joy and peace of believing: yet there, be it where it may, these duties must remain unperformed—the members must go down to the grave, leaving them undone—they must arise with us at the resurrection of the dead, and appear with us, as deeds done or not done in the body, at the Judgment Seat of God. The true faith which we received—the right rule of life which was expounded to us—the fellowship of the Holy Ghost which we supposed we enjoyed—as well as all our joy and peace in believing—these, and all the other privileges of light and knowledge which we may have possessed and enjoyed, can only serve to render us inexcusable for the neglect of these duties, and aggravate our guilt. There they stand, in the Lamb's books, written against our names, as things left undone, which we ought to have done. It will then be found that we had bestowed upon others that which God had required for Himself. We had conferred upon others that honor which He required to be paid to His servants. We had scattered where He would gather together into one Fold. We had multiplied and encouraged divisions, instead of laboring and praying, as He did, that His disciples might be one, and that as the Apostle says He designed, "there might be no schisms in the body."

I do not wish to magnify the importance of these things at all. I aim simply to call attention to them, as indubitable facts tending to show the importance of the Identity of the Church. Let each judge for himself of their importance, and as he judges so let him act. To his own Master he standeth or falleth; for we shall all stand before the Judgment Seat of Christ, and every one of us shall give account of *himself* to God. But I refer to these facts as being in part the reason, and as being in themselves a sufficient reason for the importance which we attach to the Identity of the Church and for our esteeming one church, better than another, even though they should seem, in the judgment of men, both equally orthodox, both equally holy in the lives of their members—both, so far as we can see, equally salutary in the influence which they exert upon the morals and welfare of the community. To man they may present the aspect of equal value and equal holiness. But in their relation to God they cannot be considered as on the same footing.

The reader will not therefore understand me as seeking to prove either directly or indirectly—Episcopacy and the Apostolic Succession. I am aiming to find that Church to which we owe so many duties, and in which we may enjoy so many privileges. As

Christians, we must have membership somewhere. We must assemble for Public Worship—for keeping the Christian Sabbath—for observance of the Sacraments—and for the performance of other commanded duties, which require, or imply, a *visible* association, or church, of professing followers of Christ.

And I aim at tracing the history of the Church, irrespective of the peculiarities of its organization, or to the doctrines which it may have taught. In writing a history of the descendants of Shem, for instance—the oldest son of Noah—we should not need to inquire into the forms of government under which they may have lived, or into the peculiarities of religious belief which they may have entertained ; but we follow them historically, showing from history where they started from, whither they wandered, and the places in which they located. And then again from each such settlement we might find colonies removing to become the founders of a nation or distinct community, somewhere else. Wherever they might go, whatever changes might be made in their mode of life, their form of civil government, their opinions and usages on religious subjects—still if they should keep themselves aloof and distinct from intermarriage with the other branches of the Noachian family, we could trace their descent and identify them as the family and descendants of Shem.

So undoubtedly the Church may be traced and identified. It began in the little flock which our blessed Lord gathered around Him during His sojourn on earth. Into this family new members received adoption by embracing and professing the Faith. As a body of professors they kept themselves distinct from all others, by their discipline and the administration of their Sacraments. And they extended themselves from Judea and Jerusalem, in all directions, as the Lord had commanded them. Their history is before us. It is from this that we propose to draw our materials for identifying the Church.

The Church of which we are in pursuit, and which we are endeavoring to identify, is properly distinguished from all others by the title, *Catholic*. It is THE CATHOLIC CHURCH OF CHRIST. The word "*Catholic*" means, *whole, general, universal*. "It is so called," says an ancient Father, "because it is spread over the whole habitable globe, from one end to the other."

We may then speak of this expanded and diffused society of Christ's Disciples, as a whole, and call it the *Catholic Church*. Or we may speak of it in any particular nation, and call it the Catholic Church in that nation; as the Catholic Church in France, the Catholic Church in England, &c. But in either case, whether we use it of the whole, or only a part, we mean, if we speak of the whole body, that Church which has, visibly and apparently, existed ever since it was founded by our Blessed Lord and His Apostles; and if we speak of a part or local division, then that of which we speak is the part or local division of that Church existing in any particular place. But the title, Catholic, as I shall use it, is intended to indicate only this one fact, or idea, namely: the Church, or Society, instituted by our Lord and continued in its existence to this day, or some part of it, as distinguished from all others of a different and more modern origin.

CHAPTER II.

THE MODE OF HISTORIC IDENTIFICATION STATED AND ILLUSTRATED.

Now, in order to identify the Church, it is obvious that we may take two different methods. We may ascertain from the Scriptures, what are to be regarded as its essential Notes, and then institute a comparison between those notes, or features, and any given body claiming, at this day, to be the Church, or a branch of it. Or we may go back to the first planting of the Church, and trace its existence down the current of time, in its spread over the face of the earth, until we find it extending itself into our own country. The former method is the most common in our day—and has involved us in interminable discussions upon the preliminary matters, which are merely Notes of the Church, and thus keep us back from the subject itself; and even when the question has been decided, it leaves the appearance of making the whole matter depend upon a question of mere form.

§ 1. I shall take the last of the two methods indicated above. This would be very easy if the infirmities, the follies, and the wilfulness of men had not encumbered the subject with embarrassments which render a more cautious procedure and a more careful investigation necessary. *[The Historical Method stated and illustrated.]*

Let us, then, endeavor to get a definite idea of the Identity of the Church. And for this purpose, perhaps a few illustrations from other subjects will be of the most important service.

There is, for instance, such an institution as *Masonry*. I say nothing of its merits, or demerits, but simply refer to its existence as an illustration in point. It has existed, through several centuries at least, one and the same institution. It is spread extensively over the face of the earth. It is the same institution, in all the nations where it has an existence at all. In separate towns and villages there are distinct Lodges, each with its officers, its Lodge-room, &c. He that joins any one of these Lodges is a Mason, there and everywhere. In any other Lodge, in any other nation, he would be received, as a free and accepted Mason, to the same standing and degree as that which he had at the place where he resided. This is because of the *identity* of the institution. It is one and the same everywhere.

If, now, several individuals, in a settlement where there is no lodge, believing the institution to be a good one, become desirous of joining the Masons, and having a lodge where they reside, there are certain rules and principles of extension by which they can obtain their object. They must first go in sufficient numbers and be regularly initiated into some Lodge already in existence; and having been initiated themselves, they may obtain a charter or dispensation, and go to work under it. In this way they become truly Masons—their association is a Lodge. They derive all the benefits, whatever they may be, of this ancient institution, from their connection with the Lodge which they have founded. And they are Masons the world over. In any Lodge, in any city or nation, they would be received to the same standing, and entitled to the same privileges. But if they had gone to work otherwise than as these principles of extension require, or got up a clandestine lodge, they would not have become Masons—their association would not have been recognised as a Lodge at all—nor would they themselves have received any of the benefits which would result to them from being Masons—for, in fact, the course which they took did not make them Masons, but only imitators of Masons.

The same illustration may be derived from the Odd Fellow's institution—from that of the Sons of Temperance—the Rechabites, &c.

As this is an important point, I will venture one or two more illustrations: and especially so because each individual will understand it the better if I give as an illustration something that he has known in his experience or that has occurred to his own thoughts.

Take, then, for another illustration, the American Bible Society; an association which, while it is chiefly designed for doing good to others, confers benefits and privileges upon its members. This society was, I believe, first established in New-York. It has a written constitution, established modes of operation, and established principles or provisions, for extension by means of auxiliary associations, which may be formed in every county, town, or parish. If individuals, residing in a place where there is no auxiliary society, are desirous of establishing one, they have only to ascertain what are the rules that are laid down by the parent society, and strictly conforming themselves to those rules in their organization, they become thereby members of the American Bible Society. They are entitled to all the benefits arising from such membership, and can do all the good which it enables them to accomplish.

But if they proceed otherwise than according to those established rules, they may indeed form themselves into *a* Bible Society—one that may confer benefits upon its members, and enable them to do good by the circulation of the Bible—but still they will not be members of *the American Bible Society*, nor will their association be one that is auxiliary to, or a part of, that older and more extensive institution, but only an imitation of it.

Now this same thing must hold true with regard to the Church. Our blessed Redeemer contemplated founding a Church, that should extend over the whole earth and last as long as the world stands.[1] But it is evident that He did not Himself establish it in all places. Neither was it established in all places and nations by His immediate Apostles, during their lifetime. There must therefore, be certain principles on which its extension depends, and by which it may be extended; so that where a number of persons, who are already Christians, or who are desirous of becoming so, are found, a society may be formed in accordance with those principles, and becomes thereby part of His Church, and not merely an imitation of it.

Every society that is intended to outlast the generation in which it is instituted, and to be extended

[1] Matt. xvi. 18.

beyond the immediate locality where it was first organized, must have principles of extension, by which it can be expanded and located elsewhere. Else of course it could not be extended at all. By ascertaining these principles, we are able to follow the society in its spread, and identify its existence in each particular place. The Church, like a vine, the root of which is at the place of its first establishment—Jerusalem—puts forth its branches into each city, province, or nation, until they spread over the face of the whole inhabited globe, and its tendrils reach every human heart. Now a vine is one. Though it may have many branches, yet we find no difficulty in identifying them We can trace each one back till it articulates with the main stalk and so through that stalk to the original root, in a continuous line of unbroken succession. Or, in case we start with a branch that does not belong to the same vine, we can trace it back to its separate root and tell where it started from, ascertain, perhaps, by whom it was planted, and at any rate, we can thus prove that it is not a branch of the same vine. In tracing the vine, however, we may find here a branch crushed and deformed by violence, there one overlayed by mildew and rust—here one blighted by dearth or choked by the growth of noxious weeds—and then, again, we may possibly find one on which man has grafted scions of a different stock so as to produce fruits of a different character. But through all, its identity can be traced: it is the same vine still. So with the Church—violence has been at work upon her sacred principles and lineaments; superstition has overlaid her simple truths and simple forms; apathy and worldliness have blighted her fruits, and the invention of man has been busy with efforts to engraft its own multifarious schemes upon that which is the only life-giving stalk. But the Church's historic identity can be traced through them all.

§ 2. It is comparatively easy to trace the identity of the Church in those places where it was established by the inspired Apostles, and continues with an uninterrupted succession to the present day. The admission of members from generation to generation, so as to keep the numbers good—the keeping of Sundays and other Holy Days, in religious worship—the observance of the Sacraments—meeting habitually in the same place—calling itself always by the same name—and various other notes, guide us, without fear or danger of mistake. And as a matter of fact, though we find the enemy has always been busy at work in creating divisions and schisms, yet, in the places of which we now speak, there has never been any difficulty in deciding which was the old Church, and which the new sect. There may have been much difference of opinion as to which was the soundest and best, the old Church or the new one, but none as to the fact, which was the old and which the new. In other words, the Identity of the body has never been a matter of doubt or dispute. In all the earlier controversies—the Arian, the Donatist, the Pelagian, and the Nestorian—there was no doubt, no question raised that, these sects were the more recent bodies. They, of course, all claimed to be right. But no one of them claimed to be the Church that had existed from Christ and the Apostles.

Their plea was, that the Church had fallen into error and corruption, and that they were reformers. And so they were, if they had truth on their side, so long as they continued in the Church. But when they left it to form a new one, that which they formed *was* a new one, and that which they left *was* the old. So, also, with the modern sects—the Presbyterians, the Independents, and the Methodists—in England. There is no pretence that any one of them is the Church that existed in England before the Reformation. It is fully and freely acknowledged that they are new churches, formed by individuals seceding from the old.

§ 3. Now such facts do not at all embarrass us in our attempts to identify the Church in those countries where it was planted in the earlier ages—that is, in ages so early as that no mere sect that then existed, has lasted down to our own. *This method attended with difficulty only in its application to countries recently converted.* The Church that was planted there, and has outlived all schisms, and sects, and oppositions, is undoubtedly and unquestionably the one of which we are in pursuit. It may be somewhat—nay, sadly —changed in doctrinal character and general appearance, but, historically, and lineally, it is the same.

The difficulty presses upon us only when we come to identify the Church in these latter ages, when sects are abundant, and where, until lately, the name of Christ had not been heard. Though late in reaching us, a branch of the Vine may have found (and we trust has found) its way to our country. In studying the history of the Church, we shall find that it was never inactive. The Vine was always growing, always putting forth new branches. The Northern nations of

Europe—Sweden and Norway—were not converted until the tenth or eleventh centuries. Yet at length a branch of the Vine reached them also. So with us. Therefore we want some clue, or guide, by which we can trace the connection and identify the body.

Now, to accomplish this object, I propose to ascertain, in the first place, what are the fundamental principles of the extension of the Church, as we find them in the Scriptures, and apply those principles to the facts of history. I propose to inquire, first, how the Church was extended and expanded by the Apostles, into other countries than that where it was first established.

The method now preferred adopted and used in all similar cases.

§ 4. The method which I propose to pursue is one with which we are familiar in similar cases. For instance, the Baptist sect was first established, in the United States, at Providence, R. I., A. D. 1639. Since that time it has spread over almost the whole country. Yet we have no difficulty in identifying it. We are willing to go by *the name*, until we learn that there are several sects claiming the same name. We then resort to their principles of extension, and to the acknowledgment of communion. They have principles by which their church can be extended indefinitely. Persons residing in a place where there is no society of that communion, have only to ascertain those principles, organize accordingly, and they are acknowledged by the general body of Baptists, and received by them into communion, and become thereby identified with them—a branch of the same vine, a church of Baptists or a part of the Baptist church.

The same may be said of any other denomination

in this country. It has its principles of extension. When in the formation of new religious societies, designed to belong to any existing communion, the people forming it conform to the rules and organic principles of that denomination, they become a part of it, and as a religious body are identified with it. But if they do not conform to those principles, they form a new denomination—at first by themselves: but, in the course of time, others may adopt their rules and principles, build on the same platform, and then they will become a part of the same church. And in writing the history of that denomination, we must first learn, from a study of its principles of extension, what we are to regard as a part of it, and what not; that is, we must identify it.

Now this is what I propose to do with regard to the Church of Christ—the visible society of believers which He founded. We cannot always be guided by the name; for that is not always an infallible guide. We must then follow the Vine historically, and trace its progress as it extends itself into different countries and thus identify its existence irrespective of its name. And in order to do this, we must, in the first place, ascertain the manner in which, or the principles by which, it was extended.

§. 5. I have said that this method is one with which we are already familiar. All denominations use it in their own case, and therefore no one can object to its use here. There is not one of the fifty or sixty denominations of this land that is not extending its communion, or at least seeking to do so, by establishing societies in places

This method cannot be objected to by any.

where there are none of their order. And when such a society is established, they ascertain, in some way or other, that it has been established on their own principles, and in conformity to their general usages, before they receive it into their communion. They all have representative bodies, or councils, under the name of Conference, Presbytery, Convention, Association, Convocation, Synod, Classis, or something of the kind; and when any newly formed society seeks admission to their deliberations, &c., they examine, (if they have not been sufficiently assured before,) and see if the society has been organized in conformity to their principles and usages. If so, they gladly grant the admission which it seeks. But if not, the admission is withheld. If it yields up the points of difference, and conform, it is well. But if not, and its members persist in their peculiarities, they constitute thereby a new denomination—a new church. Their act becomes a fact of history. It neither violates the identity of the denomination previously existing, nor does it throw any serious difficulty in the way of our efforts to identify it.

Whatever, therefore, we may think of *the result* of our application of the organic principles of the Christian Church to the facts of history, we are, all of us, prohibited by our own acts—acts indispensable to our distinct existence—from pronouncing the method unsound or unjust. And in taking this course, it seems to me no small gain that we avoid all of the appearance, as well as the reality, of making Church-communion depend upon a mere form, or incidental fact. It carries all along with it the impression that it is not a mere form that we are seeking, but the Church itself—the mystical body of Christ—the fellowship of the Apostles and Martyrs—the communion of those who have been sanctified—the Temple of His Worship—the participation of His promised presence—the Flock that He feeds, and the Fold of His watchful care.

§ 6. The principles by which the Church was extended over the face of the earth, must be inferred partly from the acts of the Apostles, in extending it, and partly from the precepts and principles scattered through the New Testament, more or less directly applicable to the subject. *The principles by which the Church is extended must be derived from the Scriptures.*

The principles that I shall call attention to, are, (1) that the Church must be extended by living members, (2) going into a place where the Church was not previously established, (3) for the purpose of preaching the true Faith, and establishing the Communion of the Church there. Of these principles we will speak in order.

§ 7. The charge or commission which our Saviour gave His Apostles, just as he was leaving the world—"Go ye into all the World, preach the Gospel to every creature, teach or make disciples of all nations, baptising them in the name of the Father, and of the Son, and of the Holy Ghost, teaching them to observe all things whatsoever I have commanded you,"[1]—raises the presumption that the Church was to be established and extended by persons who had previously been re- *First Principle: the Church must be extended by persons who are in its Communion.*

---

[1] Mark xvi. 15; Matt. xxviii. 20.

ceived as members, and acknowledged to have authority in it. No question will be raised, I presume, that this commission, and the duties assigned the Apostles, did at the least include the establishing or extension of the Church which He had before declared that He would build.[1] He did not send the Apostles to preach the Gospel and leave the converts to organize a church or not, as they might choose, and in such a way as they might choose. He did not charge them to commit the Gospel to writing and leave the people to study it for themselves, and then act as they might think it required. The duties of the new life to which the converts were called, required some society, association, or organization. The Church was not a mere matter of choice or expediency: it had an end in view: it was a necessary element of His religion. It was for the support of Public Worship; the administration of the Sacraments; the comfort, fellowship and edification of its members. Therefore the Apostles were to establish it, and enlarge its extension as fast and as far as converts should be made to resort to it, and live in its communion. It was a voluntary association, only as all duties are voluntary. We may perform them or not as we choose, but if we do not perform them, we must abide the penalty of disobedience. They are not, and cannot be indifferent in themselves; nor does this obligation arise from our consent to perform them. They are duties, because some one having authority so to do, has commanded or required them. So the Church originated in the will of God, and union with it is a

---

[1] Matt. xvi. 18.

part of the duty that He requires of us. It depends upon *our* wills whether we do as He requires or not. In this sense, the Church is a voluntary association, and in no other.

1. The thing to which I wish first to direct attention, is, the fact that the Apostles went and did the work of founding and extending the Church themselves.

It is unnecessary to follow them as they went, preaching the Gospel, and ordaining Elders in every Church[1] where converts to the faith had been made in sufficient numbers to sustain the continued worship of God. The fact that the living Preacher went first with the Gospel—not in his hand, for it was not then committed to writing, but in his heart—is the conspicuous and the prevailing rule. Nor is this commission confined to the Twelve; for St. Paul, the chief Apostle of the Gentiles, was converted after the commission was first given, and became more efficient than any of the rest, and in no respect a whit behind the very chiefest Apostles.[2] We also find Barnabas, Timothy, Titus, and others, laboring in the same way and sphere, though manifestly in an inferior capacity.

There are, also, instances on record in the Scriptures in which an Apostle did not precede other efforts to spread the Gospel.

2. After the persecution that arose at the time of Stephen's martyrdom, Philip, who, as we read, had previously been appointed to some inferior offce in the Church,[3] went down to Samaria and preached the

---

[1] Acts xiv. 23.   [2] 2 Cor. xi. 5.   [3] Acts vi. 1–6.

Gospel. And the people gave heed to Philip, hearing and seeing the miracles that he wrought. And when they believed and were converted, they were baptised in large numbers. The Apostles yet abode at Jerusalem: but when they heard that Samaria had received the word of God, they sent down Peter and John, two of their number, who laid their hands on the newly baptised converts, and they received spiritual gifts.[1] These gifts had not before been received by the Samaritan converts.

3. But again: We find that they which were scattered abroad upon the persecution that arose about Stephen, travelled as far as Phenice, Cyprus and Antioch, preaching the Gospel. Now who these men were we do not know. We know only that they were not Apostles. But be this as it may, the narrative proceeds to say, that when tidings of this came to the ears of the Church which was at Jerusalem, they sent forth Barnabas, that he should go as far as Antioch, the most distant place from Jerusalem that is mentioned, and so over the whole country spoken of. When he came and saw the grace that had been given them, he exhorted them to cleave unto the Lord. And, as we read, much people was added unto the Lord. Immediately Barnabas went for Saul—or Paul—and brought him to Antioch, and they remained there for a whole year, and "assembled themselves with the Church, and taught much people."

Hence we see that the Church was extended by individuals previously in its communion—sometimes

[1] Acts viii. 5–7.

alone, as in the case of Philip, and sometimes in companies—going into places where they would be as seed scattered in the soil to spring up and bring forth a harvest, or like leaven hid in a lump until the whole be leavened. Thus always each branch and part of the Church had a historic and visible connection with that which existed before, and through that Church received the persons who were to do the work of the ministry, among them. Wherever the Apostles went, they were men who had been set apart for the Ministry themselves. And in other cases—as Samaria and Antioch—the mother Church sent forth Apostles as soon as they had heard of the conversions in those places: to the one Peter and John, and to the other Barnabas and Paul.

But in no case do we find a society starting up independently of that which existed before, and organizing themselves as "a voluntary association," called or recognized as a part of the Church of Christ; the gathering and organizing energy in all cases proceeded from Christ through the Church itself, to each separate branch and member.

§ 8. The second principle of the extension of the Church seems to be, that, besides perpetuation by additions in places where it already exists, it must be extended by establishing new branches in other places, and not by establishing different branches in the same place. *The Second Principle: Persons extending the Communion of the Church by establishing a new Branch must go into a place where it is not already established.*

We might follow the Apostles, as they went from one nation or province to another, laboring for a time in the central places of population and influence, and see how in every case, this rule was observed. In this way a great number of distinct and independent branches of the Church were established, all having the same faith, the same hope, the same rule of life, and all partaking of the same fellowship, and forming one and the same communion.

In each place the Church had to start anew, and begin from nothing. At first, therefore, it would be but small in point of numbers. They could all be accommodated in one place of meeting and worship, and they would need no more. As they increased in numbers, however, they would need more than one place of worship. Other places were provided. But there were then no divisions into parishes and separate congregations, each with its appropriate minister, as at the present day. This division forms what is called the "*Parochial System*," and was introduced after the Apostles' days.

But with or without the Parochial system, there could be no occasion for forming another religious communion, or denomination, in the same place. With it, the Church or communion already established might be extended as far as occasion should require, as is done, by each denomination at the present day, by forming new congregations and organizing new parishes. Without it, all that would be required would be to add to the number of places of worship, and to the number of the Clergy, as fast as the increasing wants of the community might require, and leave the members to attend at which ever place they might choose.

The feelings of brotherhood, and brotherly love,

which are so strongly inculcated in the Scriptures, and which the religion of Christ is so peculiarly calculated to produce, would dispose all the Christians in each place, to belong to the same society, or church. They would also remember the Lord's prayer that they might all be one, that He might dwell in them and they in Him.[1] They would be familiar with such precepts as these: "Let brotherly love continue,"[2] "Let us walk by the same rule, let us mind the same thing,"[3] "Be of the same mind one toward another,"[4] "Love as brethren,"[5] "For as the body is one and hath many members, and all the members of that one body, being many, are one body, so also is Christ; for by one Spirit we are all baptised into one body."[6] "There is one Body and one Spirit, even as ye are all called in one hope of your calling, one Lord, one Faith, one Baptism, one God and Father of all, who is above all, and through all, and in you all,"[7] "That there may be one Fold and one Shepherd."[8]

And, as enforcing these precepts of Divine truth, we are to consider what is said of the nature and danger of divisions; "For ye are yet carnal—for whereas there is among you envying and strife, and divisions, are ye not carnal, and walk as men? For while one saith, I am of Paul, and another, I am of Apollos, are ye not carnal?"[9] "Mark them that cause divisions and offences contrary to the doctrine which ye have learned, and avoid them, for they that are such serve not the Lord Jesus Christ."[10] "There must also be

[1] John xvii. 21. [2] Heb. xiii. 1. [3] Phil. iii. 16.
[4] Rom. xii. 16. [5] 1 Pet. iii. 8. [6] 1 Cor. xii. 12, 13.
[7] Eph. iv. 4, 5. [8] John x. 16. [8] 1 Cor. iii. 3.
[10] Rom. xvi. 17.

heresies among you, that they which are approved may be made manifest."[1]

We need go no farther to see that all the believers in one place would endeavor to "speak the same thing, that there should be no divisions among them, but that they should be perfectly joined together, in the same mind and in the same judgment."[2]

If, then, one Apostle after another should go into the same place, it would be, as St. Paul says, only to build on the same foundation, to enlarge the borders and edify the same Church. Each would not be the founder of a sect, to be called by his name, as the Corinthians seem to have thought. And how many soever the brethren might be, they would make but one communion and fellowship—"many members in one body."

Such then must be the result, so long as only those who were truly the Apostles and Ministers of Christ, labored among them. False Prophets, false Apostles might come. Against these they had been sufficiently warned. They might deceive many and would do so. But the society of followers which they could establish, most clearly would not be a part or branch of the Church of Christ.—As a visible society it would be totally distinct.

And if one should come, though not a false Prophet or Apostle—nay, though he were an angel from heaven—and should preach *another gospel*—either in the Church already existing or for the purpose of founding another—he must be rejected. In the strong

---

[1] 1 Cor. xi. 19.   [2] 1 Cor. i. 10.

language of St. Paul, twice repeated, "let him be accursed."[1]

This must evidently be the meaning of the apostle. He was not speaking of those who professed to teach a new religion, altogether distinct from and independent of Christianity, but of those who inculcated a view of Christianity inconsistent with the doctrine of Justification by Faith, which he had taught them. By "another gospel" therefore, he must have meant another view of the same gospel; for he says of it, that it "is not another," but another view, or a perversion, of the same.

There was then no possible way in which another church which should be a distinct visible society, or communion, and yet a true branch of the Church of Christ, could be established, in a place where one already existed, so as to produce two in a community. (1.) It could not be produced by a division, or secession, for that is condemned as carnal, and not serving the Lord Jesus Christ. (2.) It could not be by the coming in among them of false Apostles or Prophets; for no society which they could establish would be any part of the Church of Christ. (3.) It could not be by a person's coming among them to preach another gospel—another view of Christianity—even though that person were an Apostle, or an angel from heaven; for whoever should come on such an errand or undertake such a work, must be held "*accursed.*"

And indeed another gospel would be necessary, to constitute another church. For the rites which the

---
[1] Gal. i. 8–9.

Apostles were to teach the disciples to observe, were commanded them by our Lord no less than the doctrines which they were to teach them to believe. This appears from the broad terms of the mission, as recorded by St Matthew,[1] "teaching them to observe all things whatsoever I have commanded you;" and so long as this was done, by all the disciples under the influence of those commands for unity, brotherly love and fellowship, and of those warnings against divisions—some of which we have quoted—there would be no separate communions, or distinct denominations, of the accepted disciples. And all others, whether they were those that were seduced by false prophets and apostles, or those who had given heed to some one coming among them preaching "another gospel," would of course have no claim, nor pretension, to be considered a branch of the Church of Christ.

Hence, then, we may lay it down as a rule that the Church was expanded or extended, not by establishing different denominations in the same place, but by establishing the same denomination in different places.

§ 9. In the third place, the persons going into an unoccupied field—purely missionary ground—to establish the Church, must go for the purpose of establishing a branch of the Catholic Church of Christ, on the same basis, and for the same object, as the Church itself. This *basis* is, the Christian Faith. And the *object* is, the glory of God in the salvation of sinners. These being essential

<small>THIRD PRINCIPLE: Each new Branch must be established on the same Doctrinal Basis and for the same End as the Church itself was originally established.</small>

---

[1] Matt. xxviii. 20.

elements of the Church and of Christianity, they must of course, therefore be essential to its Identity.

St. Paul says, "other foundation can no man lay than that which is laid."[1] This foundation is the Christian Faith, as the Apostles taught it, and the Church at first received it.

I do not mean to say that every error or mistake in point of fact, will nullify or invalidate the labors of the missionary who makes it. Such mistakes are incident to human infirmity, and inseparable from whatever is to be done by fallible man. But when a missionary, or a band of them, go about to build a church on a basis or foundation materially different from that which was the acknowledged Creed, or Confession of Faith of the Primitive Church, the design itself shows that they intend to found a new church—a new religious communion, rather than to extend the old one. And such a step would lead to two results, which would make the fact that a new church had been established conspicuous and generally admitted. (1.) The new church would not be likely to claim communion with the old, but would be likely, on the other hand, to entertain some feelings of hostility towards it. (2.) Nor would the old Church admit the claims of the new one to be received to communion and fellowship, if such claims were made. So that the fact of non-intercommunion—and perhaps of hostility—would be a sufficient indication that there was no identity or affiliation between them.

One may err in his apprehension of some points of

[1] I Cor. iii. 11.

the Primitive Faith. Education may have accustomed him to some modifications of the Primitive rites and customs. But these things, so long as they do not lead him to seek, by a conscious intention, to engraft them upon the Primitive Faith and customs; or so to narrow down the Christian Platform, and restrain the liberty of conscience allowed to Christians by the Law of Liberty in Christ Jesus, as that its members are not allowed to hold the Faith in its purity—do not necessarily constitute the church so established, an entirely distinct one. It may teach and practise error—but it does so unintentionally. It was not founded for the purpose of binding over its members to the errors which it inculcates. The door is not closed against the light. It has interposed no obstacles to the return to the truth, in its purity and simplicity, but everywhere professes the design so to teach that truth to its members.

The design of the heresiarch—that is, the person who founds a new sect or church—is, to found one that shall embody and represent his own peculiar views. These views are of course diverse from those entertained by the Church or churches already existing—else there could be no desire to establish a new one. Now we have seen, under the Principle last specified, that this desire or design can not be indulged in a community where the Church already exists. The operation of the Principle now under discussion, is to prevent this design or desire from taking effect *in any other community*. The result would be no less a new and distinct church in the one case than in the other. The founder lays a new foundation in the doctrines and usages which he advocates, and his followers are built upon that foundation, with himself, perhaps, for 'the Chief Corner-stone.' And his church, instead of being an extension of the Church of Christ, is most evidently another and a new one.

We have now considered the three Principles of Church extension, which encompass the whole subject. I do not profess to have enumerated all the principles involved—I have selected only those which are the most general in their character—the most obviously true, and the most easily applied to the facts of history. With these principles, we can follow the Church from its establishment at Jerusalem, in the days of the Apostles, to its extension and final triumph in all the remotest corners of the earth. Be it Episcopal or Presbyterian, Baptist or Papal—be its form and its doctrines what they may—the same Principles of Extension will enable us to follow it in its growth, and identify its existence. We need not even know what are its doctrines or its forms—these may all be left as a matter for subsequent investigation. But the Church itself, in any place, and for any country, or any age, we can find and identify—postponing all secondary and subordinate questions until we are able to contemplate them from a more advantageous position, and settle them more satisfactorily.

§ 10. The application of the foregoing principles would in all cases lead to the correct result. But it would require an extensive investigation of Church history—and it is possible that in many cases there are no documents extant from which the precise state of the facts can be ascertained. *Another mode of arriving at the same result.*

We may then direct our attention to two other tests which can be applied with a less minute research into history, and yet lead to the same result.

1. The first is indicated by the answer given to the inquiry—*Does the society in question claim to be a part of the Church that has always existed from the Apostles' days, and to be now in communion with it, or any part of it?*

Most sects frankly acknowledge the fact and the occasion of their origin as distinct and visible societies, and make no claim to be any part of the Church that was in existence before them. Thus the Methodists claim to have been founded as a church by John Wesley. They do not claim to be a part of the Church of England—from which their founders seceded, nor do they claim now to be in communion with it. Of course, therefore, they are not to be considered as a legitimate branch and part of the English Church.

On the other hand, the Protestant Episcopal Church in the United States, does claim to have been founded by the English Church, as a true and legitimate branch of itself. She claims to be, and in point of fact now is, in full and reciprocal communion with the mother Church.

2. This, then, leads us to the second part of our test. *Does that which is claimed to be the parent Church acknowledge the one in question to have been duly founded as a branch of herself?*

We have seen in the case of the Methodists, that they do not claim to be a regular branch of the English Church, or in full and reciprocal communion with it. So it is true, likewise, that the English Church does not acknowledge any such relationship, and would not, if it were claimed.

But in regard to the Protestant Episcopal Church, the relationship claimed by it is fully acknowledged. Members go from one Church to the other by letters of transference—the clergy of each Church are mutually and reciprocally acknowledged by the other, and received to a full participation in the ministry..

So, with regard to the Church of England itself. Go back to a period anterior to the divisions of the East and the West, and we find it claiming to be a true and legitimate branch of the Catholic Church of Christ, and it was so acknowledged to be. After the division, it of course adhered to the Romish Bishop and party until the Reformation caused a further division in the Church, and then the English Church adhered to the Reformation.

That it is, therefore, a branch of the original Vine, may be safely inferred from the application of these two tests; and the only question in regard to it is, whether it became apostate by the Reformation or not. Up to that time it was fully acknowledged to be a branch of the Church of Christ, by that Church itself.

And, in fact, the two tests which I have last laid down, are the ones in most common use. You meet a man in the streets, and ask what church he belongs to—you are seeking for the first test named. What church does he claim to be a member of? Suppose he answers the Methodist. If we have no special object for inquiring further, and have no reason to doubt his word, we rest upon his assertion and inquire no further. But if we doubt his word, or have need to be very certain, we go to the Methodist church of which he claims to be a member, and ascertain if they acknowledge him as such. If so, it settles the question in our mind, as fully as though we had compared all the facts of his admission with the established rules and usages of that church.

Now, this is what I mean by the application of our tests to particular churches. We first ask of any one, was it founded by an Apostle? If answered in the negative, we ask by what Apostolic Church it was founded—from which branch of the original Vine is it an offshoot; and if we find that Church acknowledging its claims, we need not doubt that the younger Church was founded in conformity with the fundamental principles of the extension of the Church, any more than we should if we had carefully examined into the facts of its early history. We presume that the Church knew the principles of her own identity and extension; we know that she knew the facts of the case under consideration, and we are willing to abide in her judgment, expressed by the acknowledgment of communion. A traveller meets a clergyman and asks him to what denomination the parish to which he ministers belongs. He says the Presbyterian, (Old School,) and on inquiry it is found that he and his parish are acknowledged regularly to belong to the Presbytery within whose geographical limits it is situated. The traveller never doubts after this that the minister and his people are a true and legitimate branch of the Presbyterian church.

So, if the Protestant Episcopal Church claims to be a branch of the English Church, and the English

Church claims to be a branch of the Apostolic Church, and to have been founded by the Apostles, and those claims were admitted by the rest of the Church from the first, then we could not doubt that all that was essential to their integration with the Church founded by the Apostles, has been duly observed in regard to their origin as separate branches of it.

§ 11. The Church is an outward and visible institution. By the word we sometimes mean, the people who constitute the Church. At other times it is used to indicate those rites and elements of organization by which the members are associated and united in a body or church; but, in either view, it is a visible and tangible object.
The Church can be identified only by outward signs.

There are those, however, who think that wherever the Gospel is preached, and the Faith received, there we are to acknowledge the existence of the Church.

But evidently the Church and the Faith are not the same thing. The Faith, as a system of truth, may be intellectually received, and dogmatically taught, when the rites and sacraments which were designed to unite those who receive it and constitute them a church, are not used. The Church is not a mere multitude of believers. In order to be a church, they must have been baptized and live in some sort of fellowship, join in a worship, and be bound together by some common tie.

I have shown in the first chapter, that those elements of organization, which constitute the believers a church or society by themselves, have a value of their own. I have by no means exhausted that branch of the subject. Nor can I go into it fully here without going further into points that are purely theological in the stricter sense of the word, than I design to do.

If by the Faith, we mean simply the articles of truth that are to be believed, then manifestly the faith is not all of Christianity that is generally necessary to our salvation.

Without repeating what has already been said bearing directly on the importance of the Church; and without pausing to consider what the Scriptures say of certain rites, as Baptism and the Lord's Supper, which are parts of the Church; we will look, at present, only at its moral design. That design is the promotion of OBEDIENCE.

All the antecedent history of God's dealings with man point to this fact. All His Institutions and commands were to test, to secure and to promote, obedience. Moses declares that God led the Israelites through the wilderness forty years, that "He might prove them and know what was in their heart, whether they would keep His commandments or no."[1] The prosperity and the adversity of the Jews depended upon their obedience or disobedience. And when Saul had broken the law of God and saved a portion of the spoil of the Amalekites, only that he might offer it to God, Samuel thus reproves him: "Hath the Lord as great delight in burnt offerings and sacrifices as in obeying the voice of the Lord? Behold, to obey, is better than sacrifice, and to hearken, than the fat of rams."[2]

So in the Christian Dispensation. The primary

---

[1] Deut. viii. 2.   [2] 1 Sam. xv. 22.

duty of the Apostolic commission was to preach the Gospel.[1] Yet, as St. Paul says, the preaching of the Gospel itself was only a means to a further end, namely *"for the obedience of the Faith."*[2] And he assures us that he was called to the Apostleship " for *obedience to the faith* among all nations."[3] St. Peter writes to those who were "*Elect according to the foreknowledge of God, the Father, through sanctification of the Spirit, unto obedience* and the sprinkling of the blood of Jesus Christ."[4] Our Blessed Lord became the Author of salvation only to those that *obey* Him.[5] St. Peter asks "What shall the end be of them that *obey not* the Gospel?"[6] And finally, St. Paul speaks of our Lord's taking vengeance at His second coming, on them " that *obey not* the Gospel."[7]

Now, in all these passages and in many more like them, the importance is attached, not to hearing or believing the Gospel merely, but to obeying it.

The faith, therefore, is not the only thing that is essential, either for the identity of the Church or for the salvation of its members. Obedience to the positive institutions and commands of the Gospel is essential also: and the Faith itself is promulgated for the promotion of this obedience.

The first act of sin committed on the face of the earth, was (so far as we can see, or are informed) simply an act of disobedience to a positive command or institution. In the act itself, aside from the commandment of God respecting it, there was nothing that is repugnant to human nature. Nor could any

---

[1] Mark xvi. 15. [2] Rom. xvi. 26. [3] Rom. i. 5. [4] 1 Peter i. 2.
[5] Heb. v. 9. [6] 1 Peter iv. 17. [7] 2 Thess. i. 8.

evil consequences be foreseen to flow from it except those that depended upon the divine threatening. It was, therefore, purely a test of obedience. And all the dealings of God with man since that time serve to enforce this precept of Holy Scripture already quoted, "BEHOLD, TO OBEY, IS BETTER THAN SACRIFICE, AND TO HEARKEN, THAN THE FAT OF RAMS."

Hence all the orders and subordinations of men. Children are commanded to obey their parents[1]. Servants are commanded to obey their masters[2]. Wives, their husbands[3]—citizens, their rulers,[4] and Christians, their pastors.[5] Nor are the recognized limits of the obligations to obedience always coincident with the justice and right of the thing commanded. Children and servants are commanded to obey "in all things."[6] St. Peter says, "Servants be subject to your masters, with all fear: not only to the good and gentle, but also to the froward; for this is thankworthy, if a man *for conscience toward God* endure grief and suffering wrongfully. For what glory is it if when ye be buffeted for your faults, ye shall take it patiently? but if when ye do well and suffer for it ye take it patiently, this is acceptable to God."[7] So too, in religious matters, notwithstanding all the corruptions and hypocrisy of the Scribes and Pharisees, our Lord commanded "the multitude," "All, therefore, whatsoever they bid you observe, that observe and do, but do ye not after their works, for they say and do not."[8] And the reason

---

[1] Eph. vi. 2. Col. iii. 20.
[2] Col. iii. 22.
[3] Eph. v. 22. Col. iii. 18. 1 Peter iii. 1.
[4] Rom. xiii. 1–5. Tit. iii. 1.
[5] Heb. xiii. 7, 17.
[6] Col. iii. 20, 22.
[7] 1 Pet. ii. 18, 19, 20.
[8] Matt. xxiii. 3.

given for this commandment is, that "the Scribes and Pharisees sat in Moses' seat," that is, in the place of office and authority over them.

Now, most manifestly the spirit of obedience is one of the most essential things in Christianity—so essential, (as is evident from what has been quoted,) as to be a justification, on the part of those who obey, for many things, which otherwise are not as they ought to be. JEREMY TAYLOR remarks, "neither can I be confident that I am wise in any thing, except when I obey; for then I have the wisdom of Him whom God has placed over me for my warrant if I am right, or my excuse if I am wrong."

Now the Church is most intimately connected with Obedience. The Church implies positive institutions—an outward visible existence. It implies not merely the preaching and hearing the Gospel, but the keeping the commandments of God—the public profession before men—the denying one's self and taking up his cross, that he may walk in the way of the Lord's appointing, and not in the way of his own choosing. It implies meekness, humility, submission, and obedience. It implies the exercise of those virtues on which depend the harmony, the peace, and the happiness of Heaven. And each positive institution that enters as a component part of the Church's constitution on earth, is designed to train us to take our place with the Cherubim and Seraphim among the orders and subordinations of the Church in Heaven. His Bible alone—whether read in the privacy of his own closet or preached to him by the chance visitations of some one gifted with utterance in divine things, is not all that man needs—is not all that his Saviour has provided for him. He needs a home—a communion of saints—a fellowship of kindred minds—a co-operation of sympathising hearts. There is a trial of his humility, his submission, and of his self-denial, which His Lord calls him to make—a testing of his fitness for Heaven, as well as a school to train him in that fitness. Man needs not only to be forgiven, but to be brought back to the state of obedience from which he has rebelled. Obedience can be tested only by outward institutions and commands, to which the conscience shall bend and habituate the will and the affections. It cannot be tested by mere subjective emotions or internal desires.

That the Church has an importance, therefore, independent of the importance of the Faith, is undeniable. The Church is Christianity located and put in practice. It is a body of men believing the Doctrines, and observing the Rites and Duties of Christianity. It is the fellowship of the Disciples—the test of our faith, and of our obedience to God.

Let it then be distinctly kept in mind, that we are seeking to identify the Church, and not the Faith. We should identify the Faith by first seeking out the earliest *Creed*, and then follow that creed in its adoption or rejection through the lapse of ages, carefully noting every variation in its language, and in the sense in which it was understood and believed. But in identifying the Church, we start with the idea that the Church is a visible society of men and women, capable of a visible historic existence through successive generations, as they pass over the stage of human action.

And when we have thus outwardly and historically

identified the Church, we may entertain a presumption almost as strong as certainty itself, that we shall find in its teaching "the Faith once delivered unto the Saints." At all events we have found the casket in which the jewel was placed—the keeper and witness to whom the Truth was entrusted, and whose testimony we are bound to take into consideration in all our inquiries after the Truth itself.

CHAPTER III.

THE CHURCH BEFORE THE REFORMATION AND ITS CONDITION AT THAT TIME.

The full execution of my plan would require me to go over the whole history of the planting and extension of the Church from the day of Pentecost up to the present time, and show the application of the principles laid down in a previous chapter throughout. But this, as will be seen at once, would require a great deal of dry detail which would have no immediate bearing upon the immediate practical result to which I design to bring my present undertaking. It will be borne in mind, that while I have laid down the principles by which to identify the Church in general, I am aiming to give to the present discussion of the subject such a shape as to enable one with certainty to identify the Church *here* in these United States, from amidst so many claiming sects. I shall select my portions of the history of the Church for the application of my principles with this view; leaving out all others as having no immediate connection with the object more immediately before us.

The Apostles, in executing their mission of preaching the Gospel, first settled in the principal towns and cities, establishing a Church in each, which was left to

CHAP. III.] CHURCH BEFORE THE REFORMATION. 65

grow until it should extend the dominion of Christ's Earthly Kingdom over the surrounding country, and meet the efforts of the Church planted in the next city spreading the Gospel in like manner over its surrounding territory. These Churches were at first independent of one another. And if we would follow out the history of their planting, we should find the three Principles already laid down fully and exactly followed.

§ 1. But instead of following the long detail of the history of their planting, it may be both more satisfactory and more interesting to quote a few passages from the early Christian writers to show that the principles to which I have called attention, were then substantially regarded in the same light as I have aimed to place them. Of course, it will not be expected that they were then stated in the way that I have stated them; for there was then no occasion for such a statement. The principles were not disputed nor denied, and needed not to be stated in either an argumentative or didactic way. All that we can expect therefore, is to find them recognised or assumed as unquestionably true. The evidence of the regard for these principles would be, perhaps most clearly manifested in such a work as EUSEBIUS's *Ecclesiastical History*, where he gives an account of the spread and perpetuation of the Church down to his own time, that is, through the first two centuries. In each case we find the historian carefully specifying the facts which show the conformity to these principles: and yet not in a way to imply that there was any dispute or doubt about them. But rather in such a way as to imply

<small>General proofs that the Principles laid down above, in Chapter II. were adhered to.</small>

that these were the essential facts, which it was well and important to put distinctly on record.

§ 2. The first passage that I will quote is from TERTULLIAN, who was converted to Christianity towards the close of the second century. In writing against Heretics, or, perhaps I had better say—concerning the rule by which we are to decide who are Heretics, he says: *Quotations from Tertullian.*

"Immediately, therefore, the Apostles (whom this title intendeth to denote as 'sent') having chosen by lot a twelfth, Matthias, into the room of Judas, on the authority of a prophecy which is in a Psalm of David, having obtained the promised power of the Holy Spirit, for the working of miracles and for utterance, first having throughout Judea borne witness to the faith in Jesus Christ and established Churches, next went forth into the world and preached the same doctrine of the same Faith to the nations, and forthwith founded Churches in every city from whence the other Churches thenceforward borrowed the tradition of the Faith [received the Faith] and the seeds of doctrine, and are daily borrowing them, that they may become churches. And for this cause they are themselves also accounted Apostolical, as being the offspring of Apostolical Churches. The whole kind must needs be classed under the original. Wherefore these Churches, so many and so great, are but that one primitive Church from the Apostles, whence they all spring. Thus all are the primitive, and all are Apostolical, while all are one."[1]

---

[1] DODGSON'S *Tertullian.* De. Præscrip Her. § xx.

And then in reference to others, he says :—

"If there be any heresies [sects] which venture to plant themselves in the midst of the age of the Apostles, that they may therefore be thought to have been handed down from the Apostles, because they existed under the Apostles, we may say, let them then make known the originals of their churches: let them unfold the roll of their bishops so coming down in succession from the beginning that their first bishop had for his ordainer and predecessor some one of the Apostles, or of the Apostolic men, that continued steadfast with the Apostles. For in this manner do the Apostolic Churches reckon their origin : as the Church of Smyrna recounteth that Polycarp was placed there by JOHN; as that of Rome doth, that Clement was in like manner ordained by PETER. Just so can the rest also show those, whom being appointed by the Apostles to the Episcopate, they have as transmitters of the Apostolic seed. Let the heretics invent something of the same sort. But even though they invent it, they will advance never a step : for their DOCTRINE, when compared with that of the Apostles, will of itself declare, by the difference and contrariety between them, that it had neither any Apostle for its author nor any Apostolic men: because, as the Apostles would not have taught things differing from each other, so neither would Apostolic men have set forth things contrary to the Apostles.   * * *
To this test, then, they will be challenged by those Churches, which, although they can bring forward as their founder no one of the Apostles or of Apostolic men, (as being of much later date, and indeed being founded daily,) nevertheless since they agree in the

same Faith, are, by reason of their consanguinity in doctrine, counted not the less Apostolical. So let all heresies when challenged by our Churches *to both these tests*, [to wit, their origin and their faith] prove themselves Apostolical in whatever way they may think themselves so to be. But in truth they neither are so, nor can they prove themselves to be what they are not, nor are they received into union and communion by Churches, in any way Apostolical, to wit, *because they are in no way Apostolical*, by reason of the sacred mystery which they teach."[1]

The "*mystery*"[2] here referred to is the Creed, which in other places the same author calls THE RULE OF FAITH. On this point he says:—

"An adulteration by the sense imposed [on the Scriptures] is as much opposed to the truth as a corruption by the pen." "To the Scriptures, therefore, we must not appeal: nor must we try the issue on points on which the victory is either none, or doubtful —or too little doubtful, [since the very doubt is their victory.] For though the debate on the Scriptures should not so turn out, as to place each party on an equal footing, the order of things would require that this question which is now the only one to be discussed, should first be proposed, namely: ' *To whom belongeth the very Faith; whose are the Scriptures; by whom, through whom, and where, and to whom was that Rule whereby men become Christians* [*The Apostles' Creed*] *delivered?*' For wherever both the true Christian

---

[1] *Tertullian* as above, § xxxii.
[2] *Musterium*. Σύμβολον, or CREED. Such were the names by which the *Apostles' Creed* is very generally denoted in the ancient writers.

Rule and Faith shall be shown to be, there will the true Scriptures be, and the true expositions and all the true Christian traditions."[1] And again, "If these things be so, so that THE TRUTH be adjudged to belong to us, as many as walk according to this Rule, [the Apostles' Creed,] which the Churches have handed down from the Apostles, the Apostles from Christ, Christ from God, the reasonableness of our proposition is manifest, which determineth, that heretics are not to be allowed to enter upon an appeal to the Scriptures whom we prove *without the Scriptures* to have no concern with the Scriptures.[2]

The reader will please bear in mind that I am not quoting TERTULLIAN for the sake of expressing my own ideas in another man's language, nor for the sake of approving all that he says. My object is to show that the Principles of Church extension which I have laid down, were constantly kept in view and regarded as sacred by the Church generally before the Reformation. For this purpose I continue my quotations a little farther.

§ 3. The next author that I shall quote is CYPRIAN, who had also been a heathen of eminence before he was converted. He died a Martyr, A.D. 258, Sept. 14.

Cyprian quoted.

"The Church is likewise one, though she be spread abroad, and multiplies with the increase of her progeny: even as the sun has rays many, yet one light; and the tree boughs many, yet its strength is one seated in the deep-lodged root; and as where many

---

[1] TERTULLIAN as above, § xix.   [2] § xxxvii.

streams flow down from one source, though a multiplicity of waters seem to be diffused from the bountifulness of the overflowing abundance, unity is preserved in the source itself. Part a ray of sun from its orb, and its unity forbids the division of light; break a branch from the tree, once broken it can bud no more; cut the stream from its fountain, the remnant will be dried up. Thus the Church flooded with the light of the Lord, puts forth her rays through the whole world, with yet one light, which is spread upon all places, while its unity of body is not infringed. She stretches forth her branches over the universal earth, in the riches of plenty, and pours abroad her beautiful and onward streams, yet is there one head, one source, one Mother abundant in the results of her fruitfulness."[1]

Again, the same author speaking of Novation, who had tried to get up a new church, says:

"He attempts to make a human church, and sends his new apostles through very many cities that he may establish certain recent foundations of his own institution." "And does any think that there can be, in one place, either many shepherds or many flocks? The Apostle Paul, likewise intimating the same unity, solemnly exhorts I beseech you brethren, by the name of our Lord Jesus Christ, that ye all speak the same thing, and that there be no schisms among you; but that ye be joined together in the same mind and in the same judgment. And again he says, 'forbearing one another in love, endeavoring to keep the unity of the spirit in the bond of peace.' Think you that any can

---

[1] CYPRIAN *De Unitate*, Oxford Trans. § 4.

stand and live who withdraws from the Church and forms himself a new home and a different dwelling?"[1]

§ 4. St. Chrysostom, a.d. 395, in writing his Homilies on the Epistle to the Galatians, on the expression "*churches of Galatia,*" thinks that St. Paul was referring to the sects that had been founded by the preachers of another Gospel. He notices that the Apostle does not call them "*the beloved,*" or "*the saints,*" nor even "*the churches of God,*" but simply "*churches of Galatia.*" "Here at the outset, as well as elsewhere, he attacks their irregularities and therefore gives them the name of '*churches*' in order to impress them and to reduce them to unity. For persons split into many parties cannot properly claim the appellation '*church,*' for the name is one of harmony and concord."[2]

Chrysostom quoted.

This exposition, as will be seen at once, is based upon the idea, that there could be only one Church in a place that could "properly claim the name." He seems not to have thought of the possibility of there being more than one in the same community, and therefore he gives the explanation which we find above.

Again he says:

"For this is, if anything, the subversion of the Church, the being in divisions. This is the Devil's weapon, this turneth all things upside-down. For so long as the body is joined into one, he has no power to get an entrance, but it is from division that the offence cometh."[3]

---

[1] Epist Lv. § 20 and *De Unitate* § 7.
[2] Commentary on Gal. i. 2.   [3] Hom. xxxii. on Rom. xvi. 17, 18.

My extracts are getting to be lengthy. But I must beg the reader to bear with me a few moments longer. I now quote from CYRIL, Bishop of Jerusalem, A. D. 350.

CYRIL of Jerusalem quoted. § 5. "While the Kings of particular nations have bounds set to their dominion, the HOLY CHURCH CATHOLIC alone extends her illimitable sovereignty over the whole world." "Now it is called *catholic* because it is throughout the world, from one end of the earth to the other, and because it teaches, universally and completely, one and all the doctrines which ought to come to men's knowledge, concerning things both visible and invisible, heavenly and earthly; and because it subjugates in order to godliness, every class of men, governors and governed, learned and unlearned; and because it universally treats and heals every sort of sins which are committed by soul or body, and possesses in itself every form of virtue which is named both in deeds and words and in every kind of spiritual gifts. And it is rightly named '*Church*,' because it *calls forth and assembles together* all men."[1]

The same author says also:

"But since the word '*Church*' or '*Assembly*' is applied to different things (as also it is written of the multitude in the theatre of the Ephesians, Acts xix. 41, and since one might properly say that there is a *church of the evil doers*) the Faith [the rule of Faith, or Apostle's Creed] has delivered to thee, by way of security, the Article, and in *One Holy Catholic Church*,

---

[1] Catchet. Lect. xviii. § 27, 23, 24.

that thou mayest avoid their wretched meetings and ever abide with the Holy Church Catholic in which thou wast born again. And if ever thou art sojourning in any city, inquire not simply where the Lord's House is, (for the sects of the profane also make an attempt to call their own dens '*Houses of the Lord*,') nor merely where the Church is, but where is the Catholic Church. For this is the peculiar name of this Holy Body, the Mother of us all, which is the Spouse of our Lord Jesus Christ, the Only Begotten Son of God."[1]

Here I close my quotations from individual authors, not, however, from want of much more like this, (for I could easily fill a volume,) but for want of room, and because I deem it unnecessary to proceed any farther.

§ 6. I will next call attention to another class of testimony, namely, the Canons of the Church. We have a series of Canons that were adopted some of them very early—and all of them received the sanction and approbation of the whole Church. From these only shall I quote. And I will begin with their definition of Heretics: *[side note: Canons quoted and referred to.]*

"And we include under the name of heretics those who have been formally cast off by the Church, and those who have since been anathematized by us, and in addition to these, those also, *who do indeed pretend to confess the sound Faith, but have separated themselves and founded congregations in opposition to our canonical Bishops.*"[1]

---

[1] Lect. xviii. § 26.   [2] Can. vi., Constantinople.

These Canons make provisions for persons going from one city or province to another, and being there received. But they never speak of going from one religious communion to another in the same community in that way. This shows first, that all the Churches in different places were in one communion, and secondly, that they recognised none as Churches of Christ that were not in the same communion with them, and finally, that there was but one Church in the same city.

They abound in laws prohibiting any of the clergy from separating from the Church to form separate congregations, distinctly repudiating all such from being in the communion of the Church.

They are full of restrictions preventing the people from praying, marrying, or having any religious associations with heretics.

I had designed to quote these Canons at length. But that will be unnecessary; as it is not from isolated Canons or here and there a pointed expression, that we can best judge of their bearing in this respect. The whole tenor and frame work of them is based upon the Principles of identification that I have already stated. To show this fully would require far more lengthy quotations than I have room for in this place, or than the reader's patience would hold out to examine.

I have not quoted or referred to these passages *as authority to give weight to what I have said*, but to show that these Principles were regarded in the Church so as that no society or assembly of persons calling themselves Christians, could have been received and acknowledged to be a part of the Church in violation of them. They would have been at once put down as heretics or schismatics—a new church on a human foundation not holding to the Head, and therefore not of the Body.[1]

§. At the time of the introduction of Christianity, the Roman empire included nearly the whole of the known world. This Empire was divided, in the first place, into *Dioceses*, which were the largest divisions. Each Diocese contained several *Provinces*, and these Provinces were again subdivided into *Parishes*. Each city was under the immediate government of certain magistrates within its own body, at the head of which was an officer called *Dictator* or *Defensor-civitatis*, and whose power extended not only over the city, but over all the adjacent territory, commonly called the προάστεια or παροικία [Parish,] the suburbs or lesser towns belonging to its jurisdiction. Such for the most part were the cities spoken of in the New Testament, in which we read of Churches being established. Each such city had a separate government by itself, and was, to a very great extent, independent of all others. This constitutes what in modern ecclesiastical language, is called a *Diocese*. Several of these divisions of the Empire conjoined into one, made the next larger division, or a *Province*, subject to the authority of one chief magistrate, who resided in the *metropolis*, or chief city of the *Province*.

The necessities of the Churches, to say nothing of

[1] Col. ii. 19.

the intention of their Founder, soon led to an association of the several Dioceses in a Province for purposes of mutual edification and helpfulness. All the early records of the Church speak of the Diocesan Churches as having one man at their head, called by a variety of names, "*Apostle*," "*Angel*," "*President*," "*Papa*," &c. &c., but more generally, and always in the Canons or laws of Discipline "*Bishop*," that is, "*overseer*"—to whom alone was reserved the right of ordaining the clergy. The very oldest canon or Church law, in existence, requires that for the Ordination of one of these Bishops, there should be at the least two or three Bishops present and assisting, while each Bishop was allowed alone and by himself to ordain the other clergy of his Diocese. In the same code, which, as I have already said is the earliest code that has come down to us—reaching back, as some of its Canons doubtless do, to near the time of the death of St. John the Apostle, it is ordained as follows:

" Let there be a meeting of the Bishops [in a Province] twice a year, and let them examine amongst themselves the decrees or canons concerning religion, and settle the ecclesiastical controversies which may have occurred."[1]

The Bishop of the metropolis of the Province was called *Metropolitan* or *Arch-Bishop*.

Hence the Council of Antioch, A. D. 341, ordains:

" It behoves the Bishops in every Province to own him who presides over the Metropolis, and who is to take care of the whole Province ; because all who have

---

[1] Apost. Can. xxxvii.

business come together from every side to the Metropolis. Wherefore, also, it has been decreed that he should have precedence of rank, and that the other Bishops should do nothing of consequence without him, according to the ancient Canon, which we have received from our Fathers: or at any rate, only those things which belong to each particular parish [Diocese in the modern sense of the word,] and the districts which are under it. For each Bishop is to have authority over his own Parish, [Diocese,] and to administer it with that piety which concerns every one, and to make provision for all the Districts which is under his City, to ordain Presbyters and Deacons, and to determine everything with judgment; but let him attempt nothing further without the Bishop of the Metropolis; and let him not do anything without the consent of others."[1]

Ere long, however, there was occasion for a still more extensive association, and the Bishops and Churches of several Provinces began to meet together. And then the several provinces in one of the larger divisions of the Empire, called a Diocese, as they then used the term, were associated in a sort of ecclesiastical union, and the Bishop of the chief city was called a "*Patriarch*," or "*Exarch.*"

Of this subdivision of the Church we find many proofs in the early Canons. The Council of Chaledon [A. D. 451,] decreed that

"If any [Bishop] is wronged by his Metropolitan, he is to be judged by the Exarch of the Diocese," or by the Emperor.[2]

---

[1] Can. ix.
[2] Can. ix. xvii.

Yet even among these Patriarchs there must needs be some order of precedence. The first Council of Constantinople, A. D. 381, therefore decreed—

"That the Bishop of Constantinople shall have the Primacy of Honor, after the Bishop of Rome, because that Constantinople is New Rome."[1]

The Council of Chalcedon, A. D. 351, also decreed that—

"Following in all things the decisions of the Holy Fathers, and acknowledging the Canon [of Constantinople just read,] they do also determine and decree the same things respecting the privileges of the most Holy city of Constantinople, New Rome. For the Fathers properly gave the primacy to the Throne of the Elder Rome, because that was the imperial city."[2]

The Emperor JUSTINIAN decreed to the same effect:

"We decree according to the decision of the Canons, that the most Holy Archbishop of the elder Rome, should be altogether first of all the Priests, and that the most Holy Archbishop of Constantinople, which is New Rome, should have the second rank after the most holy Apostolic throne of the elder Rome."[3]

What was here conferred upon the Bishop of Rome, was, however, only a *"primacy in honor,"* and *"precedence in rank;"* it was no superiority of jurisdiction and conferred no authority over those of whom it gave him the right to take the precedence.

§ 8. The jurisdiction of the Bishop of Rome at this time, was bounded on the North by the Patriarchate of Milan,[4] that is, about the parallel of North

---

[1] Can. iii. [2] Can. xxviii. [3] *Novell* 131. c. 2.
[4] Theodoret Eccl. Hist. B. H. c. XV. compared with Athanasius Epist. ad Solitar, in Bingham, B. IX. c. 1.

Latitude, 44 degrees, and extended south, including the Peninsula of Italy, and the Islands of Sardinia, Corsica, and Sicily. Beyond these limits he was not acknowledged to have any more authority than any other foreign Bishop whatever. *The limits of the Jurisdiction of the Bishops of Rome in the early ages.*

At the latter end of the fourth century the Church was thus subdivided, according to Bingham.[1]

I. The *Patriarchate* of Antioch with	15 Provinces	&	15 Arbps.
II. Alexandria	6	"	6 "
III. Ephesus	11	"	11 "
IV. Cæsarea	11	"	11 "
V. Heraclea, afterwards Constantinople	6	"	6 "
VI. Thessalonica	6	"	6 "
VII. Sardica	5	"	3 "
VIII. Milan	7	"	4 "
IX. Rome	10	"	3 "
X. Sirimium	6	"	uncertain.
XI. Carthage	6	"	6 "
XII. Spain, Exarchate uncertain	7	"	7 "
XIII. Gallia, Exarchate uncertain	17	"	17 "

XIV. Great Britain, Exarchate York, if any, with five provinces, and probably three Archbishops, York, London, and Caerleon.

The foregoing table shows the subdivisions of the Church at that early period, and it will be useful to

---

[1] Antiquities, vol. iii. p. 7.–12.

bear it in mind when we come to read the following Canon with respect to encroachments made by any ambitious Bishop over other parts of the Church than those which rightly belonged to him.

<small>PATRIARCHS *prohibited* from extending *their jurisdiction*.</small> § 9. In almost every Council anterior to that at Ephesus A. D. 431, there had been something said to prevent the ambition of the Bishops from going beyond their limits to extend their authority over others. In this state of things the Council of Ephesus passed the following law :—

" The most beloved of God and our fellow Bishop Rheginus, and Zeno, and Euagrius, the most religious Bishops of the province of Cyprus, who were with him, have declared unto us an innovation which has been introduced contrary to the laws of the Church and the Canons of the Holy Fathers, and which effects the liberty of all. Wherefore, since evils which effect the community [i. e. the whole Church] require more attention, inasmuch as they cause greater hurt, especially since the Bishop of Antioch has not so much as followed an ancient custom in performing ordinations in Cyprus, as those most religious persons who have come to the holy Synod have informed us, by writing and by word of mouth, we declare that they who preside over the holy Churches which are in Cyprus, shall preserve, without gainsaying or opposition, their right of performing by themselves the ordinations of the most religious Bishops, according to the Canons of the Holy Fathers, and the ancient custom. The same rule shall be observed *in all the other* Dioceses, and in the Provinces, *everywhere*, so that none of the most religious Bishops shall invade *any other* Province which has not heretofore *from the beginning*, been under the hand of himself, or his predecessors. But if any one has so invaded a Province, and brought it by force under himself, he shall restore it, that the Canons of the Fathers may not be transgressed, *nor the pride of secular dominion be privily introduced under the appearance of a sacred office, nor we lose by little and little the freedom which our Lord Jesus Christ, the Deliverer of all men, has given us by His blood.* The holy and œcumenical Synod has therefore, decreed, that the rights which have heretofore, and from beginning, belonged to each Province, shall be preserved to it pure and without restraint, according to the custom which has prevailed of old, each Metropolitan having permission to take a copy of the things now transacted for his own security. But if any shall introduce any regulation contrary to what has been now defined, the whole holy and œcumenical Synod has decreed that it shall be of no effect."[1]

Towards the close of the ninth century, Leo Sapiens the *Emperor*, caused a catalogue of the Bishoprics to be made. This is given by Bingham.[2] The order of precedency of the Patriarchates is—1. Rome; 2. Constantinople; 3. Alexandria; 4. Antioch; 5. Ælia, or Jerusalem. Even so late as this, England was not included within the Patriarchate, or jurisdiction of Rome. But of this we shall see more when we come to speak of the Reformation in England.

§ 10. Thus was the Church of Christ—while it

---

[1] Can. viii. [2] Vol. iii. p. 186, et seq.

In what sense constituted one Church and in what sense many Churches. constituted one Body, one Church, divided and subdivided, each part being in perfect union, communion, and harmony, with each other. And when, therefore, the ancient writers spoke of *Churches* in the plural number, they always meant these subdivisions, one, and one only, of which existed in the same place, and not as we now do, the several denominations or churches in the same place.

Sketch of the Extension of the Church before the Reformation. § 11. In accordance with the Principles already discussed, and which as we have seen, were entertained by the Church universally, the communion of the Church was extended from its first establishment up to the time of the Reformation with a progressive growth from century to century, until it covered the whole of Europe—the Western part of Asia, and the Northeastern part of Africa.

Thus the Church was established in Asia Minor by the Apostles A. D. 40-50. St. Mark, the Evangelist, established it in Egypt. In the fourth century Frumentius was consecrated by St. Athanasius as the first Bishop of Ethiopia. And in the same century the Gospel was preached in Armenia, Iberia, Thrace, Moesia, and Dacia. Two missionaries, Columban and Wilibord—the former from Ireland, and the latter from England, planted the Church to a considerable extent in many parts of Germany—Batavia, Friesland, Westphalia and Denmark in the seventh century. In the eighth century Nestorian Missionaries from Chaldea converted the Tartars. In the ninth century the Church made its way into Austria, Sweden and Russia.

In the tenth it became established in Poland, Hungary and Denmark. Of course it did not reach the Western Continent until the sixteenth century, or afterwards.

Thus we see that the Church was never stationary—but always progressing in its extension. Many of the nations which we have named above were not wholly converted at the time specified, and the work of their conversion continued many years (in some cases more than a century) before it was completed.

§ 12. The ravages of Mahometanism had obscured and greatly marred a part of the Church, and the strifes between the Bishops of Rome and of Constantinople for the supremacy or precedence had led to a division or schism. Russia and the east of Europe, including Greece and the west of Asia, and the northeast part of Africa were on the one side, and Europe, from Austria west was on the other. The former part is usually known as the Greek Church. The latter as the Western or Roman Church. *[The Church divided at the commencement of the Reformation into two Grand Divisions.]*

The Roman Communion therefore consisted of several national or provincial Churches, which had been brought in some way to acknowledge the supremacy of the Bishop of Rome as Pope. He and they had arrogantly appropriated to themselves the title of "*Catholic,*" and declared obedience and submission to the Pope indispensable to God's favor.

Among those Churches which had been brought into this subjugation was the Church of England. Planted in that Island in the days of the Apostles, and probably by an Apostle's own labors—ST. PAUL—it maintained its perfect freedom from all foreign jurisdiction or interference for four or five centuries—until after the Saxon invasion. The Island was then reconverted in part, by Missionaries, sent thither from Rome, who, of course, brought with them a Roman influence, which, by one means and another, was increased, until near the time of the Reformation. Of course, therefore, the Church of England partook of the darkness and corruptions of the middle ages. While the Eastern Churches which had never acknowledged the Papal Supremacy, had not become nearly so corrupt.[1]

At the Reformation then, we have the Church in what, for convenience sake, may be called two communions—the Eastern or Greek, and the Western or Roman—nearly equal in point of numbers—and both equally parts of the original vine, planted in accordance with the Principles to which our attention has been called. They were divided by events that occurred long after they were established, and not by the very fact of their origin. The Reformation—which took place in a part of the Western or Roman part of the Church—constituted still another division, as we shall soon see, so as that after that event the whole Church Catholic will be found divided into three parts or communions, the Greek, the Roman, and the Reformed.

§ 13. It would be unnecessary, so far as the practical result of our present undertaking is concerned, to refer to any of the sects which existed before the

---

[1] The independence of the English Church of the Romish Supremacy in the first centuries, and the means by which that supremacy was acquired, will be considered more at length in a future Chapter.

Reformation, were it not for the fact, that some of our modern sects refer to them, and especially to the *Waldenses* and *Albigenses*, as the link of visible union and connection between themselves and the Primitive Church Catholic. These sects have also served many modern speculators another very convenient turn. After having come to the conclusion that the Churches in the Roman Obedience are apostate, it is necessary to point to something that might be regarded as the continuation of the Church, notwithstanding this apostacy; and, as if forgetting the whole Eastern half of the Church, these writers have fixed upon the Waldenses and Albigenses as answering the demands of their theory. It becomes necessary, therefore, for these two reasons, to give these Sects a passing notice. *All the early sects had become extinct or nearly so.*

§ 14. And here it becomes important to call attention to the distinction between sects *in* the Church and sects *out* of the Church. A sect *in the Church* is a class, or number of persons, holding and advocating peculiar views of their own, but without separating themselves from its communion, or attempting to hold meetings, form congregations, and have a ministry, and, in fact, becoming a church by themselves. They may be denounced, excommunicated, and persecuted with inquisitions, fire and sword; and though, in the common use of language, they must be called a sect, yet, notwithstanding all this, they *may be* only the meek, uncompromising adherents to the Faith once delivered to the Saints; and when the awards of the final day shall show every man's work what it is—they will be *A distinction between sects in the Church and sects out of it.*

seen with the crowns of confessors and martyrs upon their heads shining forth forever, like stars in the firmament of God's eternal glory. But when a class or number of persons, holding peculiar views, forsaking the communion and fellowship of the Church, set about originating one of their own, with separate meetings and congregations, separate ministers and ministrations, claiming to be a church by themselves, they are a sect outside of the Church. And though their faith and usages may be in perfect accordance with the Apostlic pattern, yet they, as a church or society, are new and distinct from that which existed before them.

There were sects of both kinds before the Reformation; and we shall probably find the Waldenses a sect answering to the former description, and the Albigenses one answering to the latter. Those of the earlier centuries had passed away and become extinct: there were also some divisions among the branches of the Greek or Eastern Church. But with neither the sects of the earlier centuries, nor with the divisions and alienations of the Greek Church do we need now to concern ourselves. The Albigenses and Waldenses seems to be the only ones that demand our attention.

The ALBI- § 15. The *Albigenses* seem to have been a GENSES. sect who were at first called *Paulicians*, and are said to have been *Manichæans* also in their religious opinions. The Paulicians are a sect " said to have been founded in Armenia [a country in Asiatic Turkey] by two brothers, *Paul* and *John*, the sons of *Callinice*, of Samosata, and said to have received its name from them: some, however, derive it from one

Paul, an Armenian, who lived in the reign of Justinian II."[1] About the middle of the eighth century, (752. *Cedrenus*,) *Constantine*, surnamed *Copronymus* by the worshippers of images, had made an expedition into Armenia, and found in the cities of Melitene and Theodosiopolis a great number of Paulicians, his kindred heretics. As a favor, or a punishment, he transplanted them from the banks of the Euphrates to *Constantinople* and *Thrace*; and by this emigration their doctrine was introduced and diffused in Europe."[2] "From *Bulgaria* and *Thrace*, some of this sect, either from zeal to extend their religion, or from weariness of Grecian persecution, removed first into Italy, and then into other countries of Europe; and there they gradually collected numerous congregations, with which the Roman Pontiffs afterwards waged very fierce wars."[3] "*Albigesium* was the name given to the whole territory of the Viscount of Albi, Beziers, Carcassone, and Rasez. Hence *Albigenses* became, from this time, the name,—at first for all those who fought against the crusaders, and then—for the *Cathari*,[4] or *Puritans*, as they called themselves."

I will now proceed to give some of their characteristic doctrines: That there are two Gods and Lords, the one good, the other evil; that the creation of all things visible and corporal was not by God the Father Almighty and the Lord Jesus Christ, but by the Devil

---

[1] Mosheim. Book III. cent. ix., Part II., cap. v., sec. 2.
[2] Gibbon's Decline and Fall. Ch. LIV.
[3] Mosheim. Cent. xi., Part II., cap. v., sec. 2.
[4] Giesler. Text Book of Ecc. ist. Ed. Philadelphia, 1836. Vol. ii. p. 385, 7.

and Satan, the evil god, who is the god of this world; that all Sacraments are vain and unprofitable. As to the Eucharist, they believe that there is nothing in it but mere bread. They condemn Baptism by water, saying that a man was to be saved by the laying on of hands upon those that believed *them*. They allow of no ministry. They say that marriage is always sinful and cannot be without sin. They hold that our Lord did not take a real human body, nor real human flesh of our nature; and that He did not really rise with it, nor do other things relating to our salvation. They affirm that the Virgin Mary was not a real woman, "but their church, which is true penitence; and that this is the Virgin Mary." They deny the resurrection of the body, and hold that human souls are spirits banished from heaven on account of their sins.[1]

I will not go farther into an account of this sect. The "*Facts and Documents*" collected by MAITLAND, show beyond question, that they were, as he says, "either hypocritical impostors, or misguided fanatics," or both, aiming at no good for mankind; and so far from being characterized for true piety and zeal against the errors of their times, they were given to sensuality and selfishness.

After what has been said, it will hardly be necessary to add anything more to show that no modern sect can gain anything in point of respectability or ecclesiastical identity with the Church of Christ, from an alliance with the Albigenses. They neither claimed, nor were acknowledged, to be a part of that identical,

---

[1] Abridged from LIMBORCH, in Maitland's Facts and Documents, p. 233–241.

visible society which had existed from the days of the Apostles, and was planted by their labors.

§ 16. "The early history of the Waldenses *The Waldenses.* is, indeed, involved in some obscurity; but it seems clear, beyond all reasonable doubt, that they owed their name, and their origin as a sect, to a certain citizen of Lyons, [Peter Waldo,] who lived at the latter half of the twelfth century [1160.] It appears, also, that he caused the Scriptures to be translated into the vulgar tongue; that he and his immediate followers drew upon themselves the censure and persecution of the Church, not only by taking upon them the office of teaching, but by some of the doctrines which they taught."[1] "It does not appear that *Waldo* and his *immediate* followers contemplated a separation from the Church, but rather a revival of personal religion within its pale, and a removal of some abuses and superstitions. * * * It seems clear, from the statements, or (what is even more important) the silence, of their persecutors and their own confessions, (that is, from all the sources of information that we possess,) that opposition *was not* directed against *some* of the peculiar doctrines of the Romish Church."[2] For instance, they held firmly to the doctrine of Transubstantiation, and believed that each individual could perform the service of the Mass. There is reason to believe that Waldo designed to form a new religious Order, like the Monks or Friars, under the sanction of the Romish See, but failed in his object.

We have before us, then, the Waldenses, or a sect

---

[1] Maitland's Facts and Documents, p. 467.   [2] p. 469.

within the Church, differing in many respects from its doctrines, yet agreeing with it in many of its peculiar characteristics—submitting to its opposition and persecution. But besides these, many of them were scattered abroad by the persecutions, became associated with the Albigenses, and were dispersed over the greatest part of Europe. There they remained until the Reformation, and were among the first to join that movement. This fact will go far to account for the confusion of names which so often occurs in speaking of these people.

Of that part of the followers of Waldo which joined the Albigenses, and by which the doctrines of the latter were much modified, we need not say anything further. Ecclesiastically they became the same "*people*," a part of the same sect, bearing the same relation to the identity of the Church as the Albigenses themselves.

But, of the other part of the Waldenses, we need say nothing further than that, as a sect *in the Church*, they had ceased to exist before the commencement of the Reformation. But if they had not, they would not require to be considered as a distinct branch of the Church, since they formed no church by themselves.

So far, then, as our present purpose is concerned, we may regard these two sects, that is, the Albigenses and the Waldenses, except that portion of them which never separated from the Church of Lyons, as being but one. Shall we now claim for them the name and character of a Church, properly so called? They were not the Church of Albigesium—that Church was established long before the emissaries from Thrace came thither with their peculiar doctrines; they neither claimed nor received communion with the Church of Albi—were in no way merged in or identified with it while they remained—but always continued to be a distinct, a rival, and an opposing body. They were a sect of human origin at the first, and that they continued to be, until they were lost in the sects which arose at the time of the Reformation.

§ 17. It is evident, therefore, that nothing can be gained by any modern sect in the point of identity with the Church of Christ, from a connection with the Albigenses or Waldenses. They constituted no distinct part of the Church—no branch of the original vine. As a church they had not existed from the Apostle's days, in a distinct individual capacity; and therefore they were not of Apostolical origin. They never were in communion with any part of the Apostolical Church for a moment, from the very commencement of their existence as a sect. They never held or claimed the ecclesiastical jurisdiction of any one portion of the habited globe; but were always a sect living within the limits of, and in opposition to, a branch of the Church whose catholicity was unquestioned by them, and whose right to jurisdiction is undeniable.

These Sects formed no Legitimate Branches of the Church.

The efforts of Waldo and his immediate followers, so far as they aimed only at a reformation, and the restoration of pure religion, cannot fail to elicit our most cordial sympathy. But we must not attribute to him an infallibility, nor let our admiration and approbation of his course follow him any farther than he followed the only infallible Standard and Guide of human actions. I readily concede, that his views were a vast improvement upon the Church dogmas of the age and country in which he lived. But when he consented to become the founder of a sect—to lay an "other foundation" whereon for others to build—he violated a fundamental law of God, which every sect and denomination of our land sanctions by its own use. It is the law of unity. Take the case of any village or community in which there is a parish of Presbyterians, Baptists, Methodists, or Congregationalists even, sufficient to accommodate all the persons of that way of thinking in that place, and where there is no prospect of an increase of numbers, and what they have are only sufficient for the support of the ministrations of the one parish: and none of these denominations will allow their members to form a new parish in that place—necessarily weakening, as it will the old one—presenting an occasion for inevitable rivalry, opposition, and contention, between those who are thus unnecessarily divided. The organized seceders would not be recognized in such a case as a church of their denomination, nor allowed a seat in their Council, Presbytery, Conference, or whatever may be the name by which they designate their deliberative body next above the parish.

Now, assuredly we cannot deny that the Church of Christ has the power which these sects claim for themselves to preserve its unity, and protect itself from the identification with itself of other bodies heterogeneous to its own, and containing principles fundamentally repugnant to those on which its existence depends.

I am aware that I have given an account of the

Waldenses and Albigenses somewhat different from those which are the most popularly received. The truth of the case is, that but little has been known about these sects until quite lately. And writers who felt the awkwardness of their position in advocating the ecclesiastical character of churches unconnected with the past, as well as those, who, though they were in no such position, were nevertheless bent on making out the theory that regards the Church of Rome as the Anti-christ spoken of in the Scriptures, and needed these sects for the "*two witnesses*," have seized upon here and there, a fact or an isolated expression, and in some cases even drawn upon their fancy for facts, to make out such an account of them as would best subserve the purposes of their respective theories. But the publication of "*the Facts and Documents*" relating to them by Mr. MAITLAND, has revealed a state of facts which yields but little support to those theories, and has completely dissipated the hopes of their advocates. It is from this source that the foregoing account of those mediæval sects has been chiefly derived.

§ 18. Before proceeding any further in our attempt to identify the Church since the Reformation, in order to make our way perfectly sure before us, we must pause and consider whether the Church had become apostate at or before the time when the Reformation commenced. That darkness, gross darkness, corruption, and superstition, had covered, as it were, the face of the earth, admits of no denial. It is the opinion of some, that "there was a time when the Church was so essentially cor-

<small>The Church had not become apostate.</small>

rupt, that she ceased to be a Church of Christ, and her officers ceased to be ministers of Christ." If so, then, any connection with the past, through that channel, can be of no avail.

We might here enter a plea of exception in favor of the Eastern Churches, on the ground that they were not involved in the same corruptions as the Churches as in the Roman Obedience. But it is unnecessary to attend to that suggestion here, for several reasons. Those that bring this charge against the Churches in the Roman Obedience, extend it also to those in the East. And besides, none of the sects that we shall notice claim to have been derived from the Eastern Church.

Now, looking at the Church simply as a visible society, we may say that it is not apostate, or extinct, so long as it has within itself the powers of recovery and reformation. If it has the Ministry and the Scriptures, it is competent to all the ecclesiastical fuctions necessary to life and vigor. Now, that the Churches in the Roman Obedience were capable of reformation, is a position that has never been denied, that I know of, and I presume it never will.

That the Church was not apostate, proved from the Scriptures. § 19. In the Book of the Prophet DANIEL[1] is a prediction that, at a time then sufficiently indicated, "the God of Heaven would set up a kingdom, which shall never be destroyed; and the kingdom shall not be left to other people, *and it shall stand for ever.*"

Now, when we remember that the time indicated

---
[1] ii. 44.

in this prophecy was the time of our Saviour—that, in the Gospels, the religious society, or estate, which He had come to establish, is called the kingdom of God—how He began by preaching that the kingdom had come[1]—how he declared to His disheartened followers, for their encouragement, "Fear not, little flock, for it is your Father's good pleasure to give unto you the kingdom,"[2]—and how, as He left the world, he appointed unto His Apostles a kingdom as His Father had appointed unto Him[3]—there seems to be no room left to doubt that the kingdom spoken of by the Prophet DANIEL was the one established by our Lord and His Apostles, and is what we and they generally call the Church. If so, the declaration of the Prophet is conclusive proof of two points:—namely, that the Church will not be destroyed, become apostate, or cease to exist as Christ's Church; and secondly, that it will not be left or given to another people—that it always will exist, and always may be traced or identified, by following the history of "*the people*" to whom it was at first given, and of whom it then consisted.

I might enlarge upon the bearing of this text, upon the importance of the identity of the Church, and upon the mode of identifying it which I have pointed out in the foregoing sections, and intend to pursue in those that follow. But leaving all this, I will refer only to its bearing on the one point before us. It proves that the Church had not become extinct, or lost its ecclesiastical character at the time of the Reformation, and will never become apostate.

---

[1] Mark i. 14.   [2] Luke xii. 32.   [3] Luke xxii. 29.

Again: Our Lord declared of His Church, that the gates of Hell should not prevail against it.¹ This passage implies, at the least, that the Church should not become extinct. If the language refers merely to a function of the Church, namely, that it should conduct to final salvation all souls that should be committed to its care and guidance, despite all the powers of Hell to the contrary—yet it must continue to be the true Church of Christ, in order to perform that function, as long as the function itself is to be performed; that is, until the Second Advent.

Once more: As our Lord was ascending to Heaven, He promised, "Lo, I am with you *always*, even unto the end of the world."² "*Always*" in the Greek, is "*every day*"—πάσας τὰς ἡμέρας.

In other connections, a very important question might here be raised, whether this promise was made to the Apostles, or to the Church at large. But, for our present purpose, the question is of no consequence; for if the promise was to either, it was to both; since the Ministry, as long as they were to continue at all, must remain in the Church, and inseparable from it.

If then the Lord has promised to be with the Church or its Ministry, "*always, every day*," unto the end of the world, it has not become apostate. It is not apostate, while He is with it; and His promise is for "every day unto the end of the world."

We may then admit that the Church had become very corrupt, at the commencement of the Reformation, without entertaining any fear that it had become

---

¹ Mat. xvi. 13. ² Mat. xxviii. 20.

apostate, or ceased to be the Church of Christ—the people to whom the Kingdom was given, and against which the gates of Hell should not prevail, and with whom He would be alway, even unto the end of the world.

§ 20. I am aware that it has sometimes been said that the promise has been fulfilled by the springing up of a new church whenever the old one had become apostate. Thus it is said that the *Albigenses* and *Waldenses* came into existence, as the deadening influences of apostacy were creeping over the Church, and when these sects became extinct, the *Baptists* and others arose in their place—and thus the divine promise has been fulfilled, and there has always been a church professing the pure doctrines of the Gospel. The promises to the Church cannot be fulfilled by transference.

The doctrinal purity of these sects is not a point that I wish now to discuss. But the divine declaration is, that "the Kingdom shall *not* be left to other people." And our Lord spoke of that Church which was established in His days, when He said that "the gates of Hell shall not prevail against it," and He promised to be "with it alway, (every day,) even unto the end of the world." The promise could not, therefore, be fulfilled by these sects rising up in the place of the Church after it had become apostate. Nay, it was to guard the minds of Christians against admitting the idea that the Church *could* become apostate—or that any sect *could* arise up to take its place, in the Divine Economy, that these declarations were made. "The gates of Hell," says our Blessed Saviour, "shall never prevail against that Church which *I* build upon *this* Rock—I will be with you alway even unto the end of the world, and when others come in my name doing many wonderful works [1] and saying, 'Lo here is Christ or Lo there,'[2] you will not believe them, neither go after them, for false prophets and false Christs will come and show great signs and wonders insomuch that, if it were possible they will deceive the very elect." The promise implies the identity of the Church to which it was made. It cannot be transferred to any other without utterly disregarding the language in which it was made. Nay, the very promise proves that the Church never can become apostate, and therefore no sect can arise to fill its place in the Divine Economy. Such a thing would show that the divine purpose had failed, the Omniscient Foresight had erred in its predictions, and the Arm of Omnipotent Power had not been able to defend His Church against the gates of Hell.

§ 21. The analogy of the Jewish history seems to me to be in point. That Church became very corrupt at several periods in its history; but, notwithstanding, it did not cease to be God's covenant people. We might mention several periods when it was, perhaps, fully as corrupt as the Churches in the Roman Obedience at the commencement of the Reformation, and yet it ceased not to be the Church of God.

The analogy of the Jewish Church.

Thus in the reign of King Ahaz, B. C. 728, the idolatrous religion of the Syrians was introduced even into Jerusalem itself Altars were erected to the

---

[1] Matt. xxiv. 24.   [2] Mark xiii. 21.

Syrian gods, or idols. The Temple itself altered in many respects according to a Syrian model, and finally it was shut up entirely.[1] Manasseh, B. C. 644, upheld idolatry by all the influence of regal power, erected idolatrous altars even within the Temple itself, set up an image which was worshipped with obscene rites, maintained a herd of necromancers, astrologers, and soothsayers of various kinds, and even sacrificed his own son to the idol Moloch.[2] And it appears that at the commencement of the reign of Josiah, B. C. 611, "the book of the law of the Lord,"—that is, the Scriptures—was almost wholly forgotten, and its contents unknown. Hilkiah appears to have discovered it among the rubbish in the Temple, and brought it to Shaphan the scribe, who examined its contents, and then brought it to the king, and read it before him. "And it came to pass, when the king had heard the words of the book of the law that he rent his clothes."[3] The whole account seems to imply as gross and as total an ignorance of God's revealed will as could possibly have prevailed in the Christian Church before the commencement of the Reformation. Even Hilkiah the high priest, seems to have known almost nothing of it.

The New Testament gives hardly a better account of the state of religious knowledge and opinion among the Jews in our Saviour's time. It is represented as "teaching for doctrines the commandments of men,"[4] and "making the word of God of none effect through their traditions."[5]

---

[1] JAHN's *Heb. Commonwealth*, Book V. § 41. [2] § 42.
[3] 2 Kings xxii. 11.   [4] Matt. 15. 9.   [5] Mark 7. 13

And yet the Jews were recognised and treated by our Saviour as the covenant people and Church of God. For this reason the Gospel was first preached to them; and it was not until after they had rejected the Messiah, crucified Him, and even refused to believe after He had risen from the dead and sent the Holy Ghost, thus completing all the evidence that could be given—that they became apostate from God, and cast off by Him. Then, and then only, were they abandoned to their impenitence and hardness of heart.

It was not, therefore, by their ignorance, as in the days of Josiah, nor by their idolatry, as in the days of Ahaz and Manasseh, that they became apostate, (though for these things they were sorely punished by the Babylonish captivity.) It was not by their superstition and hypocrisy, as in the days of our Saviour—it was not even for crucifying Him as a malefactor, that they fell from the estate to which they had been called. But it was for refusing to believe in Him after the fulness of evidence had been rendered complete by the miraculous gifts poured out on them that believed, on the day of Pentecost, that they ceased to be the chosen people of God.

Apostacy defined. § 22. From the foregoing reference to the case of the Jews, we shall be able to derive some idea of what is properly an apostacy. And in fact it will be necessary to get a pretty definite idea of what is an apostacy, before we can satisfactorily settle the question now before us.

Apostacy is not merely a great declension in doctrine and in manners. It is something more, and implies a total falling away from the Christian estate, or covenant with God. A writer of great authority, has defined *apostacy* to be "willingly casting off, and utterly forsaking both profession of Christ, and communion with Christians."[1]

And this definition, I apprehend, is as good as can be found. It corresponds with the etymological meaning of the word, and with its use in the New Testament. The word itself indicates an outward act, rather than an inward change of opinions or character.

Thus, people may apostatize *from the Church*, by separating from it, and forsaking its communion altogether. They may carry with them the Scriptures—they may (possibly) hold all the articles of the Christian Faith—they may administer Baptism and the Lord's Supper among themselves—and whatever may be their condition before their final Judge, they are none the less apostates from the Church than if they had not made any pretence of holding to the Faith.

But when a Church, or any branch of it, refuse to receive the Bible as the word of God—and to acknowledge the Christian Faith altogether—or if, instead of the Christian Scriptures, they should substitute the Alcoran, or the writings of Plato, as their chief authority and guide to faith and practice, they would of course apostatize from Christ.

But there may be much corruption and sin, much ignorance and degrading superstition, without apostacy.

§ 23. It cannot therefore be contended that the Church was apostate before the Reformation. It is probable that we have been so much accustomed to

---

[1] Hooker's *Two Sermons.* Serm. I. § 11.

The state of the Church in respect to apostacy - before the Reformation. dwell upon its errors and corruptions that these features in its character have contributed more than their proportion to the impression that we have received of it. At all events, we, for the most part, have heard but little said of those facts and features which go to show that it was not apostate.

Now, how much soever the legends of the saints, and the fabulous accounts of miracles may have usurped the place of the Scriptures in their public services—yet the Church had never professed to reject the Scriptures as the Word of God—they rather used these legends and notions because they supposed that they enforced what was contained in the Scriptures. They set up images and pictures in their churches and chapels—but it was only because they supposed that these things helped the devotions of the unlearned and were deserving of some reverence on account of their connection with what was truly the proper object of worship. Baptism and the Lord's Supper were not repudiated, nor neglected in their essential elements, though grossly misunderstood, and the administration of them loaded down with superstitious and foolish ceremonies. The Creed which had been adopted, and had received the sanction of the whole Church, before the division of the East and the West, known at the present as the NICENE CREED, had never been repudiated, nor had any *professed* departure from it been made, or proposed as a thing that was allowable. And the *Council of Trent*, 1546, begins by "setting forth a confession of faith," and recites the Nicene Creed, "as that symbol of Faith which the holy Roman

Church makes use of as being that principle wherein all who profess the Faith of Christ, *necessarily* agree, and that firm and only foundation, against which the gates of Hell shall never prevail." [1]

Likewise, in the ordination of the Ministry, though many unworthy men were doubtless ordained, yet the Church took good care to secure the outward forms of ordination, so as that the succession should not be lost.

But perhaps the strongest proof, on the whole, that they were not apostate, is the fact that a consciousness of their errors and corruptions, and a desire for reformation were so prevalent, and so frequently and so forcibly expressed. When a people are apostate, they have forsaken God, and He has forsaken them. Their prayers are no longer heard. Their sacraments are unaccompanied by any spiritual grace. Their discipline is without authority, and all the ordinary influences of the Spirit, are withholden. But the grace to confess their sins, and to repent, is always proof that the Spirit of God has not ceased striving with a people. There were doubtless hundreds and thousands who notwithstanding all their errors and ignorances, did nevertheless, in meekness and sincerity of heart, devote themselves to do the Lord's will. The accounts of the Church in that age with which we have been most familiar, have come to us through an unfriendly channel just as at the present day we often receive accounts of the English Church by persons unfriendly to it, which would lead us to suppose that there could be nothing good in it, if we did not know from other

---

[1] Sess. III.

sources that those accounts are an inadequate representation of the subject. The humble, the meek, the self-denying, who labor to be quiet, and do their own business as the Lord hath appointed them, seldom occupy a conspicuous place on the page of the historian or the traveller.

I freely grant that there was great ignorance of the truth as it is in Jesus—that their use of pictures and images was idolatry—their prayers to the saints a bestowing upon the creature the glory that was due to God alone—that their view of the Mass was inconsistent with the Atonement—their doctrine of Purgatory unscriptural—their views of absolution, of works of supererogation, and many others that we might name, were such as tended to render the commandments of God of none effect. But still they were not worse than the Jews had been—they had not *willingly and confessedly forsaken God*, and they had the grace to see their need of repentance and reformation, and many of them, at least, to set about it.

§ 24. There is one important consideration in relation to this subject to be derived from the history of the Council of Trent. This Council was not held until after the Reformation had commenced. The English Church took no part in it, and never assented to its doings. Now, until this Council, the Churches in the Roman Obedience were not committed to many of the worst abuses and corruptions which were then incorporated into their Rule of Faith. These abuses and corruptions were in existence, and had been approved and allowed by Provincial Councils; but their formal adoption of them,

The position of the Roman Church materially changed by the Council of Trent.

as necessary to salvation, at the Council of Trent, put the whole Roman Obedience into an entirely new position in its relation to the Catholic Church of Christ. And it would certainly be much more difficult to defend it against the charge of apostacy since that Council than before; that is, since the Reformation, than before. Until that time, they were historically a part of "*the people*" to whom the Kingdom was given— they had the Ministry and the Scriptures, and they had not formally and professedly set forth any new Rule of Faith peculiar to themselves, and excluding from the Christian estate, or condition, all who do not adopt their Rule.[1] But this Creed was not adopted until after the Reformation;—and whatever may be its effects upon the position of those that have adopted it, its adoption by the unreformed does by no means involve the reformed branches of the Church in its legitimate consequences.

§ 25. In conclusion, I will use the language of the Rev. Dr. LATHROP, late of West Springfield, Mass. The origin of the passage is worthy of note. He and his people had been imposed upon by a man claiming to be a minister of Christ. The Doctor wrote two sermons on Matt. vii. 15, 16, ["Beware of false prophets," &c.,] in which he occupied nearly the whole of the first Sermon in proving that "they who refuse to enter into the ministry in the way which the Gospel prescribes, are to be rejected: they have one plain mark of false teachers." The doctor considers "the way which the Gospel pre-

Dr. Lathrop quoted.

---

[1] I refer to the Créed of Pius IV., A. D. 1569, which will be given in a subsequent Section.

scribes" to be, ordination by those that were in the ministry before them. Perceiving that this position implied the necessity of an Apostolic Succession, and that the validity of such a succession depended upon the Church's not having become apostate before the Reformation, he adds to his sermons an Appendix, in which he discusses these points:

"Did the first Reformers, distrusting their past ordination, receive one from their lay brethren? The contrary is most evident. The Protestant Reformers in England early drew up a confession of their faith, in which, as Dr. Burnet says, 'they censure any who should take upon them to preach, or administer the sacraments, without having lawfully received the power from the *ministers*, to whom *alone* the right of conferring that power doth appertain.' Certainly they had no apprehension that the ministerial succession was at an end. . . . .

"Though corruptions early began in the Christian Church, yet their progress was gradual and slow. In every age many dissented from them; great opposition was made to them, and large councils of Bishops or ministers condemned them. The Western, or Roman Church ultimately carried her corruptions to a more extravagant height than the Oriental, or Greek Church; but even in the former, they never came to their crisis, until the famous Council of *Trent*, which was opened more than twenty and closed more than forty years after the beginning of Luther's Reformation. That Council, called by the Pope's bull, and supported by the Emperor's arms, in opposition to the Reformers established, as Dr. Tillotson says, 'several articles which had never before been acknowledged by any general council. Those new articles, if avowed by some, yet had not been generally received in their full extent, as now declared. If they had been decreed by one council, it was but a partial one, and they were soon after condemned by another; and, therefore, were not to be considered as the received and acknowledged doctrines of the Church. . . . .

"Luther and his associates, in their first opposition to the errors of the Roman Church, did not consider her as having *essentially* departed from the Gospel, or as being utterly disowned by Christ; for their primary object was not to withdraw from her, but to effect a Reformation by means which might preserve the general union. They never renounced her, until they and their adherents were excommunicated, and all hopes of union were cut off; but, on the contrary, demanded a *free* and *general* council, to deliberate on means of accomplishing the Reformation so much desired. When Luther was constrained to disclaim that Church, Dr. Mosheim observes, 'he separated himself from it, only as it acknowledged the Pope to be infallible; not from the Church, considered in a more extensive sense; for he submitted to the decision of the *universal* Church, when that decision should be given in a general council, lawfully assembled.' 'This,' says Dr. Maclaine, ' was a judicious distinction; for though the papacy was confounded with the Catholic Church [Roman,][1] they were in reality, different things. The

---

[1] It is surprising to see how generally writers have agreed in applying to the Roman branch of the Church the title "CATHOLIC" which belongs to the whole Church, as though the Roman were the whole and *only* Church.

papacy had, indeed, by degrees, incorporated itself into the Church; but it was a preposterous supplement, and as foreign to its genuine constitution as a new citadel, erected by a successful usurper, would be to an ancient city.'

"One cannot but feel the striking contrast between those ancient reformers who labored to correct the errors, without breaking the union of the Church, and certain modern pretenders, who in the first instance separated themselves from the churches, and then exclaiming against them as corrupt, promote and *encourage divisions in them.*

"It will, perhaps, be asked, 'How do we know but the first Reformers had been ordained by some of the vilest men in the Roman Church?' But let me ask, How do we know, or is it probable this was the case? The Reformers themselves appear to have entertained no scruples on this head. Let it still be remembered, that irregularity in ordinations was not made matter of complaint against her; and that her corruptions had not so recently risen to their height; and that she had not yet established, by a general council, her grossest errors, nor expunged her purest members.

"But admitting that a man of corrupt principle and morals, acts in an ordination, will his character nullify the transaction? As long as the Scribes sat in Moses' seat, Christ acknowledged them as officers of the Jewish Church; nor did He deny the authority of the High Priest, though his personal character was far from recommending him.

"The person ordained derives his authority to preach from Jesus Christ; not from the men who ordain him. They indigitate the person to be vested with this authority, and officially instal him in the regular exercise of it; but it is Christ's Gospel, not their will, which must direct him in the execution of his office. If they are corrupt in principles or manners, it will not thence follow that *he* must preach heresy or immorality. He is ordained to preach the Gospel; and whoever may ordain him, the charge which he receives, and the vow which he makes, bind him to teach not the commandments of men, but all things whatsoever Christ has commanded."[1]

I am sure my readers will pardon this long quotation from one, of whom it has justly been said, "Perhaps there was no minister in the whole circle of the Congregational churches of New England more respected by his cotemporaries, or who exercised greater influence among them," when he says so much that is to our present point so much better than I could say it myself.

§26. Suppose, now, that it be admitted that when it was first established, the Church was materially different in its constitution from what it was at the time of the Reformation, yet it is impossible to regard these departures— if they are to be considered as departures from the original plan at all—as apostacy—or ceasing to be the Church of Christ—for that Church, as we have seen from the Scriptures, cannot become apostate, Christ is *with it*, always, *every day*, even unto the end of the world.

There may be changes in the form of Church government without apostacy.

I am well aware that the great body of the Re-

[1] WAINWRIGHT's Ed. 1844, pp. 111—119.

formers, and, indeed, of the Protestants generally, have regarded the Pope as the Anti-Christ. Without either admitting or denying the correctness of the opinion in this place, I will only say that, if it be correct, it does not involve the conclusion, or admission, that the Churches subject to him are apostate. Whether the Pope be Anti-Christ or not, it is evident, from the Scriptures, that the Anti-Christ was to manifest himself in the Church; and, perhaps, I may say that it is equally as manifest, on a careful inspection of the prophecies concerning him, that the Church, over which he should usurp his authority, would not thereby become apostate, though subjugated to an antichristian power. The sheep which the wolf worries and rends, do not thereby become wolves. Nay, if the Pope is Anti-Christ, the very Reformation, which was a refusing to hear and obey him, is proof that the part, at least, which reformed, was not apostate, or involved in his condemnation.

The comparative size of the two Grand Divisions of the Church. § 27. We now come round again to the point that we occupied at the close of a preceding section. At the commencement of the Reformation the Church of Christ was separated into two communions. The Oriental Church prevailed in *Russia, Liberia, Poland, European Turkey, Servia, Moldavia, Wallachia, Greece, the Archipelago, Crete, Cyprus, the Ionian Islands, Georgia, Circassia, Mingrelia, Asia Minor, Syria, Palestine, and Egypt.*[1] The Western Church, or the Roman Obedience included, therefore the whole of

---

[1] PALMER's Treatise on the Church, Vol. I. p. 176, N. Y. Ed. 1841.

Europe, west of *Russia, Poland, and European Turkey.*

PALMER in his *Treatise on the Church*,[1] has entered into an interesting calculation of the relative portions of the Church that adhered to the two heads of this division. As the result of his computation, he says: "It is impossible to determine precisely, the number of Bishops on each side; but there is neither proof nor presumption, that *the majority* of the Church took part with the Roman Pontiff against the Greeks: and it is impossible to affirm with any certainty that the Western Churches were greater than the Eastern, up to the period of the Reformation."

[1] Vol. I. p. 198, et seq.

CHAPTER IV.

THE REFORMATION IN ENGLAND AND ITS EFFECTS UPON THE CONDITION OF THE CHURCH.

AMONG the separate and distinct subdivisions of the early Church, that of England was one. Nothing in history is more certain than the perfect and entire independence of the English Church of any foreign Bishop or Church for the first five hundred years. The best proof of this is found in the history of the missionary labors of *Augustine*.

The Church planted in England by St. Paul. § 1. It is not perfectly certain who first introduced the Gospel into England. The earliest and most reliable testimony refers to St. PAUL.

In the first century, Clement, (of whom mention is made in Philippians iv. 3,) the friend and fellow laborer of St. Paul, says: "St Paul published righteousness through the whole world, and in so doing, went to the utmost bounds of the west."[1]

Stillingfleet[2] has shown that this expression was very generally used to include England.

In the second century, Irenæus, who had seen

---

[1] Ἐπί τὸ τέρμα τῆς Δύσεως. *Ep. ad. Cor.*
[2] *Origines Britannicæ.* Ed. 1841, pp. 38, 39.

St. John, and was a disciple of Polycarp the disciple of St. John, said that the Apostles propagated Christianity among "the Celtic nations," that is, Germans, Gauls and Britons.

But perhaps the best and most explicit testimony is that of *Eusebius*, the great and the earliest Church historian, who was familiar with and wrote an account of all that was done up to his time, that is, through the first three centuries. He says, that some of the Apostles passed over the ocean "to the British Islands."[1]

Jerome, in the fourth century, says that St. Paul having been in Spain, preached the Gospel "in the Western parts;" an expression, as I have just remarked, generally used to denote Great Britain. Theodoret and Venantius still later, testify to the same point.

This is but a small part of the testimony, more or less direct, to this point. It is sufficient, I apprehend, to establish the point that the Gospel was established in Britain in the Apostolic age, and probably by St. Paul himself.

§ 2. On this point I will quote the following very pointed argument from the Rev. J. A. Spooner's "*Catholic saved from Popery.*" The Independence of the early English Church.

"On this point, of the independent character of the Church of England, I will be content with quoting the testimony of only a Roman Catholic writer. It is the testimony of *Lingard*, given in his '*History of the Anglo-Saxon Church;*' and when it is known that

---

[1] 'Επί τὰς καλουμένας Βρεττανικὰς νήσους. Dem. Evang. Lib III. c. 7.

Lingard is of highest literary fame as an accurate historian, and that he is of the highest repute among Romanists, the last ground of doubt as to the weight of the *testimony* is removed. Testimony of overwhelming amount might be drawn from Church historians, and from historians unbiased by *any* religious partialities; but if, foregoing all those, the point can be established by Romish testimony alone, there needs no further dispute. The edition of Lingard from which I quote, is an American copy, printed by the Romish house of Fithian, Philadelphia, 1841; and the two points which I shall establish from that history are, 1. That the Church was established in Britain before the visit there of any Romish missionary; and 2. That the Church in Britain was independent of Rome after the establishment in Britain of the first Romish missionary, Augustine.

"1. THE CHURCH WAS ESTABLISHED IN BRITAIN BEFORE THE VISIT THERE OF ANY ROMISH MISSIONARY.

"(*i.*) Lingard, page 23, states that the first missionary from Rome, the Monk Augustine, found, on landing in Britain—1. The *Queen* an avowed and earnest Christian. 2. A church edifice outside the walls of Canterbury, which had been built by Christians at an early day, and recently renewed by the Queen. 3. A Bishop, Liudhard, in possession of that church by the appointment of the Queen. 'And the saintly deportment of Liudhard,' says Lingard, 'reflected a lustre on the faith which he professed.' All the foregoing was found on the very spot where the first Romish missionary made his first attempt in 597. Of all the farther Church arrangements, which, from the presence of so faithful a Bishop, and from the known interest of the Queen, may well be supposed to have been in other parts of the Island, and of which, much indeed is said by early writers, Lingard, in the outset, quietly says nothing: but he says enough to reveal the existence of the Church in Britain before the Roman missionary went there.

"Of that which is said by the early writers, showing the *extent* of the Gospel in Britain, we may take that one declaration from the venerable Bede, a Saxon ecclesiastic and historian of the eighth century, where he is speaking of those who attend the council to meet Augustine. Among others who came, (Book ii. ch. 2,) he says, 'Seven Bishops of the Britons, and many most learned men came; particularly from their most noble monastery.' And Bede adds, that monastery had 'so great a number of monks that, being divided into seven parts, none of those parts contained less than 300 men.' This is called 'the most noble monastery,' showing there were others. This was in Mercia, a hundred miles from Liudhard; and if one monastery contained so many when Augustine came, how prevalent through Britain must have been already the influence of the Church!

"(*ii.*) Lingard states, page 19, that a *synod* of British Christians was held at Verulam, and that for the purpose of checking the heresy of Pelagius; and Pelagius was a Welshman, flourishing between 400 and 420. Not only at the landing of Augustine, then, in 598, but as long as 200 years before, the Church was so prevalent in Britian that the Christians held a synod, and which synod successfully repressed a great heresy.

"(*iii.*) Lingard states, page 18, that the Christians in Britain were *persecuted* by *Dioclesian*. Now, the persecuting edicts of Dioclesian were issued about A. D. 300. Not only 200 years, then, but so long as 300 years before Augustine, the Christians were so numerous in Britain as to excite the jealousy of the Pagan government, and to beget its persecuting hostility.

"(*iv.*) By whom was Christianity introduced into Britain? On "the testimony of an ancient and respectable historian," Lingard, page 1, rests the plea, that THE APOSTLES planted the Church in Britain. Lingard says, 'see Eusebius (Dem. Evang. l. i. c. 7,) who informs us, that the apostles not only preached to the nations on the continent, but passed the ocean and visited the British Isles.' And Lingard adds, 'Theodoret appears to assert the same (Theod. tom. 4. p. 610.') Not only for 300 years, then, before Augustine, but for *six hundred* years before Rome sent its agents to Britain, the Church was fully established and existing there.

"(*v.*) But *which* of the apostles planted the Church in Britain? The Romish polemics have been naturally anxious to prove that *St. Peter* founded the Church in Britain. Catholic writers, the Church writers, have been assiduous in proving that the Church was founded in Britain by *St. Paul*. Lingard, page 1, sums up the matter by saying:

"'The former' (the Papists) 'relied on the treacherous authority of Metaphrastes: the latter,' (Churchmen,) 'on the ambiguous and hyperbolical expressions of a few more ancient writers.'

"Lingard has here said the best for Rome and the

worst for its opponents that truth permitted—and how much? For St. Peter, *one* author; a late one; and he 'treacherous,' that is, perfidious, not to be trusted. For *St. Paul*, several authors; they, ancient writers; given to stating things 'hyperbolically,' that is, figuratively, or in a large way; and whose statements were 'ambiguous,' that is, about which doubts *might be* entertained. And Lingard has said the worst against the Church that facts would allow. Thus: for St Peter, one writer; for St. Paul *several*. For St. Peter, a modern or *late;* for St. Paul, *early* writers. For St. Peter, a writer *not to be* believed; for St. Paul, a writer whose statements only *might be* doubted. By Lingard, then, all authority that exists is in favor of St. Paul; in favor of St. Peter, *none*.

"So, according to Lingard, not only was the Church existing in Britain 600 years before the Romish monk was sent there; not only was it existing there quite as early as it did at all at Rome, that is, from the very days of the Apostles, but it was also established, not by St. Peter, but by him 'who was not a whit behind the very chiefest Apostles,' viz., by St. Paul. It therefore was not only begun from the earliest day, but it was begun, too, in entire independence of Rome.

"(*vi.*) And from St. Paul, up to the time of Augustine the monk, *i. e.* for the first 600 years, the Church in Britain *continued* independent of Rome. One fact given by Lingard establishes that point. Augustine was sent from Italy to Britain in the year 596. Lingard pictures that work as the going forth of a missionary to convert *a heathen land.* The following are his words:

"'Scarcely had the Saxons obtained the undisputed possession of their conquests, when a private monk conceived the bold but benevolent design, of reducing those savage warriors under the obedience of the Gospel.'—Page 21.

"So does he paint Britian as heathen, and Augustine as going forth to convert it. And Lingard does but echo in those words the opinion held by Gregory himself, (the pope,) and by whom the mission was set on foot. The following is the manner in which Gregory appears in this undertaking:—

"'Gregory,' says Lingard, 'on whom the veneration of posterity has bestowed the epithet of *the great*, chanced (at Rome) to pass through the public market at the moment in which some Saxon slaves were exposed to sale. Their beauty caught his eye, and he exclaimed with pious zeal, that 'forms so fair ought no *longer to be excluded from the inheritance of Christ.*'— Page 21. How Gregory came to know the country of those slaves, and that their land was heathen, does not well appear from Lingard's narrative. But Lingard quotes from Bede, and the full narrative as usually given, and as given by that historian, does interpret the matter, and it is as follows:—

"'Some merchants,' says Bede, 'having just arrived at Rome on a certain day, exposed many things for sale in the market-place, and abundance of people resorted thither to buy: Gregory himself went with the rest; and, among other things, some boys were set to sale, their bodies white, their countenances beautiful, and their hair very fine. Having viewed them, he asked, as is said, from what country or nation they were brought? and was told from the island of Britain, whose inhabitants were of such personal appearance. He again inquired whether those islanders were Christians, or still involved in the errors of paganism? and was informed that they were pagans. Then fetching a deep sigh from the bottom of his heart, 'Alas! what pity,' said he, 'that the author of darkness is possessed of men of such fair countenances; and that being remarkable for such graceful aspects, their minds should be void of inward grace.' He therefore again asked, what was the name of that nation? and was answered, that they were called Angles. 'Right,' said he, 'for they have an angelic face, and it becomes such to be co-heirs with the angels in heaven. What is the name,' proceeded he, 'of the province from which they are brought?' It was replied, that the natives of that province were called Deiri. 'Truly are they *De ira*,' said he, 'withdrawn from wrath, and called to the mercy of Christ. How is the king of that province called?' They told him his name was Aella; and he, alluding to the name, said, 'Hallelujah, the praise of God the Creator, must be sung in those parts.'—BEDE, *Eccl. Hist. Book II.*, *chap.* i.

"Of this account by Bede, Lingard (page 21) says, 'I see no reason to dispute the truth of this anecdote. Bede asserts that he received it from the fathers; and no nation could be more interested than the Saxons to preserve the memory of the accident which led to their conversion.' That last word, 'conversion,' again shows Lingard's sympathy with the feeling that Britain was heathen. But not only does Lingard—not only did the Pope, reckon Britain barbarous—the missionary Augustine and his party did the same. After the Pope had selected the missionaries, Lingard (page 22) says of them:

"'Animated by the exhortation of the pontiff, the missionaries traversed with speed the north of Italy, and arrived at the foot of the Gallic Alps; but the enthusiasm which they had imbibed, in Rome, insensibly evaporated during their journey; and, from the neighborhood of Lerins, they despatched Augustine, their superior, to Gregory, to explain their reasons for declining so unpromising and so dangerous an enterprise.'

"By this extract from Lingard, it is not quite seen why the mission appeared to Augustine and his companions to be 'unpromising and dangerous;' but Bede's history, from which Lingard again quotes, makes the point clear. Bede says of the missionaries: (Book I. chap. 23.)

"'Having in obedience to the Pope's commands undertaken that work, they were, on their journey, siezed with a sudden fear, and began to think of returning home, rather than proceed to a *barbarous, fierce* and *unbelieving* nation.'

"It was the supposed heathenism and wickedness of the land, then, which terrified and stopped them.

"Now the one fact given by Lingard, in these last pages, is this, viz: that Augustine and the Pope *considered Britain as heathen land*. And the point I press is this, viz: *Could* it have been so considered, if for 600 years the British Church had been *under the control of the Pope?*

"*The fact that the Pope did not even know of the existence of the Church in Britain, shows that he could not have had there any jurisdiction. The Church existed fully and by God's Spirit without him.*

"The first fact which I asserted then, is established by the Romish writer, Lingard, viz: that the Church existed in Britain, and independently of Rome, before Rome sent its agents there in 596. And the further fact is also established, that the Church was founded in Britain by St. Paul—the English Church is therefore an Apostolic Church; and in its origin and continuance, independent of Rome.

"While you are now most ready to acknowledge and to reassert this, let me present the next proposition, viz:

"*2. The British Church was also independent of Rome after the visit of Augustine.*

"'All,' says Lingard, (p. 35.) 'were not animated with the spirit of the pontiff. The Scottish monks (who had produced the conversions which Augustine found) had been taught to respect as sacred every institution which had been sanctioned by the approbation of *their ancestors,* while the Roman missionaries contended that the customs of an obscure and sequestered people ought to yield to the consentient practice of the principal Christian Churches.' '*Each party,*' concludes Lingard, '*pertinaciously adhered to their own opinions.*'

"Is not here, in the very first movement of Augustine, a distinction from Rome, and even a 'pertinacious' independence of Rome? All had *not* the spirit of the Pontiff. One body was led by the Pope, the other

6

stood arrayed with their ancestors, and 'pertinaciously adhered to their opinions.' Again:

"'The British Christians,' says Lingard, (p. 37.) 'scattered along the western coasts of the island, observed in the computation of Easter a rule peculiar to themselves; and when it was asked how *they*, buried in an obscure corner of the earth, dared oppose their customs to the unanimous voice of the Greek and Latin Churches, they boldly but ignorantly replied, that they had received them *from their forefathers*, whose sanction had been proved by a multitude of miracles, and whose doctrine they considered as their most valuable inheritance.'

"Here again the British Christians stand with their forefathers *against intruders;* they recognize the nationality of their Church; and they not only feel but they assert its independence of Rome. The very contempt with which Lingard speaks of them, all along, only heightens the certainty of his testimony to their undeniable independence. He himself felt it.

"But the controversy between the monk Augustine and other Romish agents on one side, against the native British and Scottish Christians on the other, became more and more earnest, and more and more absorbing. Therefore Lingard, on page 39, says:

"'If uniformity was desirable, it could only be obtained by the submission or retreat of one of the contending parties; and certainly it was unreasonable to expect that those, who observed the discipline which universally prevailed among the Christians on the continent, should yield to the pretensions of a few obscure churches on the remotest coast of Britain.'

"About this point as to which should yield, the sons of the land or intruders, I offer here no word; I quote Lingard only to make clear one fact, the professed and acted *independence* of the British Church. That, Lingard still farther exhibits by showing (p. 38.) that a council was at length called and held at Whitby in Northumbria, for the very purpose of settling the differences. In Northumbria, which, says Lingard, 'had received the doctrine of the Gospel from the Scottish missionaries;' and it was therefore truly their own ground. But into that ground, the Romish missionaries had forced themselves; had won to their notions, not the king, but the queen and her son; and then urged a council to bring about 'a uniformity,' i. e. to subject to *themselves* that country *which they had not converted.* The council was held; and Wilfrid defended the Roman customs, while Colman, Bishop of Lindisfarne, a Briton, defended the national customs. But no unanimity was attained. For, says Lingard:

"'When Daganus, a Caledonian Bishop, arrived at Canterbury afterwards, in the days of Lawrence, the successor of Augustine, he pertinaciously refused to eat at the same table, or even in the same house, *with those who observed the Roman Easter;* and St. Aldhelm assures us that the clergy of Demetia carried their abhorrence of the Roman discipline to such an extreme that *they punished the most trivial conformity with a long course of penance, and purified with a fanatic scrupulosity every utensil which had been contaminated by the touch of a Roman priest.*'

"The very epithets themselves, abusive as they

are, which Lingard here employs, only serves to show the more strongly the *real* and *inflexible* independence of the British Church. The Britons seem to have been so strongly irritated by the papal encroachments and overbearing, as to have come to hold the papists in real religious abhorrence.

" ' Gregory,' the pope, ' lamented,' says Lingard, page 41, ' and sought to remedy these disorders; and *invested* Augustine with an extensive jurisdiction *over all the Bishops* of Britain.' But, he adds, ' those degenerate ecclesiastics *determined to refuse all connection with him.*'

" Still, you see the same independence. And it was worthy of Britons. It was worthy of Christians, begotten in the Gospel by St. Paul, of whom the Spirit had declared that he ' was not a whit behind the chiefest Apostles.' (2 Cor. ii. 5.) But that act of marked rejection was not all. Augustine persevered, says Lingard, and by the influence of the king, ' prevailed on some of the British prelates to meet him ' in conference. ' To facilitate their compliance,' continues Lingard, ' Augustine had reduced, (he had insisted on more than showing the thorough and felt difference between Britain and Rome, but Augustine) reduced his demands to three: that they should observe its orthodox computation of Easter, should conform to the Roman rite in the administration of baptism, and join with him in preaching to the Saxons.' Join with him; that is, submit to the control which the Pope had proposed for him. But Lingard adds, ' *each request was refused* and his *metropolitical* authority *contemptuously rejected.*' And this last, his ' metropolitical authority,' shows what his 'three' demands were; one embraced the submission of the British Church to Roman control in the headship of Augustine; and the result shows the yet maintained and unstooping independence of the Britons—they rejected each request; they had their own metropolitan; they constituted by themselves a free national Church.

"That independence of the British Church is shown, too, (by a casual remark of Lingard on page 44,) to have been then *known* and *acknowledged*. Speaking of the supervisory authority given by the Pope to Augustine, he says:

"'Its jurisdiction at first extended no farther than *the churches founded by Roman missionaries.*'

"There were, then, other and independent churches. They had been discovered. And by that limitation, we see, the Pope *recognised* that freedom from his jurisdiction.

"But the Church existed on the very spot where Augustine landed; yet instead of withdrawing, over that Augustine *obtruded Roman authority*. The Church was already planted, too, in Northumbria, and by Scottish missionaries, yet *Augustine forced Roman authority upon it*. And, in spite of the first modest instructions of the Pope, that the Roman jurisdiction was to be *limited to churches founded by themselves*, (instructions which tell plainly that the independence of the British Church was known at Rome and recognised by Rome,) yet the days before Henry VIII, tell how *entirely* that British independence had been *suppressed*, and how over *all*, that papal jurisdiction, by little and little, had been pushed. But the independence of the British Church was a fact—a fact known and recognised even at Rome, (or why did the Pope refrain from interfering with their jurisdiction?) a fact daily and annoyingly seen by Augustine and his successors; a fact which the indignant *acts* of the Britons constantly asserted.

"Yet if by being overpowered the British Church grew less and less independent, still you may note, and as an Englishman you may note it proudly, that its independence never ceased to be asserted. In satisfying proof of that, look at the times of Wighard, the sixth after Augustine. He had been sent to Rome by the kings of Kent and Northumbria to consult the Pope concerning the controversies which had arisen among the bishops of the party of Augustine. He died in Rome. Then, says Lingard, the Pope Vitalian, '*seized the favorable moment* to place in the see of Canterbury a prelate of vigor and capacity;' that is, one of his own reliable countrymen. Lingard continues —'He sent Theodore of Cilicia, an aged monk. The authority which Theodore claimed was almost unlimited. At his arrival he assumed the title of ARCHBISHOP OF BRITAIN.' (Had Roman missionaries now 'founded' *all* British Churches? You see the wicked and unscrupulous encroachments by little and little.) 'The murmurs of opposition (Lingard states it softly, but still '*opposition*') were silenced by the veneration that his character inspired, and *by a new decree of the Pope in favor of Canterbury*;' that is, the Pope bought in adherents.

But that claim of Archbishop of all Britain *was not allowed*. With all their yet remaining strength, the

Britons *opposed* it. There were not only " murmurs," but "after the death of Theodore," says Lingard, page 44, " different Bishops *attempted to assert their independence;* and the *successors* of Augustine had more than once to contend with the ambition of their suffragans. The first who dared to refuse obedience was Egbert of York." We see it; Lingard cannot keep back the fact, that British resistance to Roman intrusion never ceased to be manifested; that their well known and sacred independence never ceased to be declared.

Again. That not to be eradicated feeling was exhibited not only by the Bishops, but it was as strongly asserted and maintained by the Kings. Let us turn our thoughts to that point. Lingard, page 48, shows how the State preserved the independence of the Church.

" As soon as any church became vacant," says he, " the ring and crosier, the emblems of Episcopal jurisdiction, were carried to the King by a deputation of the chapter and returned by him to the person whom they had chosen, with a letter by which the civil officers were ordered to maintain him in the possession of the lands belonging to his church."

At the hands of *the King*, then, and not from the Pope, the *sanction* of Episcopal *jurisdiction* was received. The Pope did oftentimes try, unsuccessfully, to interfere with that remnant of independence before he overcame it. Witness that kingly exhibition of British independence, in the case of Aldfred, King of Northumbria, given by Lingard, page 115. A provincial Synod had removed Wilfrid, a bishop of

Northumbria, from his episcopate, for certain alleged faults, and the king had given his sanction. Wilfred gained the ear of the Pope;—the good will of the Pope;—the *mandate* of the Pope for his restoration; and certain of the Northumbrian clergy brought that mandate to the King.

"'My brothers,' said the King, 'ask for yourselves, and you shall not be refused. But ask not for Wilfrid. His cause has been judged by myself and the Archbishop, the envoy of the Apostolic See; *nor will I change that judgment* for the writings as you call them of that See.'

"A Christian and kingly answer; and one that told not only of a consciousness of independence, but of will and ability to assert it. But mark here a note of Lingard's.

"'From this period,' says he, 'the use of *appeals* was established in the Anglo-Saxon Church.'

"From this period: what, then, let me call your attention to ask, was the state of things before, but that of a still preserved independence under their own Kings and under their own Synods? This last vestige of independence, it was, that Wilfrid by appealing to the Pope was instrumental in destroying. Wilfrid of Northumbria; Northumbria, from the first unconnected with Rome, the longest in maintaining independence, and the last to be subdued. The Italian divided it into factions; got one party to appeal to the Pope; and so subdued it.

"In thus exhibiting to you, my brother, the independence of the British Church, and its opposition to Rome *after* the visit and the encroaching efforts of St. Augustine and his co-operators, I have confined myself to extracts which exhibited the fact in its large and general aspect,—Britons on their own ground, resisting the aggressions of Rome, a foreign power. You have seen the Papists in their approach resisted; in their customs resisted; in all their propositions of fellowship resisted; in the social matter even of eating at the same table, indignantly and religiously rejected. You have seen a great English unanimity in that feeling of hostility to Romish intrusions; people and synods, counties and dioceses, Bishops and kings, moved by a sometimes despairing, yet always noble, and never-dying sense of original and rightful and God-given independence."

Thus it appears that about the middle of the sixth century, the Saxons, a heathen people from the continent, overrun the whole of the North and East of England. GREGORY, Bishop of Rome, sent Augustine as a missionary to convert them. On his arrival, he found that the British Church remained complete in its organization, and in full operation in what is now called Wales—or the western part of England. He called their Bishops together, seven in number, and had a conference with them. He found that their rites did not correspond with those used in the Church of Rome in all respects, and that they had never acknowledged any dependence upon the Roman See. He then proposed that they should conform and acknowledge the supremacy of the Bishop of Rome. This they positively refused.

The reply was given by DINOTH, *Abbot of Bangor*, as follows:

"Be it known to you beyond a doubt, that we are all and each one of us, obedient and subject to the Church of God and the Pope of Rome, and to every other true and pious Christian, to the extent of loving each of them in word and deed, as the sons of God: but other obedience than this I do not know to be justly [*vindicari et postulari*] claimed and proved to be due to him whom you call 'Father of the Fathers.'[i] And this obedience we are willing to give and perform to him and to every other Christian continually. But for anything further, we are under the jurisdiction of the Bishop of Cærleon upon the Uske, [now St. Davids] who is, under God, to take the oversight of us and make us pursue a spiritual life."[2]

Of course this proof is conclusive and beyond exception. The British Church up to that time, A. D. 601, had never acknowledged the Roman Primacy or Supremacy at all, in any form or to any extent—three of its Bishops were at the Council of Arles, A. D. 314. St. Anthanasius says also that there were three British Bishops at the Council of Sardica, A. D. 347.[3]

These Councils were held, the one in the South of France, the other was in what is now called European Turkey. The presence of her Bishops in these councils, proves that the Church of England was then in communion with the rest of the Church.

Augustine and his company went on with their work, and the British Church continued its separate existence until nearly a century after, when the whole

---

[1] A title which Augustine gave to the Pope.
[2] Spellman's *Conc. Brit.* an. 601.
[3] Apol. Introduc. § 1.

Island had been reconverted and the ancient British and the converted Saxons were again united into one Church, as the Heptarchy had been united under one Monarch.

§ 3. In order to understand this subject we shall need to go back a little and consider the earlier geography of England and the English Church. At the time of our earliest notices of the English Church, England was divided into *five* secular and *three* ecclesiastical provinces.

Only a small part of England converted by the Romish missionaries.

The secular provinces were:

1. *Britannia Prima*, comprehending the country south of the river *Thames* and the *Bristol Channel*.

2. *Britannia Secunda*, comprehending the country between the *Severn* and the *Dee* rivers.

3. *Flavia Cæsariensis*, comprehending the country northward from *Britannia Prima* and east of *Britannia Secunda*, as far north as the *Mersey*, the *Don* and the *Humber*.

4. *Maxima Cæsariensis*, comprehending the country north of *Flavia Cæsariensis*, as far as the wall of *Severus*, which stretched across the country from the *Solway Firth* to the river *Tine* on the east coast.

5. *Valentia*, or *Valentiana*, extended north of the wall of Severus to the rampart of Antoninus—extending across the isthmus from the Firth of Clyde to the Firth of Forth.[1]

The Ecclesiastical Provinces were then:

---

[1] See ANTHON's "*System of Ancient and Mædieval Geography*," pp. 169, 205, 206.

1. YORK, on the north, including *Valentia*, *Maxima Cæsariensis*, and *Flavia Cæsariensis*.

2. LONDON, including *Britannia Prima*, that is, the south and east of England.

3. CÆRLEON, including *Britannia Secunda*, that is, Wales, &c. in the west of England.

It is probable that the See of York had the precedence, and probably a supremacy over the others.

In A. D. 449, two Saxon leaders, Hengist and Horsa, arrived in England—and after a while made an alliance with the Scots and Picts on the north, and subjugated the whole of England, except *Britannia Secunda*, or the ecclesiastical province of Cærleon. To this, therefore, many of the early British Christians and Bishops fled for refuge.

After the Saxon conquest, all of England (except *Britannia Secunda*, or the province of *Cærleon*) was divided into seven kingdoms.

1. *Northumbria*, on the North.
2. *Mercia*, in the middle.
3. *East Anglia*, including the eastern part of *Flavia Cæsariensis*, or the present counties of *Norfolk* and *Suffolk*.
4. *East Saxony, or Essex*, also a part of *Flavia. Cæsariensis*, south of *East Anglia*, and including the present site of London, the counties of Essex, Middlesex, and part of Hertfordshire.
5. *Kent*, on the south-eastern extremity of the Island, including (at first) the present counties of Kent, Middlesex, Essex, and Surrey. Canterbury was the capital of the kingdom.
6. *South Saxony, or Sussex*, extending from the

kingdom of Kent on the east—to that of the West Saxons, on the west, including only the present county of Sussex.

7. *West Saxony, or Wessex*, extending from South Saxony on the east, westward, including the present counties of Hampshire, Dorsetshire, Berkshire, and Witshire.[1]

These kingdoms were all merged into one undivided sovereignty under Egbert, King of the West Saxons, or Wessex, in A. D. 828.

We may now proceed with our account of the conversion of England, with the prospect of conveying a distinct idea of the extent of the obligation under which the nation was laid by the Romish missionaries.

Augustine came into the small, but powerful kingdom of Kent, the capital of which was the present Canterbury. The wife of the king, Ethelbert, was Bertha, daughter of the king of Paris, and a Christian. Augustine, accordingly, seems to have found but little difficulty in gaining an ascendancy for Christianity in this kingdom, including at that time only the present counties of Kent and Surrey.

But to begin on the North: *Northumbria* was converted chiefly by the exertions of Oswald, one of the old royal family who had been educated in Scotland, and among the members of the ancient British Church. Aidan, a distinguished monk from what is now one of the Hebrides, was the principal missionary. Finan and Colman succeeded him the one after the

---

[1] The foregoing account of the Saxon Heptarchy has been derived chiefly from *Hume's* Hist. of England. Vol. I. pp. 14–86.

other. Neither of these had any connection with Rome.

Mercia was converted by missionaries from *Northumbria*, who were of course of the Old British School.

East Anglia was chiefly converted by *Fursey*, an *Irish* monk. At this time the Irish Church was wholly disconnected from Rome, and by no means under its influence or control.

Essex, or East Saxony. Sigebert, the king, had been converted at the Northumbrian court, and on his return to his own kingdom, he succeeded in gaining for Christianity a permanent establishment there.

Thus do we see that the only part of England that was really indebted to the Romish missionaries for its conversion, is that which is south of the Thames and east of the British Channel, including only a part of the old *Britannia Prima,* and, of course, only the same portion of the ecclesiastical province of London, which was in reality but a very small part of England.[1]

The following testimony of NEANDER, a German Church Historian, may be worth adding to what has been said : " the peculiarities of the Church in Britain are an argument against its deriving its origin from Rome—for that Church differed from the Romish in many respects ; it agreed far more with the Churches of Asia Minor—and it withstood for a long time the authority of the Romish Church. This appears to prove that the British received either immediately, or by means of Gaul, (now France,) their Christianity

---

[1] For the foregoing account see SOAME's Ed. of *Mosheim.* Vol. ii. pp. 65-69, and BEDE's Eccl. Hist. from which *Soame's* account is derived.

from Asia Minor, which may have easily taken place through their commercial intercourse."[1]

§ 4. With regard to the old Province of Cærleon, which had never been conquered by the Saxons—it continued to be an independent province until the reign of Henry I. (A. D. 1100–1135.) "During this whole period, the Bishops of this province, *eleven* in number, were all consecrated by the Suffragan Bishops of that province, (Cærleon,) without any profession or subjection to any other Church whatever."[2] *The Province of Cærleon remained independent for five hundred years after Augustine's arrival.*

§ 5. At the close of the eleventh century WILLIAM, Duke of *Normandy*, formed a design to place himself on the throne of England. In this he was encouraged by *the Pope*, ALEXANDER II., who was probably no less anxious to gain an ecclesiastical supremacy over England than William was to gain the crown. Accordingly they encouraged and assisted each other, until, by steps and means which I shall not now stop to specify, the Church of England was reduced to a pretty complete subjugation to the Papal Supremacy. *The Norman Conquest, and protests against the papal supremacy even until the Reformation.*

From the period of the Norman conquest, however, down to the Reformation, there were not wanting strong and positive protests against the Romish usurpation and encroachments.

In 1237, MATTHEW PARIS, a Benedictine monk, of

---

[1] Hist. Christ. Religion and Church, vol. I. p. 79 and 80, ROSE's Translation.
[2] HAMMOND on *Schism*, cap. VI. § 4, and *Spelman's Council Anglic.* p. 26, cited in Hammond's *Minor Theolog.* Works, p. 255.

St. Albans, thus announces the condition of the English Church. "Therefore a man might see sorrow of heart water the eyelids of holy men. Complaints broke out and groans multiplied, many crying with bloody sighs, it is better for us to die than to see the misery of our nation, and of holy persons. Woe be to England which once was the Princess of Provinces, the mistress of nations, the mirror of the Church, a pattern of religion, but now it is become tributary."[1]

About the same time Greathead, Bishop of Lincoln, obtained the name of "*Romanorum Malleus*," "the hammer of the Romans," for his opposition to the Papal encroachments. He called the Pope "Anti-christ," and "murderer of souls," and styles the condition of the English Church in relation to Rome an "Egyptian bondage."[2]

In 1257 the Pope pretended to excommunicate Sewalus, Archbishop of York. "But," says the historian, "he did not care to submit womanishly to the Pope's will, leaving the proper strictness of the law; *wherefore the more he was accursed by the Pope's command the more was he blessed of the people, though it was but secretly for fear of the Romans.*"[3]

As early as 1236, we find the famous "*Statute of Merton*" asserting as a fact universally acknowledged, that the canons and decrees of Rome were of no force in England.

The famous "*Statute of Carlisle*," made in 35, Ed. 1, that is, about A. D. 1305, declares "that the

---

[1] BRAMHALL Just Vindication. Works vol. I. p. 182.
[2] Bramhall, Vol. I. p. 185.   [3] Vol. i. p. 183.

Holy Church of England was founded in the estate of Prelacy, within the realm of England, and that the encroachments of the Bishop of Rome' tended to the annullation of the state of the Church."[1]

A similar declaration was made in the reign of Edward II. 1307—1327. "*The Articles of the Clergy*," as they were called, passed in the 9th Parliament of this reign, declare "that elections of the Bishops shall be free to the clergy, without papal interference or nomination,—the king's assent alone being obtained."[2]

"The Constitutions of Clarendon," A. D. 1164, declare that "if any man be found bringing in the Pope's letter or mandate, let him be apprehended and let justice pass upon him without delay, as a traitor to the king and kingdom;" and that "every man is interdicted to appeal to the Pope."[3]

The same point was re-enacted in the various laws of "*Provisions*" and of "*Præmunire*" from that time down to the Reformation. One, in Ed. III. 25, A. D. 1250, declares that "the king ought, and is bound by his oath, with the accord of his people and parliament to make remedy and law for the removal of such mischiefs." About thirty years after, the Statute 16 Richard II. declared that "the Crown of England was immediately subjected to God in all things and ought not to be submitted to the Pope," and that "they who shall procure or prosecute any Pope's Bulls and excommunications shall incur the forfeiture of their estates or be banished." Henry VI., king from 1422–

---

[1] Vol. I, p. 145.   [2] p. 146.   [3] p. 136.

1461, declares "that the English would not admit the legate of the Pope, Martin V., to England contrary to the laws and liberties of the realm."[1] And in 1420, when the Pope had undertaken to translate the Bishop of Lincoln to York, the Dean and Chapter refused to promote it, and appealed to the laws of the land protecting them against papal interference, and were sustained, so that the Pope was obliged to give up the point.[2]

In the first half of the sixteenth century, Henry VIII., King of England, having married the widow of his deceased brother, began to entertain doubts of the lawfulness of the marriage, and appealed to the Pope, notwithstanding these laws against such a step. The Pope did not readily decide in the affirmative, for fear of displeasing Charles V. of Spain, nor in the negative, lest he offend Henry. This occasioned a vexatious delay. At length, Henry, by the advice of some of the wisest divines in his country, determined to revive the old freedom from Romish authority, and declare the independence of the English Church, and decide his own question in his own realm.

The rejection of the Papal Supremacy. § 6. In the reign of Henry VIII. all those old laws were revived and put in force. They were declared to be no new laws, but only the old laws of the realm revived. This was the Reformation in its political aspect.

Corruptions in doctrine, and abuses of jurisdiction of the most gross character, had also long been calling for reformation. But these evils seemed to be insepar-

---

[1] Vol. I. p. 148.   [2] p. 141.

ably connected with the Supremacy of the Pope, and he steadfastly opposed any adequate measures for reform. Accordingly it began to be discussed in the Universities, and by the learned men of the kingdom generally—whether the Bishop of Rome had any right to that supremacy which he had so long claimed over England.

In March of 1534, the question being put by Archbishop CRANMER, both Houses [of Convocation,] came to a resolution against the Pope's supremacy. In the lower house four only voted for the Pope's supremacy, and one demurred. In June, Archibshop LEE, of York, sent the king a sort of an address from the Convocation of his province, in which they renounce the Pope's authority and expressly declare that "by the Word of God he has no more jurisdiction in England than any other Bishop." The same protestations were made by the Bishops of Lichfield and Coventry, St. Davids and Bath and Wells, by the Dean and Chapter of Bath and Wells, by the Prior and Chapter of St. Davids, by the Dean and Chapter of St. Paul's, St. Asaph, Lincoln, and of Landaff, together with thirty-four Abbots of the most considerable monasteries.[1]

This shows clearly enough how tired the English were of their papal bondage; and that the rejection of the Papal Supremacy was not made in haste and inconsiderately, or without competent authority.

It surely cannot be necessary to say anything more than has been already said to show that this step was justifiable. The Scriptures gave the Bishop of

---

[1] COLLIER *Eccl. Hist.* of Great Britain, Vol. IV, p. 266.

Rome no authority over the English Church. For the first five centuries he neither had nor claimed such authority. The extension of his jurisdiction was prohibited by the most positive laws of the Church. He did but little in fact towards the conversion of the Saxons, and his encroachments upon England were protested against and resisted more or less until the Reformation, and they were always in violation of the laws of the realm and the canons of the Church.

§ 7. Thus the Church of England was declared free and independent; and proceeded to a reformation of errors and abuses in doctrine and in morals. But no changes were made in the Constitution and organization of the Church, except merely the removal of the Papal authority, and the abuses dependent upon it. No clergymen of any order were removed from office—no new ones appointed in their places—no new congregations gathered—no new Churches built in place of the old. It was in all respects the old Church going on in a regular and orderly way, doing her work of preaching the Gospel, administering the Sacraments, and edifying the body of Christ, as before, with the exception of the Papal Supremacy.

The identity of the Church of England not affected by the rejection of the Papal Supremacy.

This rejection of the Papal Supremacy took place in 1534. There was, at that time, and for centuries before there had been, but one Church or religious communion in England. And for more than thirty years after this event there was only one—and that one before the Reformation as after it, was called and known as the Church of England. About thirty years after this date, the Puritans and the Papists began to separate from the Church and form themselves into separate sects.

§ 8. We are not to suppose that the change in opinion in the English took place all at once. More than one hundred years before, the celebrated WICKLIFFE had preached a reformation and inculcated doctrines contrary to the prevailing errors of the times, which had never been eradicated or fully suppressed. On the contrary, they had been gaining ground until the middle of the sixteenth century; they were entertained by the majority of the Church, and a favorable time had come for a reformation in accordance with them. The friends of the Reformation had, however, always remained in the Church except when the Church itself excommunicated them, and then they formed themselves into no rival or opposing communion. At the Reformation there was a minority opposed to it. Among them occur the distinguished names of FISHER of Rochester, and Sir THOMAS MORE, men of unquestionable learning, integrity and piety—as well as *Wolsey, Gardiner* and *Bonner,* of whom a different character must be given. And even for thirty years and more after the Reformation, we find many persons opposing its principles, and yet they did not separate from the English Church or form themselves into a new communion.

§ 9. As I have said, no change was made in the mode of Church government, except simply the abolition of the Papacy. In doctrines the English Church retained for their Rule of Faith, the Apostle's Creed, (which had, in fact, been the only one that they had ever acknowledged to hold that place,) though they drew up certain "ARTICLES *agreed upon by the Archbishops and Bishops of both Provinces and the whole Clergy, for the avoiding of diversities of opinions, and for the establishing consent touching true Religion,*" commonly called the XXXIX Articles. But these were never declared articles *of the Faith*, or necessary to salvation. Nor were they ever imposed upon the laity at all, as a condition of communion. They were only an agreement among the clergy on certain points then chiefly in controversy.

For their Liturgy, they revised the Books then generally in use, purging them from the errors and superstitions that had crept into them. In all this the one rule that they strictly adhered to, was to restore all things to a conformity, as near as possible to the authentic documents of the first centuries.

They also translated the Scriptures, and used them in the Churches in the English language, and made provisions for putting a copy into every family and into the hands of every individual that could read them.

In all these steps the Church herself took the lead and did the work. Sometimes a Formulary or Document was drawn by persons appointed for that purpose by the Church, and then adopted. At others, the Formulary was first drawn up, and subsequently adopted. But it was always duly adopted by the representative body of the Church before it came into use, or was considered to be duly in force.

§ 10. But the main point for our present purposes is the fact that this Reformation constituted no new

Church. *The Church of England reformed itself.* There was but one religious denomination in England before 1534. There was but one for more than thirty years afterward: and that one was the same identical body through the whole interval. There was no change in its name or form of organization, no turning out old clergy and appointing new, no gathering new congregations from the old, no separation of the clergy from the laity, but a quiet, orderly, and harmonious progress in the work of Reformation.

<small>The Church of England not formed or founded anew at the Reformation.</small>

In 1569, the advocates of the old papal abuses, having lost all hope of gaining the ascendancy in the Church of England again, left it and organized a Papal sect, which, however, was very small in point of numbers. Subsequently, the partisans of the peculiarities of the Calvinistic theory, despairing of gaining the ascendancy in the Church, withdrew also and formed another sect. But still the Church included the vast majority of the people of England. No one of these sects of seceders claimed to be the Church which had existed in England for centuries. Such a claim was too obviously absurd, and contrary to all facts, and all principles of identity to be thought of, even by those whose interests were the most concerned in making it.

Hence there was no new communion formed, no new Rule of Faith adopted, no new terms of communion proposed, no new name assumed, no new standard set up, nothing new except a *new* return to *old* truths, a renewed inculcation of the Faith once delivered to the Saints

It is desirable to show, not only that the Reformation did not establish "the Church of England" as a new sect, but also that it was not so regarded by the enemies of the Reformation themselves.

This appears from several facts, no less clearly than from declarations in express words.

After the accession of Mary, 1553, when she determined to restore Popery in England, the principal changes required, were that the Bishops and Clergy should conform to the Romish Faith and Obedience. If they would have done that, they need not have been molested or disturbed. So likewise in the early years of Elizabeth's reign. While the Pope was endeavoring to regain the ascendancy which he lost when she came to the throne, he did not declare the Church of England a mere new sect that had sprung up, but he was willing to receive it collectively as a Church—acknowledging the validity of its ordinations, if it would acknowledge his supremacy and conform in some few particulars to his will.

But most of all; after he had succeeded in getting a sect of seceders from the Church to profess their adherence to him, he did not even then call his followers in England "the Church of England." And though he sent Bishops there, he did not call them Bishops of London, of Durham, of Winchester, &c., &c., after the Sees from which the Bishops in the English Church for centuries had taken their titles, and from which they take them to this day; but he gave them a fictitious title, derived from no place whatever, as Bishop of Melipotamus [Honey-river,] &c., &c.

Now from these facts it is perfectly certain, that

the Church of Rome did not regard its adherents in England as the Church *of England*, and that it did so regard the Church which had thrown off the Papal yoke.

It appears thus from the admissions of her enemies, no less than from her own claims and from the indisputable and insuperable facts in the case, that the Church of England did not originate at the time of the Reformation, or lose her identity by the change; and by rejecting the Papal Supremacy, she only gained the independence to which, by the Scriptures and the ancient laws of the Church, she was most fully and most indefeasibly entitled.

§ 11. Since the Reformation in England, the Church of England has been in communion with the Eastern Churches. They have mutually recognized each other to be true branches of the Church of Christ, acknowledging the validity of each other's ordinations, conceding to each other the communion due from one branch of the Church of Christ to another. *The Church of England in communion with the Eastern Churches since the Reformation.*

§ 12. Although we may say that the Original Church is divided at present into three Communions, the Eastern, the Roman, and the Reformed—including, in the latter, all the Churches which she has established since her reformation, yet in fact they are but two—the Roman, on the one hand, and the Eastern and the Reformed, [being in communion with each other,] constituting the other. *The Church now divided into Three Grand Divisions.*

§ 13. In speaking of the Reformation in England, I do not intend to prejudice the *The Reformed Branches.*

character of any of the other reformations. I select England as the point of discussion for several reasons, 1. Because the Church in that country is older than that in any of the others where a Reformation has been effected. 2. Because that Church was so unquestionably independent for several centuries after its first planting. 3. Because the Reformation was there beyond the possibility of a denial—a reformation *in a branch of the Church*, and not the origination of a new church or sect; and finally. 4. Because the Church of England has done more than all the other reformed Churches put together, in extending the Church, by establishing new and affiliated branches.

In what I shall have to say in the present chapter, I shall include with the Church of England, as a class of which that is a type and representative, all other Churches which have been founded by the Church of England, or which are in communion with her.

<small>The early divisions local and not denominational.</small> § 14. The early divisions in the Church were local; each division being called, also, a Church, and taking its name from the place where it was situated. The only denominational difference known to the Scriptures or allowed in the Church, were derived from the place in which each Church was located. It was not a Presbyterian church, a Methodist church, a Congregational church, &c.; but it was the Church at Ephesus, the Church of Rome, the Church of England, &c., &c.

<small>The divisions between the East and the West.</small> § 15. We have seen how these Churches were associated for provincial and still more general purposes. As early as the middle of the fifth century, LEO *the Great*, Bishop of

Rome, had formed the design of an universal supremacy in the Church, for himself and his successors in the same See. And yet, more than a century after this, GREGORY, also called *the Great*, Bishop of Rome, vehemently denounced the idea of any such supremacy. In his letter to *Mauritius* the Emperor, he says: "I am bold to say that whosoever uses or affects the style of universal Bishop [as the Archbishop of Constantinople had done,] has the pride and character of Anti-Christ, and is in some measure his harbinger in this haughty quality of mounting himself above the rest of his order." Writing to *Anastasius*, Bishop of Antioch, he says still further: "this is a point of the last importance, neither can we comply with the innovation without betraying Religion, and adulterating the Catholic Faith?" Thus we see that in the sixth century, a Bishop of Rome could condemn as a characteristic of Anti-Christ, that for not believing in which a Bishop of the same See, in more modern centuries must declare persons out of communion with the Church, and cut off from its INVISIBLE HEAD.

Jealousies had for a long time subsisted between the East and the West, before a final separation took place.

In A. D. 1053, MICHAEL CERULARIUS, *Patriarch of Constantinople*, sent a letter to the Bishop of *Trani*, intended for the Bishop of *Rome*, complaining, as he had a right to do, of some of the rites and customs which the Bishop of Rome was encouraging in the Western Churches. LEO IX. (for that was the name of the Bishop of Rome) complained of the interference of the Constantinople Bishop. In the next year he sent three Legates to Constantinople. Among these Legates was Cardinal *Humbert*, which was evidently an unfortunate selection. His language to Cerularius was arrogant and discourteous, and he closed by threatening him with excommunication, &c., if he did not reject, what Humbert was pleased to call his errors, and conform to the Romish usages. The Bishop of Constantinople would not yield, and before the Legates left the city, they placed on the Altar of St. Sophia's, a formal excommunication of Cerularius and his adherents. This was a most direct assumption of authority over Cerularius and the Eastern Church, of which he was the acknowledged head. It led to the division of the East and the West, which exists to the present day.

<small>The division in the Western Church effected by the Reformation.</small> § 16. At the Reformation, as we have seen, another division was occasioned. The contest then, also, was with the Romish claim to Supremacy. Yet not directly: for the Church of England probably would not have rejected that Supremacy if it had been kept within the bounds of the early canons, and had not indissolubly allied itself to some of the worst corruptions in morals, as well as doctrines, that were to be found in that age. As England had the right to be free from Rome, and could not reform herself without, she exercised that right, and was anathematised by Rome for it.

This, of course, led to another division and alienation among Churches which are unquestionably Apostolic, and whose catholicity up to that day had never been called in question. We have not yet proceeded far enough in our work of historic identification to say with any definiteness how large a portion of the Churches, in the Roman Obedience, became separated from it by the Reformation. In England, Ireland, Scotland, Norway, Sweden and Denmark, the Church of Rome made no pretensions of retaining the jurisdiction. She made no show even of setting up her claims for the individuals that still cherished a preference for her doctrines and usages that they should be considered as the old Church in those countries, still in existence, though diminished in numbers. By her own confession, then, she lost the Churches in these several nations, from her obedience.

§ 17. Now, it cannot for a moment be pretended, with any show of reason, that any one of these parts of the Church lost its right, or its power, to spread the Gospel, in consequence of this alienation. If the Papal Supremacy were an essential element of the Church, then, of course, rejection *of* that supremacy—or rejection *by* it—would disable any Church from carrying on missionary operations. It might, indeed, preach and build, but it would be building on " another foundation," and what it built would not be the Church of Christ.

Neither of these Divisions of the Church became apostate in consequence of the Separation.

Or again: if any one of these three parts, into which the Original and Primitive Church is divided, has set forth another Rule of Faith different from and inconsistent with that of the Primitive Church, so as that in her missionary operations she is inculcating a Gospel different in its essential features from that preached by the immediate Evangelists and Apostles of our

Lord, this fact may incapacitate them from effectual missionary labors.

§ 18. I will not here stop to inquire how far Rome has laid a new foundation. But most assuredly the Church of England has not done it. Her Rule of Faith is the Apostle's Creed—the most simple—the most primitive, and the one that was and is now universally received. This she proposes as her Baptismal confession of Faith. This is what she requires all of her members to be taught in her Catechism, and to renew their profession and confession of, in Confirmation, and this it is which she proposes to her members when about to leave the world as the Faith in which they are to be received by their Final Judge.

<small>The English Church only returned to the Primitive Rule of Faith and Practice.</small>

Nor does she put upon this Creed any new or peculiar construction of her own. Her solemn declaration is that her

"Preachers shall take heed that they teach nothing in their preaching, which they would have the people religiously observe and believe, but that which is agreeable to the teaching of the Old Testament and the New, and that which the Catholic Fathers and the Ancient Bishops have gathered out of that very teaching."[1]

Again:

"Nay, so far was it from the purpose of the Church of England to forsake and reject the Churches of Italy, France, Spain, Germany, or any such like Churches, in all things which they held and practised, that as the

---

[1] CARDWELL's *Synodalia*, Vol. I. p. 126.

Apology of the Church of England confesseth, it doth with reverence retain those *ceremonies* [even] which do neither endamage the Church of God, nor offend the minds of sober men; and only departed from them in those particular points wherein they were fallen both from themselves in their ancient integrity and from the Apostolical Churches, which were their first founders."[1]

§ 19. It has sometimes been said, that since the English Church and Bishops derived whatever authority they had from the Pope and Church of Rome, therefore, now that the Church of Rome has withdrawn that authority they are none the better for this connection with the past.   *The Romish excommunication of no force against the English Church.*

This objection presents three distinct points, which we will consider in order.

1. Nothing occurred which can be regarded as depriving the English Church and Clergy of their authority and mission until the Bull of Pius V., dated Feb. 23; 1569. This Bull declares "that those who adhere to Queen Elizabeth in the practices aforesaid"—the Reformation—"lie under the censure of anathema, and are cut off from the unity of the body of Christ." But the Pope had no authority at that time, either in fact or by right over Elizabeth or the Church of England, and therefore, his excommunication was of no force against them. The Pope had no more right or authority to excommunicate them than any private individual whatever. This answer cannot be denied

---

[1] *Canon* xxx. of 1603.

without maintaining the *divine right* of the Pope to Supremacy over the Whole Church.

2. But, again, from the abolition of the Papal Supremacy in 1534, until the accession of Mary, in 1553, a period of nineteen years, Bishops were selected and ordained without obtaining any authority or permission from the Pope—and without even consulting him at all. After the accession of Elizabeth, 1558, the Papal Supremacy was again abolished, and from that time until the Bull of 1569, Bishops had also been ordained without consulting him at all. None of the Bishops who had been consecrated before 1534,—the first rejection of the Papal Supremacy—lived to hold their offices after the accession of Elizabeth. And none of those that had been consecrated during Mary's reign, while the Papal Supremacy was acknowledged, consented to retain their offices under Elizabeth. All the Bishops in the actual possession of Sees in England during Elizabeth's reign, and when the Bull was issued in 1569, had been ordained, therefore, either between 1534, and the accession of Mary, or during the reign of Queen Elizabeth herself. Hence it so happens that when the Bull of excommunication was issued, *there was not a single Bishop in the English Church who had been ordained under the Pope's Supremacy*, or had in any way promised obedience to him, or derived even a show of authority from him in any shape or form whatever.[1]

---

[1] ANTHONY KITCHEN, Bishop of *Llandaff*, was the only Bishop who did hold a See during *Mary's* reign, and conformed to the Papacy, that consented to retain his See under Elizabeth. He was elected March 26, 1545, confirmed May 2, and consecrated the day after. Of course, there-

If, then, it were true that the English Bishops before the Reformation derived their authority from the Pope, yet there is not the slightest shadow of a pretence that those whom he undertook to excommunicate in Elizabeth's reign, had derived any authority from him. And the Pope had never excommunicated or deprived those who had been ordained under him— who had concurred in the rejection of his Supremacy, and from whom, after its rejection, the Bishops of Elizabeth's reign had derived their orders.

This Bull was of no force, therefore, against the Bishops at whom it was aimed, on the ground that the Pope could take away what he had given.

3. But even before the Reformation, the English Bishops were not regarded as obtaining their authority to minister in sacred things from the Pope. It is true, that he had claimed the right of "Investiture," as it was called. And this right, though in violation of the laws of the land, which were revived under Henry VIII., was conceded, though with a good deal of opposition and protestation. The election of Bishops was as follows: The King granted to the Chapter,

---

fore, the Pope had nothing to do with the matter. Under Mary, 1553–1558, he conformed to the Papacy, but on the accession of Elizabeth, he took the oath and retained his See. He died on 31st of Oct., 1563, more than five years before the pretended Excommunication and Deprivation. (GODWIN De *Præsulibus Angliæ*) And it should also be remarked, that but a short time before the Bull of 1569, the Pope himself had acknowledged the English Bishops to possess Episcopal character and authority, by consenting to allow them to retain their Sees, and conceding some other points to them if they would acknowledge his Supremacy. It appears, therefore, from his confessions, that even in his own estimation, they possessed the authority of their office, though they had not derived it from him.

that is, the Cathedral clergy, of the vacant Diocese a *conge d'elire* [permission to elect.] They chose the man whom they desired for Bishop. The Bishop elect must then have the royal assent and be confirmed, that is, approved of, as Bishop elect by the Pope or his Legate. After which he was ordained by the Bishops whom the Pope named for that purpose. These Bishops, however, were English Bishops, who were residing in England, and actually in the exercise of the duties of their office. The Pope also, or his Legate, put upon the newly consecrated Bishop the pall and other insignia of his authority—which was called the "*Investiture*."[1] But his election and ordination gave the Bishop his authority as Bishop in the Church, and his right to jurisdiction in the particular Diocese. Neither of them was held to be derived from the Pope.

There is therefore no sense in which the English Church or her Bishops had derived their authority from the Pope or Church of Rome, consequently no sense in which it could be taken away by Romish authorities.

Here then we have the Church of England unquestionably a part of the identical historic Church of Christ, deriving the origin of its existence from the very Apostles themselves, reformed from the corruptions and errors of the middle ages, returning to the teachings and standards of the Primitive Church—and disowned by Rome for so doing. If now this alienation is the annihilation of one or the other of the parties to the division, as Churches of Christ, there is no rea

---

[1] Burns' *Ecclesiastical Law.* Vol. I. p. 179.

son why this consequence should result to the Church of England rather than to the Church of Rome.

§ 20. The alienation between these three branches of the Church, the *Eastern*, the *Roman*, and the *Reformed*, is undoubtedly an evil, and alike the result and the proof of sin. But most unquestionably neither the division nor the alienation terminates the visible existence of either of those branches. And I know of no reason why it should necessarily involve any one of them in apostacy from Christ. If they are apostate it must be for other reasons.

The separation between these Grand Divisions of the Church unlike a Schism in the same communion.

Such an alienation between different branches of the Church as this which we are now considering, is a very different thing from what we considered in Chapter II. when we were speaking of the rise of a new sect or second church in the place where one already existed, so as to make two different churches or denominations in the same place. It is such an alienation that the Scriptures are speaking of in all those passages from which we infer that the result would be a rival sect, rather than an affiliated branch of the Church itself.

Although an alienation between the different branches of the Church such as that which now subsists between England and Rome, for instance, is undoubtedly a great evil—a contravention of the prayer of our Lord in the night in which He was betrayed,[1] and involves a tremendous responsibility for those who are truly the causes of it, yet it does not bring in its

[1] John xvii. 21.

train the evils for which schisms are chiefly condemned in the New Testament. There being but one Church in a country still, the members of the different Churches would live in entirely different communities—move in different circles—associate in different spheres of action, and of course have but very rare occasions to come into either contact or collision. Being united among themselves in the Church in each particular locality, they would enjoy by far the greatest share of the benefits of an entire unity in the whole Church. There would be but very little occasion offered for those jealousies, contentions, rivalries, and oppositions, which inevitably result from there being several sects in the same place, and which lead, as they have led, to great decay of religion, and to the prevalence of infidelity and profanity amongst by far the greatest proportion of the inhabitants of our land.

I am not anxious to conceal the fact, though the object we have now in view does not require any prolonged discussion of it—that there are also alienations and misunderstandings existing to some extent between the different branches of the Oriental Church. And so, too, there are controversies and points of material difference, between the several Churches in the Roman Obedience, as, for instance, between those in France and Italy. From what has been said, it will appear that the Church, in any one or all of these separate or distinct nations, has a right to declare itself free and independent of the control of any foreign Bishop or Church whatever, if it should choose to do so.

Without saying, then, that there is a perfect harmony among all of the Branches in each of the great divisions of the Catholic Church of Christ—for that manifestly is not the case—I say that we may include all these Churches in three distinct classes.

1. The Eastern, including all those Branches of the Church which have never submitted to the Papal Supremacy—the Russian, the Greek, the Syrian, the Armenian, the Coptic, or Egyptian, the Abyssinian, &c.

2. The Churches that are yet in the Roman Obedience, as those of Austria, Italy, France, Spain, Portugal, &c.

3. Those Churches which were once subject to the Papal Supremacy, and are now reformed and freed from it, as England, Ireland, Scotland, Norway, Sweden, Denmark, &c., without naming now the midland nations of Europe, where, as we shall see by and by, the case is somewhat different, and omitting to mention, in this place, all those Churches that have been established by any of the Churches in this class since the Reformation.

In classing the churches of Norway, Sweden and Denmark, with the Church of England, I do by no means intend to intimate that I consider them as occupying the same position in all respects. In some of those nations, there is no doubt that the Clergy at the time of the Reformation were driven off or out of their official positions, and others put in their places in a manner which was at variance with what has always been regarded in the Church as essential to the validity of the ministerial office. This, however, is a point that we need not discuss here. They are at least Churches that separated themselves at that time from the Roman Obedience; and if their ministry is invalid or informal, the defect can be remedied, as was done with that in the Church of Scotland in 1610, when the regular succession having been lost, three Bishops were ordained for Scotland in London, and they on their return ordained others to supply the whole deficiency.

The Ministry of the English Church the same after the Reformation as before.

§ 21. But no such imperfection or invalidity attaches to the Ministry of the English Church. They were neither driven off nor rejected at the Reformation, but, on the contrary, they were themselves the chief agents in carrying it on. And, in the ordination of their successors, all the rites that have ever been deemed essential in the Church, were carefully observed.

The clergy were foremost in the rejection of the Papal Supremacy. They revised and prepared the Liturgy—they translated the Scriptures—and though they were sometimes compelled to submit to an exercise of royal authority, which they considered as an infringement of the liberties of the Church, yet in all the stages of the Reformation, they were the leading agents, and any thing that could affect the validity of its position, was duly enacted and sanctioned by the Church clergy and laity in their legitimate modes of transacting ecclesiastical affairs.

We have then, before our minds, one of the oldest branches of the Church of Christ, reaching back, in the commencement of its existence, to the very days of the Apostles, once subjugated to the Roman Supremacy—but now reformed and free,—in the full exercise of her functions as a Church of Christ, and as unquestionably a part of that identical visible society which He and His Apostles founded as any other that can be named on earth; disowned, indeed, by Rome for her Protestantism, but for that very reason owned and fellowshipped by Churches older than Rome herself, and which were *in* CHRIST before the sound of the Gospel had ever been heard in the city of the seven hills. She has had, indeed, some vicissitudes of fortune, but through them all she has been the same—the Church of England—the only body of persons that ever claimed to be called by that name in England, or to which it was ever by any body for one moment supposed to belong.

CHAPTER V.

THE ORIGIN OF MODERN SECTS, AND THEIR RELATION TO THE CHURCH.

Having succeeded in identifying a part of the Church which is free from the Romish Jurisdiction, and which has done much towards extending its communion in this western world, we will now draw our subject within still narrower limits. Before proceeding, however, to trace the introduction and extension of the English Branch of the Church into this country, and to identify its existence here, we will turn aside to consider the several sects to be found here, which have come into existence since the reformation commenced.

In considering these sects we shall see that some of them were formed by persons seceding directly from either the Roman or the Reformed Branch of the Church: some have been formed by divisions in those sects: and still another class have arisen as it were *de novo*, by some individual collecting around him a number of persons from all sects, or that had belonged to no sect. Hence we may divide them all into three classes, *Primary, Secondary, and Autothentic.*

In this enumeration I shall have regard only to the

sects in our own country. I shall in all cases take their own statements, and accounts of their origin; and when I can conveniently do so, I shall give those statements in their own language. My object will not lead me into any general account of their doctrines or of their principles of church-polity. Our attention is directed chiefly to their history as visible societies.

PRIMARY SECTS.

Under this head, I include some nine or ten. The characteristic by which they are distinguished, is, that, with one or two exceptions, they resulted from attempts at what was, or was regarded as, a reformation *in the Church*—the reformers however, failing to have their views adopted by the Church, seceded with their adherents and became a sect. I shall take up the consideration of them in alphabetic order.

§ 1. "The Baptist church in this country was founded *March*, A. D. 1639. 'Many of the first settlers in Massachusetts were Baptists, and a holy and watchful, and fruitful, and heavenly a people, as perhaps any in the world,' says *Cotton Mather*. Roger Williams having escaped the intolerance of the *Puritans* of Massachusetts Bay, came to what now is called *Providence, Rhode Island*, in 1636, founded a colony, and became its governor. He was a Baptist, and 'many of his people entertained his views.' But neither he nor any of them having been baptised, as they understood the rite, and 'there being no minister in New England who had been baptised by immersion on a profession of faith, in March, 1639, *Ezekiel Holliman* baptised Roger

The Baptists; their Origin and History.

Williams, who then administered the rite to Holliman and ten others.' Williams had been ordained in the English Church. 'Thus was founded' under Roger Williams as Governor of Rhode Island, and minister of the Lord Jesus, and by Ezekiel Holliman, Deputy Governor, with ten others, the first Baptist church on the continent of America."

For this quotation, and all my others when not otherwise indicated, I am indebted to a *History of the Baptists*, by the Rev. A. D. GILLETTE, Pastor of the Eleventh Baptist church, Philadelphia, published in Rupp's Collection, 1844.

But though this was the origin of the Baptist church in this country, it was not the origin of the communion to which it belongs. Our author claims:

That persons holding Baptist sentiments have existed always in the Church; that for the first three or four centuries after Christ, the whole Church held to such sentiments—that the *Novatians*, the *Donatists*, the *Paulicians*, separated from the Church because sentiments and practices of an opposite character were being introduced—that fleeing from the persecutions of the Church which had now become apostate, they finally settled in the vallies of Piedmont and became what was afterwards known as *Albigenses* and *Waldenses;* that at the time of the Reformation they became scattered throughout Europe and sprang up in part as a Baptist church. But the first *society* or *church* of Baptists which our author names is as follows: "The British Baptists continued to multiply; and in 1689, they, with forty of their bishops [preachers, for they had no Bishops in the established sense of the word,] assembled in an association at London and adopted a confession of Faith; the same that was adopted by the Philadelphia association in 1742."

§ 2. *Mr. Gillette* refers to nothing earlier than 1689 which can be regarded as the origin of the Baptists *as a church*—for most evidently any number of persons, though agreeing in their views, cannot be regarded as *a church* until they are gathered into some bond of union, with a formal organization. A church is a society of persons, and implies not only the existence of the persons, but it also implies that they are gathered out of the rest of the world and brought together either in some place or within some definite and visible bond of union. Mr. Gillette points out no such association, which he recognizes as a Baptist church before the one named above in 1689. I should certainly differ from him on this point, but as the difference is of no material importance to our present object, I will not take up the time to point it out.

<small>A number of persons, though holding similar views, are not a church, without some organization.</small>

§ 3. There is no need that we should go into the history of the Baptists any farther, for the purposes of our present inquiry. Their claim is that the Church or Society which Christ and the Apostles founded, early became apostate, and that the Baptist church was founded some centuries later by persons who seceded from the apostatizing Church of Christ. Of course, therefore, the Baptist church is another, and entirely distinct from that from which its founders seceded.

<small>The Baptists, therefore, claim another and more modern origin than the Christian Church.</small>

The Baptists claim in this country 4,000,000 people, 1,000,000 members, 9,000 churches, and 6,000 ministers.

§ 4. In giving the origin of this sect I shall follow chiefly the account by the Rev. E. W. ANDREWS, *Pastor of the Broadway Tabernacle*, New-York, in Rupp's Collection, p. 184.

<small>Origin and History of the Congregationalists.</small>

"The origin of the Congregationalists as a modern sect is commonly ascribed to Robert Brown, who organized a church in England in 1583. But it appears probable that there were churches formed upon congregational principles in the reigns of Edward VI. and Queen Mary, although it is impossible to speak with any certainty concerning them. But the dividing line between the supporters of the Church, and the non-conformists, was not distinctly drawn until the Acts of Supremacy and Uniformity passed in the early part of Elizabeth's reign. From this period there was little hope of permanent reconciliation between them and the Church, although it was not until about the year 1565 that separate assemblies were held. It is from this time that the *Puritans* are to be regarded as a distinct party."

Brown's church, however, seems to have come to nought, and many—perhaps a majority of the early Puritans or non-conformists—were Presbyterians in principle.

"But about the commencement of the seventeenth century appeared *John Robinson*, who has, not inappropriately, been called the Father of modern Congregationalism. We first hear of him as a pastor of a church which had been formed in the north of England in the year previous to Elizabeth's death [March 1603.]———" But not finding things to their mind in England, they left for Holland in 1608, and Mr. Robinson soon followed. "——— Mr. Robinson and his congregation, upon their arrival in Holland, first joined themselves to the church at Amsterdam [Dutch Reformed;] but owing to the dissensions that had broken out among its members, at the end of a year they removed to Leyden. In the year 1617, Mr. Robinson and his church began to think of a removal to America. Robinson remained with the majority at Leyden, and Elder Brewster accompanied the emigrants.———" They arrived at Plymouth, Mass., 1620. "To Mr. Robinson and his church at Leyden, in the old world, and at Plymouth in the new, we owe the first modern developments of the principles of the congregational polity."

§ 5. At first the Congregationalists gathered their congregations within the bosom of the Church of England, then they went to Holland, and, failing to gain their object there, obtained a grant of a large tract of land in America, and came hither to settle.

<small>The Congregational church formed from seceders from the English Church since the Reformation.</small>

Of course there is no pretence that these Pilgrims were the Church of England.

Mr. Robinson "at the commencement of his ministry among the separatists, in common with Brown, denounced that Church, as *essentially antichristian*, and would neither regard her members as brethren, nor hear her ministers preach." His opinions underwent some change after this; "yet it does not appear that Mr. Robinson was ever willing to admit that the Church of England, as a National Establishment, was a Christian Church, although he communed with its individual members."

This we are to remember, was after the Reformation—after the Church of England had adopted the Apostles' Creed, as the Rule of Faith—after the adoption of the XXXIX Articles as the standard of her teaching on all points included in them.

The grounds of their separation not such as to be essential to salvation. § 6. The complaints against the Church by the Puritans, were, at first, only against the use of the clerical garments—against ceremonies—and certain abuses of plurality, non-residence, &c., and against a general laxity of discipline. Granting that the Puritans were right in all this, these abuses did not endanger the salvation of *their* souls, so long as they remained in the Church, and were faithful to themselves: and when they had borne their testimony against them, and "refused compliance, yet without separation," as they told some of their own members, that they must do in regard to themselves, I cannot see why they had not done all that was required of them.

The Congregationalists do not claim to be a branch of the English Church. § 7. While in Holland, the Congregationalists were beyond the King's dominions, and the jurisdiction of the English Church. They claim no historic connection with a past that was before them. They do not claim to have been founded by the English Church, or any other branch of the Church, but by John Robinson, and other seceders from the Church in England co-operating with him.

The Congregationalists have 160,000 members, 1,300 congregations, 1,150 ministers, chiefly in New England.

§ 8. In speaking of this Sect I shall follow chiefly Dr. BROWNLEE's *Account of the Dutch Reformed church*, in Rupp's Collection—p. 220. The origin and history of the Dutch Reformed church.

"The Dutch Reformed church is the oldest church in the United States, which adopts the Presbyterian form of church government. Its history begins with the history of New-York and New Jersey. It is a branch of the National church of Holland. . . . . The Dutch West India Company were the first who carried the ministers of the Gospel from Holland to our shores.———" .Until 1772, they were dependent upon the *Classis* in Holland.

They receive as their Rule of Faith, the Confessions of Faith, &c., of the *Synod of Dort*.

Now upon this state of facts two questions arise, one relating to the Dutch Reformed church in the old country, and the other to its mission in this country.

§ 9. By the Bull of Paul IV., May 19, 1559, and confirmed by Pius IV., January 8, 1560, the NETHERLANDS were constituted and divided as follows: The "Dutch Reformed church" a sect of seceders from the Dutch Church.

1. Archbishopric of MECHLEM, containing the Dioceses of *Antwerp, Bois le Duc, Ruremand, Gant,* and *Ypres.*

2. Archbishopric of CAMBRAY, containing *Tourncy; Arras, St. Omer,* and *Namur.*

3. Archbishopric of UTRECHT, containing *Harlem,*

Midelburg, Leeuwarden, Groningen, and *Deventer.*[1]

Now I do not design to claim for this *Bull* any special authority. But the Church in the Netherlands or Low countries acquiesced in and adopted the new arrangement, and it became therefore a part of the Church arrangement or organization. *Amsterdam*, when the Dutch Reformed church began its existance, was in the Diocese of *Harlem* and Province of UTRECHT.[2]

The Reformation was commenced by persons in their individual capacity, and not carried on, as in England, by the Church, in her regular course of ecclesiastical proceedings. The recognized authorities of the Church did not encourage the change at all, but still adhered to their old opinions. The Protestants, consequently separated from the Church, and formed themselves into a new church on the Calvinistic foundation.

I have no means of ascertaining what were the relative numbers of the two parties—the Catholics and the Protestants. Yet from all I can learn, the Catholics have generally been the most numerous; and at present, though the Dutch Reformed religion is established by law, the Catholics have in Amsterdam twenty-two churches, and the Dutch Reformed only ten; other Christian denominations together, eight.[3]

But the relative numbers is not very important. It is always held that the identity of a society depends up-

---

[1] BRANDT's *Hist. Ref. in the Netherlands, Vol. i. p.* 133, Ed. 9, 1720.
[2] RANKE's *Hist. of the Popes*, p. 242.
[3] BROOKE's *Gazetteer*, by Marshall. 1840. Art. *Amsterdam.*

on its officers and recognized authorities. This point was clearly established in the famous case of the Presbyterian church of York, Penn. The court, in that case, held the Old School to be the Presbyterian church, on the ground, that "a popular body is known only by its government or its head," and awarded to them the name, the funds, and the property; not because the New School "were thought to be anything else than Presbyterians," but because the recognized head and government of the church remained with the Old School, or rather, the Old School remained with the recognized government, and the New School were declared seceders and their church a new one, on this ground. This, I believe, to be the established principle.

We must therefore decide that the adherents to the Romish Obedience, in Holland, were the Old Church, whether they were the minority or the majority in point of numbers. And in that case, the Protestants were seceders, as they acknowledged themselves to be, setting up a rival sect within the actual jurisdiction of the Church which Christ and His Apostles had established fifteen hundred years before.

§ 10. Finally—it does not appear that the Holland Missionaries came into this country for the purpose of building a Branch of the Church of Christ, on the broad Foundation laid by Christ and the Apostles. Their object was to establish the new Rule of Faith, adopted by the Holland seceders from that Church, and to extend the communion or church which they had formed on their own terms of com-

The Dutch Reformed came into this country to establish here the new communion which they themselves had founded.

munion. They neither took the Apostle's nor any one of the Creeds of the Universal Church for their Rule of Faith, nor did they manifest any serious regard for the acknowledged Creeds, opinions and usages of the Primitive ages of the Church of Christ. But in all respects they regarded themselves as a new sect or church—based, indeed, upon the Bible—but still, as a church, a religious society, a visible community, they considered themselves of an origin more recent than the commencement of the Reformation. They were not derived from the Church that existed before the Reformation, in any way which that Church itself or any part of it, would acknowledge to be valid.

This church is situated chiefly in New-York and New Jersey. It has 21,569 families, 96,302 individuals, 29,322 communicants, 267 churches, and 259 ministers.

§ 11. The following account is taken from Dr. MAYER, *of York, Pa.*, in Rupp's Collection. *The Origin and History of the German Reformed church.*

"The German Reformed church, as its name imports, comprises that portion of the family of reformed churches which speak the German language, and their descendants, and as such is distinguished from the French Reformed, the Dutch Reformed, &c. The founder of this church was ULRIC ZWINGLI, a native of Switzerland. After the death of Zwingle and Œcolompadius in 1531, none of their associates enjoyed so decided a superiority over his brethren as to give him a commanding influence over the whole church, and to secure to him the chief direction of her councils. This honor was reserved for JOHN CALVIN, *the*

French Reformer. Driven from his own country by persecution, he came to Basil, in 1534. On his return from a visit to the *Duchess of Ferrara* in Italy, who was friendly to the Reformation, being compelled by the war to take the route through Geneva, he came to that city in August, 1536, and was persuaded by *Farell* and *Viret* to remain there and complete the reformation which they had begun."

Thus the reformed church was established at Geneva, in 1541, with Calvin at its head.

"The German Reformed church in the United States was founded by emigrants from Germany and Switzerland. Its origin may be dated about the year 1740, or rather somewhat earlier. The principal seat of the church in its infancy was eastern Pennsylvania, though settlements were made also, and congregations formed, at an earlier period in other states, particularly in the Carolinas, Virginia, Maryland, New Jersey and New-York. Its doctrinal system is derived from Germany and Switzerland; but its ecclesiastical polity is formed after the model of the Reformed Dutch church of Holland, by whom it was nurtured and protected in its infant state, and to whom it owes a large debt of gratitude."

The *Heidelberg Catechism* is their Rule of Faith.

§ 12. It is perfectly evident, from the foregoing account of the German Reformed church, that it does not fulfil the conditions requisite to constitute a Branch of that Church which has existed since our Lord was on earth. It was established in this country by members of the German Reformed church

The German Reformed church claims to be only a Sect founded by Ulric Zwingli.

in Germany and Switzerland, and that church, as Dr. Mayer ingenuously confesses, "*was founded*" by Ulric Zwingle, and consisted of seceders from the Church that existed in those countries before his day.

Mosheim says the same thing of them:

"The founder of the Reformed church was *Ulric Zwingli*, a Swiss, an acute man, and a lover of truth." (*Cent.* xvi. *Sect.* iii. c. ii. § 3.)

§ 13. In order to judge the better of the ecclesiastical position of this religious communion, it will be necessary to recur to the history of its origin. *The history of their origin examined still further.*

As early as 1519, Leo X., Bishop of Rome, authorized *Robert Simson*, a Franciscan or gray Friar, of Milan, to preach indulgences at Zurich, in the Diocese of *Constance*. The indignation of Zwinglius was aroused, and he began to inveigh against the abuse. At first, Hugh, Bishop of Constance, approved his course, and sanctioned his opposition to the prevailing abuses and corruptions in the Church. But in a short time, the Reformer became so indiscreet and headlong—denying some most sacred truths, as well as many of the prevailing errors—that his Bishop and the other ecclesiastical authorities found it necessary to acquit themselves of all responsibility for what he might do and teach. Zwinglius was in all probability the most popular and powerful preacher among the Reformers. His indefatigable zeal against the gross and intolerable abuses of the age, gained him friends: and in 1523, the Senate of Zurich summoned the Bishop of the Diocese, and the other ecclesiastics of the Canton, to appear before them and answer to the doctrines of Zwinglius. Now the Senate neither had, nor was acknowledged to have, any authority in matters of faith. It was not an ecclesiastical or religious body at all, any more than the Legislature of New-York, or the Congress of the United States. The Bishop and ecclesiastics, constituting the lawful and recognized representatives of the Church, protested against this assumption and against the Senate's right to judge in the matter. They however, decided in favor of Zwinglius, and called a more general assembly to be held at the close of the month of October, in the same year. The Senate invited the Bishops of Constance, Chur or Coire, and Basel, and the University of the latter place, and the Twelve Cantons of Switzerland, to appear before them. I do not find that these ecclesiastical personages paid any attention to the invitation, except that the Bishop of Constance in whose Diocese Zurich was situated, "wrote to the Senate to urge them to preserve the ancient religion."[1] The Senate issued a Decree in favor of the Zwinglians.

§ 14. The Church, however, continued on as before, in all its functions and ministrations, notwithstanding the opposition of the secular authorities and the reduction of numbers, occasioned by the secession of the Zwinglians. The seceders, though but a minority, formed themselves into what is now called the German Reformed church. *The Church continued notwithstanding the secessions.*

§ 15. At *Geneva* this Sect was introduced in 1531, chiefly in consequence, as *Vidal* says, of the alliance of the Cantons of Berne *This Sect established in Geneva.*

[1] VIDAL's *Continuation of Fleury*, vol. iv. p. 518, 539, Ed. 1837.

and Friburg, in order to defend themselves against the Duke of Savoy. The inhabitants of Berne brought along with them their preacher *Farel* and made him preach daily in the Cathedral of St. Peter's, Geneva. The Discourses of *Farel* and *Viret* soon made such an impression that their views were established as the public religion by the village Council, a purely secular body, in 1535. It allowed each person, however, the liberty to embrace which religion he pleased—the new or the old. The Zwinglians compelled Peter de Labaume, the Bishop, to leave the city. He retired to *Annecy*, a village of Savoy, about 16 miles from Geneva, and established the See of the Diocese there, where it remains to this day. The number of the seceders was daily increased by immigrants from France, and thus soon gained the ascendency.[1]

As we have already seen, Calvin came to Geneva in 1536. In 1541, he was placed not only at the head of the church into which these separatists had formed themselves, but also at the head of the secular government.

The German Reformed incapable of extending the communion of Christ's Church. § 16. As at Zurich, so at Geneva and elsewhere, therefore, the German Reformed church was made up of those who seceded from the Church, rejecting its regular and acknowledged authorities—retiring from its congregations to form new ones of their own, taking a new name and proceeding in a new manner altogether, whilst the old Church continued its functions and ministrations as before. They were, therefore, merely

---

[1] VIDAL's *Continuation*, vol. vi. p. 598.

a sect of seceders, and no part of that visible society which had existed from the days of the Apostles. And therefore, although they might, and did—as history proves—extend *their* church into America, and other countries, yet the *Church* of *Christ*, whose visible communion they had left, they were entirely incapable of extending until they should return to its communion.

I enter now into no comparison between the doctrinal or moral purity of the Church, as it then existed in Switzerland, and that of the new church of the seceders. I grant, for all present purposes, that the result of such a comparison might be vastly and altogether in favor of the latter. But be that as it may, it is in vain to attempt to call them what they were not, what they never considered themselves and what they never claimed to be—a part of that continuous visible Society or Church which our Blessed Lord founded, and which had existed from its first establishment to their day. They had seceded from that Church, as they thought, for a just cause. They had done what they considered to be the best thing that they could do under the circumstances—and what they believed the necessities of the case would justify. But it was either their misfortune or their fault that they were a new sect and not the old Church of Christ.

§ 17. Nor, even in this, let any one suppose that I am saying of them what they did not admit to be true of themselves. Thus CALVIN, the very highest authority among them, said, "I know how great are our deficiencies, [in an

They did not consider their position satisfactory.

ecclesiastical point of view,] and certainly if God should call us this day to an account, it would be difficult for us to make an excuse." [*difficilis esset excusatio.*] VIRET, of whom we have before spoken, says the same: "Many things are yet necessary for us in order that we may have the full regimen of the Church." CALVIN also, in his reply to *Cardinal Sadolet* says, in behalf of himself and his German Reformed church, "We do not deny that we are destitute of the regimen which the ancient Church had." BEZA, Calvin's successor, said, "Think not that we wish to abolish that which is eternal, to wit, the Church of God. Think not that we search after arguments by which to depress you to this *our* wretched and vile condition." Writing to Archbishop Grindal of England, he says "that we are as yet far from what we ought to be, we willingly confess." The context shows beyond a question that he referred to their ecclesiastical position. The son of PETER DU MOULIN, another of their distinguished writers, says:—"But the generous and illuminate souls make no difficulty to acknowledge openly the scantiness of their church government, and that their bed is shorter than that they can stretch themselves on it, and their covering narrower than that they can wrap themselves in it. But as short and narrow as it is, they must keep it by an invincible necessity." He also says, that so far as ecclesiastical power [power to do anything as a church] is concerned, it is a perfect interregnum," i. e., there is none. In addition, I will only refer to the fact that Calvin himself made application to the Church of England, to ordain him Bishop, and thus constitute him and his followers, a Branch of the Church at Geneva. The application was intercepted by Romanists. But it is in itself a confession of the truth of all that I have said or need to say for our present purpose of the defects of the German Reformed church.

This sect claims 750 congregations, 192 ministers.

§ 18. The name officially adopted by the Lutheran reformers was the "Evangelical church." <small>Origin and history of the Evangelical Lutheran church.</small>

"As Germany was the cradle of the Reformation, she was also the primitive seat of that church which grew out of the Reformation in the land of Luther. The Germans, after they had thrown off the yoke of Rome, through the instrumentality of their countryman Luther, and others, *constituted themselves* a reformed evangelical church which has been denominated Lutheran." The Elector of Saxony early instituted measures by which the Lutheran religion was established throughout his dominions. The treaty of *Passau* 1552, in which the Elector gained some important concessions from the Emperor Charles V., after the surprise at *Inspruck*, is regarded by the Lutherans as the basis of their religious freedom. A Diet assembled at Augsburg, 1555, declared that all who adopted the Augsburg Confession [all Lutherans] should for the future be considered entirely free from the jurisdiction of the Roman Pontiff, and from the authority and supervision of the Bishops (who retained their allegiance to Rome,) that all the inhabitants of the German Empire should be allowed to judge for themselves, and to join the church whose doctrine and worship they thought most pure and Scriptural—*i. e.*, the old or the new.

The movement began by individuals in their individual capacity, and was finally established by the Civil Authority.

§ 19. This sect presents to our consideration substantially the same state of facts as the one last reviewed. The movement was commenced by an individual in the Diocese of Brandenburg, soon gained the favor of the secular arm in the person of the Elector of Saxony, and the seceders became established as a new sect; the Church still continuing, (though of course diminished in numbers by the secessions,) in the full performance of its functions as before.

The DIET is a *secular* body, and no representative of the Church in matters of faith. It consisted of laymen with the exception of the Archbishops of Mentz, Treves and Cologne, and the two spiritual benches in the second 'Chamber.'¹ From the time of Otho I., [Emp. 936,] the kings of Germany had found it for their advantage to balance the power of their nobles by endowing the Bishops with whole counties as fiefs.² This of course gave them a seat in the secular councils of the Empire, as temporal lords or nobility. The Diet was, notwithstanding, as a legislature, exclusively secular, as much so as the American Congress.

The Introduction of the Evangelical Lutherans into the United States.

§ 20. It was from the church thus reformed, indoctrinated and established, that the German Lutheran Christians in the United States, descended. After the establishment of the Lutheran church in Germany by the

---

¹ BRANDE's *Encyclop.* in voc. ² GIESLER's *Text Book*, vol. ii. p. 91.

labors of Luther, Melancthon and others, about 1525, the Lutheran doctrines were extensively diffused and adopted. The earliest settlement of Lutherans in this country was made by emigrants from Holland to New-York soon after the first establishment of the Dutch in that city, 1621. To this settlement succeeded that of the Swedes on the Delaware in 1636. The third settlements of the Lutherans in this country, was that of the Germans which gradually spread over Pennsylvania, Maryland, Virginia, the interior of New-York, and the Western States. The year 1820 has been mentioned as the date of the formation of the General Synod of the American Lutheran church. (*Chiefly from the Article in Rupp.*)

The *Augsburg Confession* is the Rule of Faith for the Evangelical Lutherans.

§ 21. The interval between the first preaching of Luther and the establishment of his church is full of events of the most interesting and important character. Luther was called out by the sale of indulgences and other abuses in the Church. At first his efforts were looked upon with favor by the Church and her authorities in immediate jurisdiction, and in more instances than one, there seemed a prospect of a substantial reformation in the Church instead of mere secessions from it. <small>The occasion of Luther's movement and its favorable reception.</small>

§ 22. But there were points in Luther's character which operated greatly to the disadvantage of such a holy cause. And still more than this, the recklessness of some of his opinions and measures greatly diminished his influence over those whose co-operation was of the utmost <small>Causes which exerted an unfavorable influence.</small>

importance. As instances of what I mean, take the following. He, a man bound by the most solemn vows, which he had *voluntarily* undertaken, made not unto man, but to God, to live an unmarried life, had married a woman, *Catharine de Bora*, under similar vows of celibacy—a step which outraged the pious sentiments of the best men of the age. He sanctioned polygamy, and consequently adultery in the Landgrave of Hesse, and he had carried his doctrine of justification by faith to such an extent that he was obliged to disparage one of the books of the Holy Scripture—the epistle of St. James—calling it "an Epistle of straw,"[1] and denying that it was written by the inspiration of the Holy Ghost. These things went far to destroy his influence with those who would have carried the Church with them if they had moved in the matter, and left him to be merely the head of a sect of followers whom he had persuaded out of its communion.

The Lutherans also confessed their deficiencies.
§ 23. I might also quote a list of confessions of deficiency and destitution of what they considered essential to the Ministry and Sacraments of the Church from the founders of the Lutheran sect, similar to those I have quoted from the founders of the German Reformed. But it is not necessary to take up the time and room to repeat them.

The Lutherans, therefore, a new Sect.
§ 24. Now, with these facts before us, we cannot doubt that the Lutheran church was a new sect founded within the very bosom of the Church, which continued still to exist notwith-

---

[1] "*Epistolam Stramineam.*"

standing its loss of numbers and opposition. Nay, the Lutherans neither then nor to this day, regard themselves as anything else than a new church, recently founded by those who had seceded from the Catholic Church in Germany.

I admit that the Church was excessively corrupt, and such cases present the question (if we choose so to consider it) whether it is better to be in the Church with the errors and corruptions of the sixteenth century, or to have the Truth and be out of it. Yet this is all that we can say of the Lutherans—all that they said of themselves—namely, that they had the Truth, but were a sect out of the Church. Of course, therefore, any religious society or communion which they can found in this country or elsewhere, cannot be identified with that Church which they left in order to be Lutherans.

The statistics of this sect are 1,371 congregations, 424 ministers, 146,300 communicants.

§ 25. This sect is probably to be regarded as more nearly the descendants and representatives of the Albigenses or Waldenses than any other now in existence. *The Menonites.*

"The Menonites fully acknowledge that they derive their name from MENNO SIMON, a native of Witmarsum, born in Friesland, A. D. 1495. In 1530 he was induced to examine the New Testament for himself, and his views were materially changed. He now commenced to travel with a view to consult some of his cotemporaries, such as Luther, Bucer, Bullinger and others. He distinctly repudiated the extravagances of the *Munsterites* or *Anabaptists*, yet assumed among them, at their earnest solicitation, the rank and functions of a public Teacher. In 1537, he commenced travelling among the Anabaptists, or descendants of the ancient Waldenses, all of whom were as scattered sheep of the House of Israel. He visited East and West Friesland, the province of Groningen, and then went to Holland, Guilderland, Brabant, Westphalia, and continued through the German Provinces, that lie on the coast of the Baltic Sea, and penetrated as far as Livonia. In these places his ministerial labors were attended with remarkable success, and added a prodigious number of followers."

§ 26. Now in all these countries the Church was established, but Meno allied himself with those who were out of its communion. Whether he found them already organized as sects, or organized them himself, or left them unorganized, it is immaterial so far as their identity with the Church is concerned.

Meno a Reformer among the Anabaptists.

His object, says his historian, CHRISTIAN HERR, of *Pequea*, a bishop of the Mennonite church, "was reformation and spiritual edification of his fellow men. He purified the doctrines of the Anabaptists—he retained some of them, and he excluded others who were tainted with the *Munsterite* heresy. He founded many communities in various parts of Europe."

Thus we see that he was a reformer *amongst the Anabaptists*, a body totally distinct in all its visible relations and connections, from the Church which we are seeking to identify.

§ 27. "From the year 1537, the Mennonites suffered great persecutions in Europe. They were compelled to flee from one country to another. Many came to Pennsylvania as early as 1683. Before 1735 there were probably rising of five hundred families in Lancaster county, Pa. In 1727, they translated and published their confession of faith.

The Mennonites introduced to this Country.

§ 28. Of course I would not associate them with the Anabaptists or Munsterites any farther than they choose such an association for themselves. Yet the common course with ecclesiastical historians, is to regard the Anabaptists as a development of the Albigenses, and both the Baptists and the Mennonites as descendants of the Anabaptists, though it is admitted on all hands, that both these sects have repudiated much of their ancestry. There is good foundation for this view. But that is immaterial to our present purpose. Whether we refer the origin of the sect to Menno, or consider him merely as a reformer in the sect; the sect itself is a body of seceders which sprung up in Germany, and has finally come to be established in this country. It claims no identity, no visible connection, union or communion with the Church that existed before them.

The Mennonites probably an offshoot of the Albigenses and Waldenses.

They claim 120,000 people, 240 ministers, 130 places of worship, 50 or 60,000 members.

§ 29. The following account is abridged from the Rev. Dr. BANGS, of New-York:—

The Methodists.

"The well-known founder of Methodism, under God, was the Rev. JOHN WESLEY, a presbyter of the Church of England, who after his own conversion, set out with a simple desire to revive pure and undefiled religion in the Church of which he was a member and a minister."

Occasion of their Rise. § 30. Dr. Bangs has not given an account of the occasion and rise of Methodism in England. I will, therefore, interrupt his narrative to speak of it somewhat.

From the Revolution in England, 1688, in consequence of important changes in the ecclesiastical management, there commenced a rapid and sad decline in the state of religion in the English Church. Daily Prayer, from being neglected and omitted, came to be regarded as not at all obligatory—then unnecessary, and even superstitious. The Church's holy seasons, for Prayer, Fasting and Repentance, were neglected. The Holy Communion was less and less frequently administered, and in some cases it was celebrated only on the three times in the year required by the laws of the land. Discipline was relaxed and worldly indifference was the prevailing characteristic. Wesley and a few others combined for the purposes of greater piety and a more faithful use of the means of grace pointed out for her members by the English Church. This procured for them the name of *Methodists*, which the sect that grew out of the movement still retain. In 1738, he visited Germany, and on his return he commenced those systematic labors which resulted in the foundation of his sect. The foundation of separate congregations in England is commonly assigned to 1739.

The Rise of Methodism in this Country. § 31. We now return to our narrative from Dr. Bangs:—

"The Methodist society in America was

established in the city of New-York, in the year 1766. A few pious emigrants from Ireland, who previously to their removal had been members of the Methodist society in their own country, landed in this city. Among their number was Mr. *Philip Embury*, their local preacher. This party soon became very dissolute in their morals, until a pious woman went into the room where they were assembled—seized the cards with which they were playing and threw them into the fire. She turned to Mr. Embury and said that he must preach to them. And accordingly he preached his first sermon in his own hired house to five persons only. This, it is believed, was the first Methodist sermon ever preached in America, Oct. 30, 1768.

"In 1784, we come to an important era in the history of this sect. Up to this time their preachers had been considered as laymen having no authority to administer the ordinances, and hence the members of the societies had been dependent upon other ministers for the rite of Baptism and the Lord's Supper. In 1770, to avoid this difficulty, some of the southern preachers had begun to ordain each other. Through the influence of Mr. Asbury this practice had been discontinued, and on the 2d of September 1784, Mr. Wesley, assisted by other presbyters, consecrated Thomas Coke, LL. D., then a presbyter in the Church of England, as superintendent, and likewise ordained two others to the office of Elders, and sent them over to America, with instructions to organise the societies here into a separate and independent church; furnishing them with forms of ordinations for deans, [deacons?] elders and superintendents, for administering baptism, and the consecration and administration of the Lord's Supper. At a Conference called for that purpose in Baltimore, December 25, 1784, the measures were unanimously approved of. Dr. Coke was recognized in his character of Superintendent, and Mr. Asbury was elected to the same office, and consecrated by Dr. Coke, on the 27th of the same month. Several others were ordained deacons and elders at the same time."

<small>The Methodists did not claim to be a Branch of the English Church.</small> § 32. The founders of the Methodist church in this country were men who had been, and were at that time, some of them at least, members of the English Church.

Yet in what they did, they did not act with the sanction of that Church; the society which they founded was not received into the communion with it, and never sought to be so received. It made no claims to be a branch of that Church. In the function of ordination which Mr. Wesley took upon himself to perform, he transcended the authority which in the view of the Church of England, he, as a Presbyter merely, possessed. Nor do even the men whom he ordained, seem to have been satisfied with their ordination; for both Dr. Coke and Mr. Asbury sought ordination from the American Bishops, SEABURY of Connecticut, and WHITE of Penn.[1]

No one, with these facts before him, would for one moment pretend that there was any identity between the Methodist church and the Church of England, by whose members it was founded.

---

[1] See WHITE's *Memoirs*, p. 168.

§ 33. It is sometimes claimed by the Methodists, that their church and ministrations are valid, because they are derived from men who were ordained in the English Church, and therefore had the right and authority to do what they did.

They were not acknowledged as a branch by the English Church.

Now in the first place, it never has been held or acknowledged in any branch of the Church, that a presbyter is competent to ordain. Without going into this question at all in this place, I will only say, that so long as the rule is held by the Church, its violation by any number of persons under such circumstances, will constitute them a new sect which the Church will not own to be a part of itself; and therefore of necessity, whether in the right or the wrong, it will be a different and diverse body.

§ 34. But again: Though it be conceded or proved that Mr. Wesley and the other presbyters were competent to ordain others, and even a Bishop, (for that was the office to which Dr. Coke and Mr. Asbury were appointed,) yet it must be done *in the Church* and *for* the Church. The ministerial authority is circumscribed to acts *for* and *within* the Church. Suppose the Ministry of Christ should undertake to preach Platonism for the Gospel, would it be attended with the same saving efficacy? Suppose they should go and administer the sacraments of Baptism and the Lord's Supper to some unconverted heathen: would these sacraments be of any efficacy to them? Surely not. So, too, with ordination. It is a power given for the purpose of supplying the

The Founders of the Methodist Sect lost their authority as soon as they left the Church, in which they received it, to found another.

Church with men "for the work of the Ministry, for the perfection of the Saints, and for the edifying the Body of Christ,"[1] all of which is to be done *in the Church*. If, therefore, those possessing this power, should exercise it for any other purpose, their act would have no validity or force whatever.

Now beyond question, such is the case, where one having authority for ordination in the Church exercises that authority in laying a foundation on which he himself or others are to build a new sect. No matter by whom performed, such acts have no validity.

Wesley never intended to be the Founder of a Sect. § 35. It is a singular fact, that as in the case of almost all the founders of the modern sects, they did not believe that they could, under the circumstances, found a society that should be a Branch of the Church, so also it was in the case of Wesley.

Thus Wesley says:—

"At the first meeting of all our preachers in conference in June 1744, I exhorted them to keep to the Church; observing that this was our peculiar glory—not to form any new sect, but abiding in our own Church, to do to all men all the good we possibly could.

"But as more dissenters joined us, many of whom were much prejudiced against the Church, these, with or without design, were continually infusing their own prejudices into their brethren.

"I saw this and gave warning of it from time to time both in private and in public, and in the year

---

[1] Eph. iv. 12.

1758 I resolved to bring the matter to a fair issue. So I desired the point might be considered at large whether it was expedient for the Methodists to leave the Church. The arguments on both sides were discussed for several days, and at length we agreed without a dissenting voice 'It is by no means expedient that the Methodists should leave the Church of England.' Nevertheless the same leaven continued to work in various parts of the kingdom."

In 1778 he says again :—

"The original Methodists are all of the Church of England, and the more awakened they were the more zealously they adhered to it in every point both of doctrine and discipline. Hence we inserted in the first Rules of our Society ' they that leave the Church, leave us.' And this we did, *not as a point of prudence, but* a point of conscience."

He died March 2, 1791, and in 1789, two years before his death, he said :—

"I never had any design of separating from the Church; I have no such design now. I do not believe that the Methodists in general design it when I am no more seen. I do, and will do all that is in my power to prevent such an event. Nevertheless in spite of all I can do many will separate from it.

"In flat opposition to these I declare once more that I live and die a member of the Church of England, and that none who regard my judgment or advice will ever separate from it."

In his sermon preached at Cork, about the same time, he declared to the preachers in his connection that they had no right to baptize and administer the sacrament of the Lord's Supper. His design was to improve the state of religion *in* the Church. But, as he said, he did not dare to leave the Church, and on the Minutes of the Conference, in 1770, he had these emphatic words entered : "*Let this be well observed—I fear when the Methodists leave the Church, God will leave them.*"

The Methodists claim 1,068,525 members, and 7,730 local preachers.

The Moravians.
§ 36. Like that of the Mennonities and Baptists, the history of this sect is involved in a great deal of obscurity. Like them too, the Moravians refer to, and make use of the Waldenses, or Albigenses. From an article in Rupp's Collection, which has the sanction of the Board of the Moravian church, I make the following abridgement :—

"United Brethren, or *Unitas Fratrum*, or sometimes called *Moravians*, were originally founded by the descendants of the Bohemian and Moravian Brethren, who being persecuted for their religious tenets and non-conformity in their native country, founded a colony under the patronage of COUNT ZINZENDORF, on an estate of his called *Berthelsdorf*, in Upper Lusatia, in the year 1722, to which colony the name of '*Hernnhut*' was given. No bond of union, however, existed for some time. But after a while, under the guidance of Count Zinzendorf, who from an early age had entertained an idea of constituting a Christian community, on the model of the primitive apostolic congregations, certain articles of union were proposed among them. All the inhabitants of Hernnhut, after mature consideration adopted this scheme, and these statutes by the name of a brotherly agreement, and pledged themselves mutually to its observance in the year 1727, and thus formed the first stock of the present Society of United Brethren. Count Zinzendorf was justly in some measure considered the founder of the society. Individuals from the Protestant denominations were from the beginning admitted among them without renouncing their original church and creed. 'The United Brethren continue strenuously to object to being considered a separate sect or denomination, because their union is exclusively founded on general Chrstian doctrines, and their peculiarities *relate solely to their social organization.*' Still, however, when called upon to point out their creed, they profess a general adherence to the Confession of Augsburg. The society early undertook to propagate the Gospel among the heathen nations. In the prosecution of their object, they planted colonies in different parts of Germany, England, Holland, America, &c., all of which together now constitute the Unity of the Brethren. Each *local congregation* is responsible to the General Board of the Directors at present seated at Berthelsdorf near Hernnhut."

§ 37. It does not appear from the above account that the Moravians claim to be a church at all. They call their society merely "a social organization," and say "it would be preposterous to conceive that the peculiar views or regulations of a society such as that of the United Brethren could ever be adopted by any large body of men." And yet they undertake to perform the functions of a church. They administer the

<small>The "Unity," regarded by its Founders, rather as a social than an Ecclesiastical Body.</small>

sacraments—exercise jurisdiction and discipline, and preach the Gospel to the heathen for their conversion.

Another account of their Origin. § 38. Although the foregoing statements are copied from a document which had the approbation of the Board, I cannot but think that it comes short of what is claimed for them. I have before me another account as follows:

"They derive their origin from the Greek Church in the ninth century, when by the instrumentality of *Methodius* and *Cyrillus*, two Greek monks, the kings of Bulgaria and Moravia being converted to the Faith were, together with their subjects, united in communion with the Greek Church. Methodius was their first Bishop, and for their use Cyrillus translated the Scriptures into the Sclavonian language. The greater part of the members in process of time were compelled to submit to the See of Rome. A few of them joined the Waldenses in 1170, and became identified with them. From this union of the Bohemian seceders and the Waldenses, arose the sect of *Moravians*."

The Moravians are Episcopalians. In 1467 three of their preachers were ordained bishops by a Waldensian Bishop in Austria by the name of *Stephen*. These on their return ordained ten other bishops. This occurred in Bohemia where the Church was already established, and consequently this step was the organization of a distinct and opposing sect.

Mosheim says:

"The *Bohemian Brethren*, as they are called, or *Moravians*, were descended from the better sort of *Hussites*, and that at the Councils of Ostorg 1620, and 1627, the two communities of Bohemians and Swiss

[Hussites] became consolidated into one, which took the name of *the church of the United Brethren*, and retained the *form* and *regulations* of the Bohemians, but embraced the *doctrines* of the Reformed."—(*Cent.* xvi. *sec.* iii. *Pt.* ii. c. 11, § 23.)

§ 39. Notwithstanding all this uncertainty and diversity of opinion and statement concerning their origin, there is no uncertainty about the main point of our inquiry, to wit, that the Moravians are a sect outside of the visible Society which has existed ever since the Ascension of our Lord. The Moravians undoubtedly, however, a Sect outside of the Church.

It is pretty certain that Moravia had been (imperfectly no doubt) converted, in a great measure, before Methodius and Cyrillus, the Greek Monks, went there, and that too by missionaries in the Roman Obedience. At all events, the Church in Moravia was soon brought into the Roman Obedience, and the few seceders only who joined the Waldenses enter in as an element towards making up the modern sect of the Moravians.

We have already seen who and what the people called Waldensians were. The Hussites were also a sect of seceders (probably from the Diocese of Constance in Switzerland) whom Huss had gathered around him. None of these things can give ecclesiastical character to them as a part of Christ's visible Church. They make no claim to such a position in the sense in which we are using the words, *i. e.* to denote the visible society which has existed since His day.

It would certainly be strange if we are called upon to allow to the Moravians what they do not claim for themselves. We have seen that in the Document written by one of their bishops, *Schweinitz*, and "sanctioned by the Board of the Moravian church," they do not even claim to be considered a church at all, but only "*a social organization*" in which each individual can have certain facilities for leading a Christian life. But it will not altogether answer to take them at their word; for they are regarded as a church by others, if not by themselves, and they perform all the functions of a church. But yet *as a church* they do not claim to have been a part of that Church which was instituted in the Apostles' days and continued its visible existence down even unto the time of the origin of the Moravians. But, on the contrary, they claim, as one great point of their merit, that they arose for the purpose of opposing the errors and corruptions of that Church. It would therefore be doing violence to all use of language and all notions of identity, no less than gross injustice to them, to say that they were that very Church, or a part of it, which they organized themselves only or chiefly for the purpose of opposing. Their right to become a church is another question, and one which we neither deny nor discuss in this place. But the fact that, as a church, they are distinct from, and not the same as the Church which had long been established where they originated, and was then in the Roman Obedience, the corruptions of which they arose to deny and protest against, is all that we are now seeking to ascertain.

The Moravians claim in this country about 6,000 people, 22 congregations, 24 clergymen, two of them bishops.

§ 40. We now come to the last in our lis **The Presbyterians** of the *Primary Sects*. I shall take my account of the Presbyterians chiefly from the article of Dr. Krebs, *Permanent Clerk of the General Assembly*, in Rupp's Collection.

"The Presbyterian church in the United States derives its lineage from the Presbyterians both in Ireland and Scotland. It is true that Presbyterianism was the form not only of the church of Scotland, but also of the Reformed churches on the continent of Europe, and indeed of the Puritans of England about the time of the Westminster Assembly [1643;] and contributions from all these sources have been made at various times to the elements of the American Presbyterian church. But still it is unquestionable that the early founders of this church were principally Scotch and Irish Presbyterians.

"In like manner, the *church of Scotland* was *more than any other*, their model in the whole arrangement of their judicatories, and in their whole ecclesiastical nomenclature, with few exceptions. And on this account the Presbyterian church in this country has always been popularly and appropriately regarded as the daughter, more especially of the church of Scotland."

We have already examined, so far as our present undertaking requires, the ecclesiastical position of those who came to this country as "elements to the American Presbyterian church," from "the Reformed churches on the Continent," and after giving an account of its establishment here, we will proceed to an account of those that came from Scotland.

The primary ecclesiastical union of the American Presbyterians occurred in 1706, when the Presbytery of Philadelphia was founded. At the meeting of the Synod in 1721, there was made a declaration that the Presbyterians in America had exercised the Presbyterian government and discipline according to the practice of 'the best reformed churches,' as far as the nature and constitution of this country would allow. In 1728, an overture was presented to the Synod of Philadelphia respecting subscription to the confession of Faith and Catechisms, &c.

" Although the Westminster Assembly's Confession of Faith and Catechisms 'always had been the only standard of faith, rites, government and discipline,' yet the Book itself had never been formally announced as the Creed and Directory of the American Presbyterians. In the next year this Book was adopted. The first General Assembly met in 1789."

Dr. MILLER, of *Princeton Theological Seminary*, N. J., who is perhaps the highest individual authority in the case, thus begins his article on the Presbyterian church in the United States, in the "Encyclopedia of Religious Knowledge," p. 966:

" This denomination is to be considered as the offspring of the church of Scotland."

Our attention is, therefore, in the first place, chiefly directed to Scotland.

§ 41. The Church of Scotland was brought

The Reformation in Scotland. into the Roman Obedience about the beginning of the twelfth century, and so continued until the sixteenth. In 1555, JOHN KNOX, who is regarded as the great Scotch Reformer, returned from

Geneva, in Switzerland, and added great vigor to the reformation which had already been begun. The Bishops and ecclesiastical authorities generally opposed the movement. The contest was carried on, on both sides, in a most unjustifiable spirit. The civil authorities were called into requisition by both parties, as it was found possible to make use of them. In 1558, the reforming party in the Parliament described themselves as "*the Nobility and Commons of the Protestants of the Church of Scotland.*" In 1560, the Parliament published by their authority, " the Confession of Faith professed and believed by the Protestants within the realm of Scotland." This Confession was confirmed by the three estates in Parliament on the 17th of August, and on the 24th of the same month, the jurisdiction of the Pope was abolished by the same authority. The Bishops and Clergy who were in Parliament seem to have acquiesced in this proceeding, though they did not approve of it. They lived and died for the most part Papists. On the 20th of December in the same year, "the Protestants of the Church of Scotland" held their first General Assembly. It consisted of *forty-six* persons, of- whom Knox was the principal. They commenced operations as an organized sect about this time, being as yet, of course, only a small minority, and in opposition to the Church and its Clergy generally.

Thus things went on; the Protestants gaining in numbers and influence. Some of the Bishops joined

---

[1] Lawson's *Hist. of the Episcopal Church of Scotland from the Reformation to the Revolution*, p. 41.

them—as for instance, the Bishops of Galloway, Orkney, Caithness and Argyll. Some of the Bishoprics soon became vacant by death or otherwise, and in 1572, a Convocation was held at *Leith* in which some very important steps were taken. It was not thought expedient, however, to alter the titles of the Archbishops and Bishops, nor the bounds of the Dioceses, but rather that they stand and continue as before the Reformation. Some of the old Bishops had conformed, and the places of the others were now filled, but without regular and canonical ordination, with Protestants.

This constituted what was called a *Tulchan* Episcopacy—a term derived, as Lawson says, from a practice then prevalent, of stuffing a calf's skin with straw, and placing it before a cow, to induce the animal to give milk, which figure was called a "*tulchan*"—a term derived from a word signifying a model, or close resemblance.

From this time [1572] the Clergy in the Roman Obedience ceased to claim or exercise jurisdiction or ministerial functions in the Church of Scotland.

This '*Tulchan*' Episcopacy continued until 1610. In 1607, James I., King of England, and VIth of Scotland, summoned a General Assembly of the Scotch Church to be held at *Dundee* on the 24th of November. Each of the Presbyteries were required to send "two of the most godly, peaceable, wise and grave" of their number, as their representatives. A Conference was also held at Falkland, in Fife, in June 1608, and a General Assembly again in Dundee, on the 26th of July the same year. In all these meetings, progress was made towards the settlement of the state of affairs in the Church, in a more satisfactory manner. In 1610, three of those persons who were actually in possession of the Sees, or had been nominated to those that were vacant, SPOTTISWOODE, of Glasgow, LAMB, of Brechin, and HAMILTON, of Galloway, went to London, and were ordained Bishops by the Bishops of the English Church. They returned home and consecrated the others, who either were in possession of, or had been appointed to the vacant Sees.

Thus the Church became again, in fact, as well as in name and form, Episcopal.

In 1574 ANDREW MELVILLE returned from a ten years' residence in Geneva, and if he was not the first to introduce a preference for the Presbyterian form of church government, he certainly added great vigor to the zeal of those who entertained such a preference.[1] His party continued to increase until 1637, when they combined and drove those of the Episcopal Clergy, who would not submit to the Presbyterian rule, out of their places in the Church.

The establishment of Presbyterianism at this period, was no act of the Church. The General Assembly—which met at Glasgow, Nov. 17, 1638—consisted, according to the laws of the Church and the Realm, of the King's Commissioner, (at that time the Marquis of Hamilton,) the Bishops, and inferior clergy and laity as Delegates. The King's Commissioner was acknowledged to have the right to dissolve the Assembly. Such an Assembly was the highest ecclesiastical authority in Scotland, and the only one that

---

[1] LAWSON'S *Hist.*, as before, p. 131.

could make any change or regulation of any kind in the Church. But on the 21st of November, before any business had been transacted, the Bishops protested against the Assembly and refused to have anything to do with it, on the ground of illegality in the election of the Deputies, and for other reasons. This protest or "*Declinature*" as it was called, occasioned a good deal of discussion—the Marquis taking sides with the Bishops. On the 29th he dissolved the Assembly and withdrew. Episcopacy was abolished and Presbyterianism established by this *remainder* of a General Assembly—after the Protest or Declinature of the Bishops—after the withdrawal of the Lord High Commissioner—and after, therefore, the Dissolution of the Assembly by what it had hitherto acknowledged a competent authority, and according to its own rules and laws.[1]

But on the Restoration of King Charles II. to the throne of England, in 1660, steps were taken to bring back those of the Episcopal Clergy that survived, to their places in the Church in Scotland, as well as in England. On the 15th of December, 1661, four persons were consecrated, for the Scottish Sees, and they, on their return home, filled up by consecration the other Sees as before 1637. *Sydserf*, of Galloway, the only Scotch Bishop that survived the Rebellion and remained faithful to the Church, was transferred to the See of Orkney. The four new Bishops were *James Sharp*, Archbishop of St. Andrews, *Andrew Fairfoul*, Archbishop of Glasgow, *James Hamilton*, Bishop of Galloway, and *Robert Leighton*, for Dumblane.

[1] LAWSON, pp. 571—590.

Thus again was Episcopacy restored to the Church of Scotland. It appears from the testimony of the Earl of Glencairne, that the Episcopalians were six to one in point of numbers at this time.[1] The Presbyterians, who were now excluded from its ministry and its Churches, many of them settled in Ireland, some came to America, and many remained at home as a sect in opposition to the Church.

§ 42. But the act which has led the Presbyterians in this country to call the Presbyterians in Scotland "*the Church of Scotland,*" is of a subsequent date, and remains yet to be related. *The Legal Establishment of the Presbyterians, as the "Church of Scotland."*

In 1688, occurred a change in the English Dynasty. James II., the last of the line of the Stuarts, left the kingdom, and William, Prince of Orange, the husband of the eldest daughter of the King, came to the Throne. James, however, had a son, who, according to the laws of England, and the oaths of all in office in the realm, was the legitimate heir to the crown. The Scotch Bishops and clergy generally, adhered to James and his son. The Presbyterians, on the other hand, readily yielded their support to William. In an interview between Compton, Bishop of London, and Rose, Bishop of Edinburg, Compton said to Rose that William was satisfied that "the great body of the nobility and gentry of Scotland were for Episcopacy, and that he had directed him [Compton] to say that if the Episcopalians of Scotland would undertake to serve him to the purpose that he

---

[1] LAWSON, p. 671.

is served in England, he would take them by the hand, support the Church and order, and throw off the Presbyterians."[1]

The Presbyterians had kept alive their animosities towards the Church, from the time of Melville's return. Their feelings had been much embittered by the proceedings of the Churchmen, at and after the Restoration: and they were ready to avail themselves of any advantage in their favor that might present itself. William, after his recognition as king, took the revenues of the Scotch Bishops and put them into his pocket, by an order published October 19, 1689.[2] Ever since that time these revenues have been paid into the Royal Exchequer.[3] An act, passed in the Scotch Parliament through the King's influence, on the 24th of April, 1690, gave to the *Presbyterian Seceders* the possession and control of the Church edifices and property; and on the 7th of June following, the Westminster Confession of Faith was declared, by *the same authority*, to be the allowed and established Confession of Faith in Scotland, and "the Presbyterian church-government and Discipline " " established, ratified and confirmed."[4]

The Bishops and Clergy, however, refused compliance, and continued their ministrations entirely distinct from the Presbyterians, as far as the tyranny

---

[1] Lathbury's *Hist. of the Non Jurors*, p. 416, where this testimony as to the comparative numbers, &c., of the Churchmen and the Presbyterians is abundantly sustained.

[2] Lawson's *Hist. of the Church of Scotland since the Revolution*, p. 100.

[3] Lawson's *Hist. of the Ch. of Scotland*, pp. 103-105.   [4] Ibid. p. 29.

of the laws and the violence of Presbyterian intolerance would permit. A large portion of the people still adhered to their communion—and thus the identity of the Church of Scotland was preserved by them, notwithstanding the dis-establishment by the secular authorities, and the violence that was brought to bear against it.

§ 43. Now this mere legal establishment of a Sect could not make it a different body ecclesiastically from what it had been before; and though the title which belonged to the Church was given to the Sect, this fact did not change the identity of either body. *This Legal Establishment did not change the Identity of the Church.*

Thus we have several distinct periods in the history of the Scotch Church—(1.) from 1560, the rejection of the Papal Supremacy, to 1572, the commencement of the Tulchan Episcopacy—(2.) from 1572 to 1610, the first consecration of Bishops in England for the Scotch Sees—(3.) from 1610 to 1638, when the illegal Assembly of Glasgow pretended to establish Presbyterianism in the Church—(4.) from 1638 to 1661, when Episcopacy was again recognized by law as the rightful government in the Church—(5.) from 1661 to 1689, when the Church property was transferred by King and Parliament into the hands of the Presbyterians, and they were constituted the "Established Church."

Thus the Scotch Church, properly so called, was never Presbyterian in its form of government.

"The first Presbyterian church that was organized and furnished with a place of worship in this country," says Dr. MILLER, "was about 1703." Their first presbytery was organized in 1704. But neither the Church of Scotland, nor the Sect which is by law entitled to that name, appear to have had anything to do with it. The agents in its formation were indeed chiefly of Scotch descent. But they were neither members of the Scotch Church when they came to this country, nor admitted to its communion afterwards. And, in point of fact they were as completely seceders from the Scotch Establishment, [Presbyterian,] as they were from the Scotch Church properly so called.

<small>The Presbyterian church in this Country, not established by the Church of Scotland, properly so called.</small> § 44. When, therefore, the Presbyterians say that the Presbyterian church in America was founded by the Church of Scotland, they mean that it was founded by the Presbyterian Sect, which since their establishment by the state, have been called "the Church of Scotland."

It is not true, therefore, in the sense required by the essential principles of the identity of the Church, that the Presbyterian church in this country was established by the Church of Scotland—but it was established by Presbyterians seceding from the Church of Scotland, for the purpose of founding a church different from that, and on an entirely different basis.

<small>The Irish Presbyterians, who come to this Country, Seceders from the Irish Church.</small> § 45. If we turn our attention to Ireland, we find the same general state of facts. In 1537, the Papal jurisdiction was abolished by Parliament, and the Bishops, Clergy, and whole Church generally assented to the Reformation. In the reign of MARY, the Papist, five of the Irish Bishops who would not conform to the Ro-

man Obedience, were expelled from their Sees. When, in 1550, the Reformation was restored, seventeen out of nineteen Bishops in Parliament approved it, and the rest of the Bishops and clergy generally, as well as the people acquiesced. But Presbyterianism was never established in the Church in Ireland. The Presbyterians were always, whenever there were any, seceders from the Church, so confessedly and nominally, as well as in fact.

§ 46. When the Presbyterians gained the ascendancy in the English Parliament, 1643, they appointed the famous Westminster Assembly of Divines—to provide for a change in religion. In consequence, Episcopacy and the Prayer Book were abolished—so far as the authority of Parliament could effect such a result, and Presbyterianism established instead. The Independents petitioned for toleration, and a correspondence ensued. From the Presbyterian replies, as given in "COLLIER's Church History of Great Britain," (Vol. VIII., p. 297—302,) I make the following quotations:— *The Principles of the Presbyterians with regard to Separation from the Church.*

"That the toleration which the Independents asked could not be granted, as it would 'be licensing perpetual division in the Church;' that 'the request supposes the lawfulness of gathering churches out of true Churches—in countenance of which there is not the least example in all the Holy Scriptures,' that 'if the Church requires that which is evil of any member, he must forbear compliance, but yet without separation,' 'that though tenderness of conscience may oblige to forbear or suspend the act of communion in a case scrupled and supposed unlawful; yet it does not bind people to a practice repugnant to the will of God; of which kind they conceive the gathering separate churches out of true churches to be an instance; that 'the notion of separation is not to be determined by the civil legislature, nor by acts of State, but by the word of God,' 'the same ground of separation may be plead by any erroneous conscience whatever, and thus by the same equity and parity of reasoning the Church may be broken into as many subdivisions as there are different scruples in the minds of men,' 'and in this new shelter, the same danger may be apprehended, and carry the scrupling persons to a further distance. And are these subdivisions and fractions in church government as lawful as they may be infinite? Or must we give that regard to erroneous consciences as to satisfy men's scruples by so unbounded a liberty? Does not this plainly import that *error in conscience* is a protection against [the guilt of] schism.' 'Scruple of conscience is no good plea against the charge of schism, the motives must have more weight in them.'"

Such is the language used, and the views held by the men who composed the Westminster Assembly—of whose *Confession of Faith and Catechism*, Dr. KREBS, "*Permanent Clerk*," &c., says that they "always have been the *only standard* [!] of Faith, Rites, Government and Discipline of the Presbyterians of this country."

I do not intend to adopt this language altogether—or to make an indiscriminate application of it. But it states with great plainness several points—(1.) that the Scriptures do not allow of the gathering of a church out of one that is already established, that is, establishing a second, where there is already one— (2.) that the civil authority or "acts of the state" can give no authority or be any justification for so doing, the matter being exclusively of a religious character— (3.) that error and evil in a Church is no justification of separation, though it may be necessary to refuse compliance in particular acts—(4.) that inasmuch as conscience may be erroneous and corrupt, *its* scruples alone are no sufficient plea or excuse for an act of separation—and (5.) that therefore, there can be no justification for a separation from a Church that is truly a Branch of the Church of Christ.

Now this is in the main, sound reasoning. When the Presbyterians used it, they supposed they occupied the position which the Church of England now occupies—that is, the position of a valid Branch of the Church, historically connected with the past, and which could be identified with the main Body. The reasoning which they then used for their own advantage, as they supposed, if it were now turned against them, completely cuts off their claim.

§ 47. In considering these Sects, I have avoided a statement of their doctrines and constitution except in so far as some allusion to them came in incidentally. But of them all it may be said:— General Observations on all the Primary Sects.

1. That no one of them has the Ministry which our Lord instituted, continued and perpetuated in the way which has always, in the Church, been esteemed essential to its identity.

2. That no one of them is based upon the Creed of

the Primitive Church, or professes to hold to it as their Rule of Faith, but each of them has a Rule of its own, and peculiar to itself.

3. That they all have been organized not by, or with the consent and approbation of the Church in which their founders were members, but always and in all cases within the jurisdiction of that Church, and in opposition to its laws and authority.

4. That no one of them has ever been recognized as a Branch of the Church of Christ by any Church which has existed from the Apostle's days, or any that has been planted by such an Apostolic Church. But they have always regarded themselves, and have been regarded by others as constituting a communion, or perhaps several, by themselves, which has arisen into being since the commencement of the Reformation.

If we look, however, at their constitution, we shall find that *two* of them—the Baptists and Congregationalists—are *Congregational* in their form of Church organization and government; *four*, namely, the Dutch Reformed, the German Reformed, the Lutherans, and the Presbyterians, are *Presbyterian;* and *three*, namely, the Mennonites, the Moravians, and the Methodists are *Episcopal*.

Yet neither upon these facts, nor on account of the Doctrines which they teach, or the Rules of Faith which they have respectively adopted, do I call them new and distinct churches. But it is because neither the visible existence of any one of them, nor that of any church which owns them as a branch of itself, can be traced back to an origin within many centuries of the foundation of the Church of Christ, or is, in its origin, identified with any Branch of that Church.

§ 48. I have no disposition to call in question the piety or motives of those who have been instrumental in laying the foundations of these sects. On the contrary I had much rather dwell upon the excuses and apologies for their error—which are to be found in the times and circumstances of their lives. The abuses and evils in the Church were great, and the influence of the preceding centuries had, perhaps on the whole, been calculated to produce views of the organization and discipline of the Church, more completely erroneous than of the doctrines of the Gospel. The reformers of whom we have been speaking felt deeply the evils under which they were suffering. But they saw no clear and satisfactory way of escape. Unlike the English Reformers, the Church and ecclesiastical authorities with which, by the Providence of God, they were connected, were against them. They considered themselves called upon to bear their testimony against the evils and corruptions of their day. In this we certainly cannot consider them in the wrong. Yet the measure was almost certain to lead to their excision from the Church by its constituted authorities. And it is now impossible to say what might have been the result if they had pursued a course not less firm and faithful, but more meek and conciliatory. The truth has a power and vitality of its own, in all cases. But religious truth is especially the object of Divine care. If they had simply borne their testimony and submitted to whatever might have been inflicted

The Motives of the Founders of these Sects, admitted to have been good.

upon them, the good seed might, and probably would have taken deeper root, and sprung up to a more wide spread growth, and Germany, instead of being, as it is, overrun with pantheism, rationalism, and infidelity, would probably have presented us with a Protestant Church, sound in the faith, unblameable in life, and embracing the great mass of the population.

But to human foresight—for man sees not as God seeth—it seemed that without some association or combination amongst themselves, their influence would be greatly circumscribed, and perhaps wholly counteracted and lost to the world. Therefore, they organized into churches, formed rules of faith for themselves, and undertook to perform ecclesiastical functions. But still as we have seen, they felt and confessed their ecclesiastical deficiencies—they acknowledged themselves to be new churches, whose visible existence could by no means be traced back to Christ and His Apostles, or identified with the Church then established: and putting their trust in Him, whose prerogative it is to bring good out of evil, they relied upon the necessities of the case for their justification in what they were doing.

With this, however, we are not now to concern ourselves. We have ascertained the fact that they are not parts of that visible and continuous Church which Christ and the Apostles founded—this they did not claim to be, and that is all that we need now to ascertain concerning them.

SECONDARY SECTS.

These, it will be remembered, are those that have split off from one of the Primary Sects.

§ 49. 1. ASSOCIATE PRESBYTERIAN CHURCH IN NORTH AMERICA. *Secessions from the Presbyterian church.*

This is a branch of the church of Scotland, [the Presbyterians] and holds the doctrines of the Westminster Assembly. It was formed in 1733. In consequence of the recognition of the Presbyterians as the Establishment in Scotland by William and Mary, in 1688, a law was passed in 1712, giving the right of patronage and presentment to lay proprietors. This led to a secession in 1733, and the seceders took the title above written. They have in the United States 105 ministers, 211 congregations, 13,477 communicants.— (*Rev. W. I. Cleland, and Rev. James P. Miller.*)

2. REFORMED PRESBYTERIAN CHURCH.

This sect also is formed of persons who seceded from the Scotch Presbyterians in 1688, in consequence of their consenting to become the Establishment, and be supported by law. They were organized into a sect in this country in 1798. They have about 30 ministers, 44 congregations—(*The Rev. John N. McLeod, D. D., N. Y.*)

3. ASSOCIATE REFORMED CHURCH.

Between 1660 and 1688, a large number [3,000 *Wodrow,*]of Presbyterians were brought to this country from Scotland and sold for slaves, chiefly in Virginia, Pennsylvania and New Jersey. The first steps towards organization into a church were taken in 1736 by the *Associate Presbyterian church, &c.* In 1751 they received a minister from the *Reformed Presbyterian church*, and in 1774 they received two more. In 1782 they became a fully organized sect. Efforts have been made to unite them with the two sects just named, derived from the Scotch Presbyterians, but they have hitherto been unavailing. They have about 160 ministers, and 260 congregations.—(*Rev. John Forsyth, D. D., Professor in the Seminary at Newburg, New-York.*)

4. CUMBERLAND PRESBYTERIANS.

This sect was founded in 1796, by the Rev. James McGready. It originated chiefly in an effort for a revival in Kentucky. It resulted in the formation of the sect in 1802. A General Assembly was formed in 1829. They have 13 Synods, and 57 Presbyteries —[350 ministers, 480 churches, and 50,000 members.]—(*Rev. Dr. Beard, President of the Cumberland College, Princeton, Ky.*)

5. PRESBYTERIANS, [*New School.*]

In 1837 there was a division effected in the Presbyterian church in this country. There had been for a long time a difference of opinion among the Presbyterians, chiefly in regard to three points, "human depravity," the "extent of the atonement," and "the freedom of the will." The party taking the extreme views on these points attempted to enforce them upon the others in 1837. The more liberal party seceded. They also claim that some measures contrary to the Constitution of the General Assembly had been used in favor of the Old School views. They have 1,551 ministers, 1,651 congregations, 155,000 members.— (*The Rev. Dr. Parker, of Philadelphia.*)

§ 50. 1. FREEWILL BAPTISTS. *Secessions from the Baptists.*

This connexion was founded in 1780. The first Baptist church was of general views, and the Baptists in several of the States were Armenian long before the Freewill Baptist connexion arose. In 1780, this portion, being in the minority, seceded. They have 898 ministers, 1,057 churches, and 54,000 members.—(*Rev. Porter S. Burbank.*)

2. SEVENTH-DAY BAPTISTS.

In 1665, a Seventh-day Baptist came from England, and in 1681 he and his followers came to an open separation from the Baptist church on the ground, as their name indicates, of their preferring the *seventh* day of the week for their Sabbath. They have forty ordained ministers, 50 churches, 6,000 members.—(*Rev. W. B. Gillett, Pastor of the Seventh-day Baptist church, Piscataway, N. J.*)

3. DISCIPLES OF CHRIST.

These are sometimes called 'Reformed Baptist' and 'Campbellites.' This sect was chiefly founded by Mr. Thomas Campbell, who had been a minister in the "Secession" branch of the Scotch Presbyterians. He and his followers were baptized again by immersion in 1812. In 1813 they were received into communion with the regular Baptists. But soon after they separated again. They claim about 200,000 members.—(*Rev. R. Richardson of Va.*)

§ 51. 1. REFORMED MENONITES. *Secession from the Menonites.*

This sect commenced in 1811—when certain members of the Menonite connexion, deploring the general decline in the piety of their sect commenced a reformation. They do not deem themselves at liberty to keep an accurate account of their members. —(*Rev. John Herr, Strasburg, one of their Bishops.*)

2. GERMAN BAPTISTS OR BRETHREN.

This sect are often called "Dunkers." They came to this country from Germany in 1718–1730.—(*Rev. Philip Boyle, Uniontown, Md.*)

3. SEVENTH-DAY GERMAN BAPTISTS.

This sect is an offshoot from the foregoing under the leading of Conrad Beissel, in 1728.—(*Dr. Wm. H. Fahnstock.*)

4. AMISH OR OMISH CHURCH.

This is a sect of the Menonites, separated from the rest chiefly on the ground of being more strict in their dress and discipline. They have about 5,000 members, and are sometimes called '*Hook* Menonites,' while the others are called '*Button* Menonites.'— (*Shem Zook.*)

Secessions from the German Reformed church. § 52. THE CHURCH OF GOD.

In 1820, the Rev. John Winebrenner commenced a revival in Harrisburg, Pa., which extended to some distance around. His movement was disapproved by the German Reformed authorities, and led to a separation, and the formation of a new sect, with the title above given. They have 83 ministers, 125 congregations, and 10,000 members.—(*Winebrenner, V. D. M.*)

§ 53. UNITARIANS.

Secessions from the Congregationalists.

Unitarian sentiments made their appearance very early among the descendants of the Puritans in New England. In 1815, a new impulse was given to the subject by the publication of Belsham's Life of Lindsey. A controversy was commenced, which led to an open separation between the two parts of the Congregational church. The Unitarians have about 300 congregations.—(*Dr. Lamson, of Dedham, Mass.*)

§ 54. 1. THE METHODIST SOCIETY.

The Secessions from the Methodists.

This Society was first composed of a number of members seceding from the Methodist Episcopal church in the city of New-York, in the year 1820, together with several of their trustees. It had its origin in the ruling elder's insisting on receiving the money collected in the different churches under his charge through stewards of his own appointment, instead of the usual and lawful way. They have three Conferences.—(*Rev. W. M. Stillwell.*)

2. METHODIST PROTESTANT CHURCH.

This sect was organized in 1830. It consists mostly of seceders from the Methodist Episcopal church "on account of her government and hostility to lay representation." It has 1,300 preachers, and 60,000 members.—(*Rev. J. R. Williams, of Baltimore.*)

3. REFORMED METHODIST CHURCH.

This sect took its origin from a feeble secession from the Methodist Episcopal church in Vermont,

1814. They believe in "the attainableness of entire sanctification in this life." No statistics are given.—(*Rev. Wesley Bailey, Utica, N. Y.*)

4. THE TRUE WESLEYAN METHODIST CHURCH.

This society was organized in 1843. It consists of seceders from the original sect, and from the Methodist Protestants. They united for the purpose of having "churches free from Episcopacy, Intemperance and Slavery." They have about 600 preachers and 20,000 members.—(*Rev. J. Timberman, Pastor, &c., N. Y.*)

This completes the list of Secondary Sects.

AUTOTHENTIC SECTS.

Under this head I include those sects which can hardly be called branches or offshoots from any of the preceding ones; but which are rather the organized body of the followers of some one or more influential individuals gathered from many sects, perhaps, and composed in a measure of those that had not previously belonged to any sect or profession of religion.

§ 55. 1. CHRISTIANS.

Sects which profess to be built upon the Scriptures alone, as the Source of Divine Knowledge.

It is claimed for this sect that they do not owe their origin to any one man. They arose nearly simultaneously in different sections of the country. In N. C., James O'Kelly and several other preachers seceded from the Methodists on account of some disagreement in regard to their church government. In Vermont, Abner Jones, among the Baptists, commenced to preach against creeds and sectarian names, and gathered a church in 1800. About the same time a number of Presbyterians, in Ky., and Tenn., began to entertain similar views, and Barton W. Stone, with several others, seceded. They are not Trinitarians, reject infant baptism, and baptize by immersion. They have 1,500 preachers, and 500 licentiates, 1,500 churches, and 325,000 members.—(*Rev. David Millard.*)

2. THE EVANGELICAL ASSOCIATION.

In 1796, Jacob Albright began to preach among the Germans, "among whom at this time Christianity was at a very low ebb." He was quite successful, and in 1800 his followers formed themselves into an association; and in 1803 they introduced among themselves "an ecclesiastical regulation." "Albright was chosen presiding Elder among them, and duly confirmed by the other preachers, and ordained by their laying on of hands, so as to authorize him to perform all transactions that are necessary for a Christian Society, and becoming to an evangelical preacher." They have between 200 and 300 preachers, and near 15,000 members.—(*Rev. W. W. Orwig.*)

3. SCHWENKFELDERS.

This sect was founded by Caspar Schwenkfeld Van Ossing of Silesia. A number of them came to Pennsylvania in 1734. They have a peculiar custom of calling their minister to pray over and for infants instead of baptizing them. They invert the words of the institution of the sacrament of the Lord's Supper, (This is My Body,) and say, My Body is this—

that is, such as is this bread which is broken for you, &c. They have at present in this country about 300 families and 5 churches.—(*Isaac Schultz.*)

4. UNIVERSALISTS.

This sect was chiefly founded by John Murray and Elhanan Winchester, from 1775 to 1780. Their first convention was held in 1785. They believe that all retribution or punishment is confined to this world. They have 646 preachers, and 990 societies.—*Rev. A. B. Grosh.*)

5. RESTORATIONISTS.

This Sect split off from the Universalists in 1831, on account of the original sect declaring against any punishment or opportunity for repentance in a future world. They have 14 clergymen, and 10 or 12 congregations.—(*Hon. Charles Hudson.*)

6. UNITED BRETHREN IN CHRIST.

This denomination took its rise in the United States about 1755, and is distinguished from the Old United Brethren or Moravians by the additional phrase "In Christ." The founder was Wm. Otterbein. The sect bears many points of resemblance to the Methodists, though gathered chiefly from among the Germans. They have 3 bishops, 500 preachers, and 65,000 members.—(*Rev. Wm. Hanby.*)

7. SECOND ADVENT BELIEVERS.

This sect was commenced by Wm. Miller, who began to lecture in 1831. They are distinguished by their view of the second Advent and their belief that the present dispensation and order of things in the world will soon come to an end. They have already fixed upon several dates which have not realized their expectations. Their numbers cannot be ascertained.—(*Most of these facts are taken from N. Southard, Editor of the Midnight Cry.*)

§ 56. 1. FRIENDS OR QUAKERS.

Sects which claim some Special Revelation or Inspiration, besides that received through the Bible.

This sect was founded by George Fox. He commenced his labors in 1647, in England. About 1655, some of the people arrived in America. They discard a Ministry, Sacraments, and outward Forms generally. Without discarding the Scriptures altogether, they believe in an "*inner light*" or "*a Spirit within*," which is recognized as the principal guide in divine things.—(*T. Evans.*)

2. FRIENDS (*Hicksites.*)

This society was founded by a secession from the foregoing in 1827. The cause of the division was doctrinal differences in opinion.

3. SHAKERS.

This sect was founded by the French Prophets in Dauphiny and Cevennes, in France, about 1688. In a few years, several hundred protestants professed to be inspired; their bodies were much agitated with various operations; when they received the spirit of prophecy they trembled, staggered and fell down, and lay as if they were dead. They recovered twitching, shaking, and crying to God for mercy for themselves and all mankind. Three of their most distinguished prophets came to London about 1705. In 1772 the society residing in Lancashire, England, received a revelation from God to repair to America. They arrived in New-York in 1774. They have 16 societies, and 4,500 members.—(*Thomas Brown.*)

4. NEW JERUSALEM, OR NEW CHRISTIAN, CHURCH.

This sect was founded by Emanuel Swedenborg, who commenced his labors in this department about 1743. He did not profess to make a new revelation, but merely to apply a new key to its interpretation. The church first received its form in England in 1783. The doctrine was introduced in the United States in 1784. The followers of Swedenborg now generally claim for him and his writings, a special inspiration. They have about 5,000 members.

5. LATTER DAY SAINTS.

"The Church of Jesus Christ of Latter Day Saints was founded upon direct revelation, as the true Church of God has ever been." Joseph Smith, the founder of this sect, was told supernaturally that "all the denominations were believing in incorrect doctrines, and none of them acknowledged by God as his." Smith "was directed not to go after them. On the 21st of Sept., 1823, a person appeared to him calling himself an angel of God, sent to assure Smith that God's covenant with ancient Israel was about to be fulfilled, and that he [Smith] was chosen to accomplish an important part of it." He received a revelation concerning the aboriginal inhabitants of this country. He was told of the existence of certain plates on which was engraven an abridgement of the records of the ancient prophets that had existed on this continent. "On the 22d of Sept., 1827, the angel delivered to Smith the records. With them was found, also, the Urim and Thummin by which he translated the records which were written in Egyptian characters." In April, 1830, was first organized the church of the Latter Day Saints. They have 150,000 members.— (*Joseph Smith.*)

This closes the list of Sects in this country, so far as I am able to make out any account of them.

§ 57. In what I have said, I have been mainly indebted to the industry and research of Mr. Rupp, whose collection I have more than once spoken of. The facts are generally given as I found them stated by the author, whose name I have appended to each paragraph. I have preferred to give them as I found them, though I would not be understood to vouch for their accuracy in all cases. But if they are not correct, the error, being made by one of their own partisans, is most likely to be in their favor; and at any rate no blame can be attached to me for it. *This Account of the Sects given on their own Authority.*

§ 58. Besides the Sects named above, there are particular congregations scattered all over our land, which are in fact, communions or sects by themselves, and of which no account has here been or can be given. A few individuals taking a dislike to something in the affairs or doctrine of the church to which *Besides this, there are many Sects that cannot be classified or described.*

they have belonged, almost without hesitation, make it a matter of conscience, withdraw and constitute themselves a new church wholly independent of, and disconnected from all others.

But, besides all this, the vast majority of our population make no profession of religion at all.

§ 59. It is, of course, unnecessary to enter at large into a discussion of the connection between these churches and that visible society which has had a continuous existence from the days of Christ. The facts of their origin present nothing that requires anything more to be said than what we have already had occasion to say, and the application of which is too obvious to need repetition here.

<small>In what sense these Sects claim to be Christian churches.</small>

I have said of the Primary Sects, and it is still more true of the last two classes that we have noticed, that they make no pretensions to be a part of the Church of Christ. Of course I would not be guilty of a misstatement or misrepresentation. Neither would I dodge or evade any fact or objection that fairly lies in my way. I therefore recur to this assertion for the purpose of explaining it in such a way as to make the whole matter perfectly clear.

When I say, then, that none of these sects make any pretension or claim to be parts of the Church of Christ, I must be understood to use the words in their strictest and most appropriate sense as indicating that society or Church which has had a visible and continuous existence from the time of its first establishment in Judea unto the present day, and which has always been known and called by that name. Now, in this sense of the words, all persons readily admit the correctness of my assertion. For there is none of these sects that professes (1) to have had a distinct visible existence from the Apostles' days—or (2) to have been founded by a Church that has had such an existence, or by its members *with its concurrence and approbation*—or (3) finally, to be in communion with any Church which has had such a distinct continuous existence, or with one which has been founded by such a Church. On the contrary they profess to have left and forsaken that Church and its branches on account of a disagreement in doctrine, discipline or worship, in order that they might found one that should be different in those respects, and more agreeable to their own opinions and consciences.

Yet, in another sense it seems they do claim to be parts of the Church of Christ or Christian churches. I confess that I am somewhat at a loss to know in what terms they would give a precise and definite statement of the grounds of this claim. It would probably include several items—such as a (1) conformity to the Scripture model—(2) a harmony with the Apostolic doctrines—(3) the fact that there have always been persons who entertained the same views as themselves—and (4) that any number of true believers, associated for the purpose of religion, are a branch of the Church of Christ.

Now we may admit all of these claims without at all interfering with our main proposition—for I have undertaken only to identify that visible Society or Church which was founded by Christ and the Apostles—I have undertaken to show that these Sects are, none of them, identical parts of that Church. This they admit, and it holds equally true, if the grounds stated above on which they claim to be considered churches of Christ be admitted. The admission, however, will raise a new issue.

It is self-evident that the first two propositions are nothing to our purpose. For, most manifestly, there may be many entirely and totally distinct churches built on the same model, and inculcating precisely the same doctrines; therefore these things do by no means prove them to be the same, or one identical body. So with the third. A number of persons, holding similar views, do not necessarily constitute a church. For instance, there may be in the Church of England a hundred persons, holding Presbyterian views, dispersed throughout the Island: but nobody would think of calling these scattered individuals a Presbyterian church. They are members of the English Church still, notwithstanding their opinions—and form no church, society, or association, by themselves.

But, if the fourth point were well founded, it would merely show that these sects were each of them *a* church of Christians—but not that they were a part of that Church which commenced its existence in the first century. They are as clearly separate and distinct from that Church, as they are from one another and among themselves.

It is no part of my design to deny that these sects are Christian churches—that is societies sincerely professing to be founded on the Christian Faith, regulated and governed by Christian principles, and aiming at the salvation of the souls of men. But as visible

Societies, they are all distinct one from another. Historically, for instance, there can be no more doubt that the Presbyterian church is a separate society—from that which our Lord and His Apostles commenced—than that the Presbyterians and the Methodists are two and distinct Societies.

§ 60. I have, in my Introductory Chapter, endeavored to show the importance of the identity of that Church which Christ founded; and, to some extent, wherein that importance consists. I shall now proceed to show that wherever the Scriptures speak of the Church, they speak of a definite visible body; and that whatever they say of any Church they say of the one then established. *The Scriptures speak of the Church as established, when they were written.*

This I do for the purpose of meeting a very common notion—that the Church is not any one particular denomination or visible body—but that it includes, and is made up of all denominations who hold to the essentials of the Faith.

This theory is also intimately connected with that of an *invisible* Church, consisting of all those who are truly converted, whatever may be their ecclesiastical relations.

I shall pursue the investigation with reference to both theories.

Among the first things which our Lord did after entering upon His public ministry, was the gathering around Him a number of disciples, for the purpose of teaching them His Gospel, and forming their character upon the principles of His religion. Soon after His Ascension, we find this body of disciples called "the

Church." Multitudes were added, both of men and women—branches were established in divers places—Gentiles were converted and added to their number;—and still, the society of those that had been converted to Christ was called "the Church."

Thus the Church was founded before any parts of the New Testament Scriptures were written, and to this they refer when they speak of the Church.

§ 61. But it will be contended that the word "*Church*," is sometimes used to denote the number (unknown to us) who are to be heirs of everlasting salvation; that all true believers are members of the Church in this sense of the word, and therefore, their associations for religious purposes, are to be regarded as parts of the visible Church. *[sidenote: Different Senses of the Word "Church" in the Scriptures.]*

This is a matter of so much importance, that we must examine it somewhat at length.

The word "Church" is not used in the English version of the Old Testament at all. But it has, of course, its corresponding words, both in Hebrew and the Septuagint. The Hebrew word means an "*assembly*," a "*congregation*," a "*multitude*," or "*mob*," a "*swarm*," (as of bees, Judges xiv. 8,)[1] The word which is used in the New Testament for church ('Εκκλησία) means nearly the same, a "*multitude assembled*," a "*congregation*," a "*convention*," an "*insurrection*," a "*family*."[2] And in the Syriac version of the New Testament, which is a sort of intermediate between the Hebrew and the Greek original, the

---

[1] GESENIUS *in voc.* [2] SCHLEUSNER *in voc.*

same word (allowing for idiomatic difference) is used where we have the word "Church" in English.

The word "Church," or its Greek original, is used in the New Testament to indicate objects other than Christians in the present state of being, as follows:—

1. The *Jews* while journeying in the wilderness between Egypt and Canaan. *Acts* vii. 38.

2. The *mob* at Ephesus, and is translated "*assembly*," and "*concourse*." *Acts* xix. 32, 39, 40.

3. The blessed company of the spiritual beings in Heaven. *Heb.* xii. 23

4. The building or house in which Christians assembled. 1 *Cor.* xi. 18, 22; xiv. 19, 28, 34, 35; *Heb.* ii. 12.

§ 62. But besides these cases, it is applied only to a visible society of Christians. I know of no way of making this point so clear and impressive as it ought to be, except by quoting the sentences from Scripture, in which the word occurs:— *The Word "Church," in the Scriptures, never used to denote an unascertainable or indefinite number of persons.*

"I will build my Church."[1] "Tell it unto the Church, if he neglect to hear the Church."[2] "Added to the Church daily such as should be saved."[3] "Great fear came upon all the Church."[4] "Persecution against the Church which was at Jerusalem."[5] "Made havoc of the Church."[6] "Then had the Churches rest."[7] "Tidings came unto the ears of the Church."[8] "They assembled themselves with the Church."[9] "Vex certain of the Church."[10] "Prayer was made

---

[1] Matt. xvi. 18. [2] xviii. 17. [3] Acts ii. 47. [4] v. 11. [5] vii. 1. [6] viii. 3. [7] ix. 31. [8] xi. 22. [9] xi. 26. [10] xii. 1.

without ceasing of the Church."[1] "Certain in the Church that was at Antioch."[2] "Elders in every Church."[3] "Had gathered the Church together.,"[4] "Being brought on their way by the Church."[5] "Received of the Church."[6] "Then pleased it the Apostles and Elders with the whole Church."[7] "Went through Syria and Cilicia confirming the Churches."[8] "So were the Churches established in the Faith."[9] "Saluted the Church."[10] "Sent to Ephesus and called the elders of the Church."[11] "To feed the Church of God which He hath purchased with His own blood."[12] "Servant of the Church which is at Cenchrea."[13] "All the Churches of the Gentiles" [give thanks.][14] "The Church which is in their house."[15] "The Churches of Christ salute you."[16] "Host of the whole Church."[17] "The Church of God which is at Corinth."[18] "I teach everywhere in every Church."[19] "Set them to judge who are least esteemed in the Church."[20] "So ordain I in all Churches."[21] "Give none offence to the Church of God."[22] "No such custom, neither the Churches of God."[23] "God hath set some in the Church, first Apostles."[24] "He that prophesieth edifieth the Church."[25] "Interpret that the Church may receive edifying."[26] "Excel to the edifying of the Church."[27] "If therefore the whole Church be come together."[28] "Peace in all Churches of the Saints."[29] "Because I

---

[1] Acts xii. 5. [2] xiii. 1. [3] xiv. 23. [4] xiv. 27. [5] xv. 3. [6] xv. 4. [7] xv. 22. [8] xv. 41. [9] xvi. 5. [10] xviii. 22. [11] xx. 17. [12] xx. 28. [13] Rom. xvi. 1. [14] xvi. 4. [15] xvi. 5. [16] xvi. 16. [17] xvi. 23. [18] 1 Cor. i. 2. 2 Cor. i. 1. [19] 1 Cor. iv. 17. [20] vi 4. [21] vii. 17. [22] x. 32. [23] xi. 16. [24] xii. 28. [25] xiv. 4. [26] xiv. 5. [27] xiv. 12. [28] xiv. 23. [29] xiv. 33.

persecuted the Church."[1] "As I have given order to the Churches of Galatia."[2] "The Churches of Asia salute you."[3] "The Church that is in their house."[4] "The grace of God bestowed on the Churches of Macedonia."[5] "Praise in the Gospel throughout all the Churches."[6] "Chosen of the Church."[7] "Brethren are the messengers of the Churches."[8] "Show before the Church the proof of your love."[9] "I robbed other Churches taking wages of them."[10] "The care of all the Churches."[11] "Inferior to other Churches."[12] "Unto the Churches of Galatia."[13] "I persecuted the Church of God."[14] "Unknown by face unto the Churches of Judea."[15] "Head over all things to the Church."[16] "Might be known by the Church."[17] "Be glory in the Church of Christ Jesus."[18] "Christ is the head of the Church."[19] "The Church is subject unto Christ."[20] "Christ also loved the Church and gave Himself for it, that He might sanctify and cleanse it with the washing of water by the word, that He might present it to Himself a glorious Church, not having spot or wrinkle, or any such thing."[21] "Nourisheth and cherisheth it even as the Lord the Church."[22] "A great mystery, but I speak concerning Christ and the Church."[23] "Persecuting the Church."[24] "No Church communicated with me, but ye only."[25] "The head of the Body, the Church."[26] "His body's sake which is the Church."[27] "Nymphas

---

[1] 1 Cor. xv. 9. [2] xvi. 1. [3] xvi. 19. [4] xvi. 19. [5] 2 Cor. viii. 1. [6] viii. 18. [7] viii. 19. [8] viii. 23. [9] viii. 24. [10] xi. 8. [11] xi. 28. [12] xii. 13. [13] Gal. i, 2. [14] i. 13. [15] i. 22. [16] Eph. i. 22. [17] iii. 10. [18] iii. 21. [19] v. 23. [20] v. 24. [21] v. 25, 26, 27. [22] v. 29. [23] v. 32. [24] Phil. iii. 6. [25] iv. 15. [26] Col. i. 18. [27] i. 24.

and the Church which is in his house."[1] "Cause that it be read also in the Church of the Laodiceans."[2] "Unto the Church of the Thessalonians."[3] "Followers of the Churches of God, which in Judea are in Christ Jesus."[4] "Unto the Church of the Thessalonians."[5] "Glory in you in the Churches of God."[6] "How shall he take care of the Church of God."[7] "The Church of the living God, the pillar and ground of the Truth."[8] Let not the Church be charged."[9] "To the Church in thy house."[10] "Let him call for the elders of the Church."[11] "Borne witness of their charity before the Church."[12] "I wrote unto the Church."[13] "Casteth them out of the Church."[14] "John to the seven Churches which are in Asia."[15] "Send it unto the seven Churches."[16] "The angels of the seven Churches."[17] "The seven Churches."[18] "To the Angel of the Church of Ephesus."[19] "Let him hear what the Spirit saith unto the Churches."[20] "The Church of Smyrna."[21] "The Church in Pergamos."[22] "The Church in Thyatira."[23] "All the Churches shall know."[24] "The Church in Sardis."[25] "The Church in Philadelphia."[26] "The Church of the Laodiceans."[27] "I, Jesus, have sent mine angel to testify unto you these things in the Churches."[28]

We, of course, admit, that the number who will finally be saved is unknown to man, and can never be ascertained by us in this life. The word " *Church*,"

---

[1] Col. iv. 15. [2] iv. 16. [3] 1 Thes. i. 1. [4] ii. 14. [5] 2 Thes. i. 1. [6] i. 4. [7] 1 Tim. iii. 5. [8] iii. 15. [9] v. 16. [10] Philemon i. 2. [11] James v. 14. [12] 3 John 6. [13] 9 [14] 10. [15] Rev. i. 4. [16] i. 11. [17] i. 20. [18] i. 20. [19] ii. 1. [20] ii. 7, 11, 17, 29. iii. 6, 13, 22. [21] ii. 8. [22] ii. 12. [23] ii. 18. [24] ii. 23. [25] iii. 1. [26] iii. 7. [27] iii. 14 [28] xxii. 16.

however, is never applied to them; but always, and only, when used of human beings at all, to the visible society of believers, or disciples, which was established by our Lord and His Apostles.

If the reader has any doubt that my assertion is true, that the word "*Church*" is never used in the Scriptures to denote what is called in the modern theories, the "*invisible Church*," I hope he will take the trouble to read over *again* all these *ninety-four* quotations, with a special view to that point. I have taken the pains to lay before him all the passages in the New Testament, in which the word occurs, either in the English translation, or in the Greek original, so as to remove all room for doubt, that we have the whole subject fully before our minds.

§ 63. That there is a visible society called the Church in the Scriptures, is admitted. We always so understand the word except when we are examining some particular passages, which seem to say, what, in our estimation, is not true of the visible Church. *The Passages in which the word "Church" is supposed to denote the invisible Church considered.*
We then resort to the admitted fact, that the number of those that are to be saved, is always an uncertainty with man, and apply to them what we think inapplicable to the visible society, and thus come to the idea of an invisible Church, as the thing intended.

Now I am not at present aiming to combat this idea; but I am endeavoring to show that the word "*Church*" is never applied, in the Scriptures, to this invisible and unascertained number of persons. 1 know of no way in which this could be accomplished, except by quoting every passage in which the word occurs, with enough of the context to show its application. I am satisfied that a careful perusal of these passages, will leave the impression, that what is called the Church, is always a visible and definite society of persons. We find it a body exercising discipline, and "as the Pillar and Ground of the truth." We read of it as "purchased by the SAVIOUR's own blood;" as "that which He loved and gave Himself for, that He might present it to Himself a glorious Church, without spot, or wrinkle, or any such thing." But still it is the Church of which the ministry are made, by the Holy Ghost, "the overseers," and which it hath pleased our Lord to cleanse and sanctify, *with the washing of water:* and therefore, it must of necessity be that visible Church whose members have been admitted by Baptism, and for whose edification the Ministry were appointed—for each of whom they have duties and responsibilities, and whom, for this reason, it is necessary that they should be able to distinguish and identify.

In one case only, I think it probable, as I have already said, that the word "*Church*," is applied to a number of persons invisible to us. (Heb. xii. 23.) And they are invisible, not because they cannot be distinguished from others, and identified as Christians, but because they are not in this world. They are the "first-born whose names are in Heaven."

It is not, however, on account of this description of them, that I consider the Apostle to be speaking of beings not on this earth—for the expression "*Church of the first-born*," may mean, either the Church of

Christ, since He is "the First-Born,"[1] or the Church of those who are *distinguished* in some way, as in Isaiah xiv. 30; and surely this is the case with all members of the Church. The expression "*written in Heaven,*" proves nothing for that theory: for the Apostles are said to have their names written in Heaven, Judas among the rest;[2] and God says, "whosoever hath sinned against me, him will I blot out of my Book.[3]

But I rely chiefly upon the connection in which the expression occurs: "We are come," says the Apostle, "unto Mount Zion [spiritual] and unto the city of the living God, the *heavenly* Jerusalem; and to an innumerable company of angels; to the general assembly and Church of the first-born which are written in heaven, and to God the Judge of all.

Now, assuredly, if St. Paul, by the expression, "*Church of the first-born, which are written in Heaven,*" had meant those persons living on the earth, who are to be heirs of everlasting salvation, he would not have placed them, in his order, between "the angels," and "God, the Judge of all," but somewhere else. He was speaking to the living saints, and includes them and himself in the pronoun "we." "We," he says, "have come, in our Christian fellowship and relations, to the spiritual Zion—the company of angels —to God—to the communion of the spirits of the holy men of old; now made perfect; to Jesus Christ the Mediator, and the cleansing influences of His most precious blood."

[1] Rom viii. 29; Col. i. 15, 18.   [2] Luke x. 20.   [3] Ex. xxxii. 33.

The "*Church of the first-born, which are written in heaven,*" are doubtless, therefore, the orders of beings extending upward in the scale of creation, from Angels to the Deity. We, as the redeemed of Christ, are brought into the same family of God with them—and if we follow on in the way of His commandments we shall come to see their blessedness, and enjoy their society.

This use of the word "*Church,*" therefore, gives no countenance to its application to the unascertained and undistinguishable number living on the earth, who will finally be saved.

§ 64. The Church contains, undoubtedly, good and bad within its communion; the wheat and the tares; the good fish and the bad; the sheep and the goats. And the Scriptures do most unquestionably, make a distinction between these two classes of persons, and direct our minds to a still more solemn and awful distinction that will be made at the Day of Judgment. But still, neither the wheat alone, nor the good fish alone, nor the sheep alone, are the Church spoken of in the Scriptures, though they are represented as being in the Church; and, together with the tares, the bad fish, and the goats, they make up the visible Society, which the Scriptures everywhere and uniformly call the Church.

§ 65. It is readily admitted that the word "*Church*" itself, does not necessarily imply an organization. Thus it is applied to the mob collected at Ephesus against St. Paul.[1]

---

[1] Acts xix. 32, 39–40.

But we go behind the bare signification of the word, and ask—not if "*a* church" must necessarily have an organization, but whether "the Church" of which we read in the Scriptures, had an organization or not.

Of this there can be no doubt. None were considered or called members of the Church until they had made a profession of the Faith and been baptized. Now here are the elements of an organization, a basis on which it was built—the Faith, and a rite of initiation, Baptism and Profession of the Faith. Baptism made members out of those who were not such before. Hence by these elements—the Creed and Baptism—those who believed were organized into a body or society distinct and distinguishable from all the rest of the world. But more than this—there was a worship in which the members engaged—there was a Sacrament in which they often participated—there was a Ministry whose instructions they received, and whom they contributed to support.

Now, these facts may not prove that there was what is called "*any particular organization.*" But they prove that there was *some* organization, or something—call it what you please—that gathered the believers into a body—a society—a church, and thus made them distinguishable from all the rest of the world, and capable of joining as a society in united and harmonious acts of duty, worship, and charity.

But there is another theory which teaches that the Church is no particular denomination, but includes many or all denominations.

We have seen that the Scriptures speak of the

Church, as only one, and as a distinct, organized body of believers. Now to say that it includes several or many such distinct and separately organized bodies or societies, is to show an utter disregard for the meaning of words. It is a violation of common sense which nothing but the stringent demands of a theory could ever occasion.

Let us inquire into the facts. Are the Presbyterian church, and the Methodist church, for instance, one and the same church? Nobody so regards them. Nobody ever so speaks of them. Then if they are not one and the same church, they cannot both of them be one and the same Church as that which our Lord instituted; for as organized bodies of professing Christians, they have organizations distinct from each other. No matter how similar in form and in principle they may be—yet historically and in fact, they are not the same, but distinct from each other. And so they are each of them distinct from that which gathered the believers and disciples in the Apostles' days, into one body.

Ask a man if there is a Presbyterian church in such-a-place, and he will say, " No—but there are a good many Presbyterians there—there is no church, and no place of worship—they have never organized themselves.——"

Such language occurs daily, and is used alike by persons of all persuasions and views, and its use shows that in the estimation of all men, there is no church where there is no organized society.

And so with the other point. Test it in any way you please, and you will find that people do never regard and speak of societies having different organizations—different officers—different places of meeting—however similar they may be in their design—in doctrine—in spirit—in forms, and in principle—as being one and the same society or church.

Ask any man if he considers the Presbyterian church as a part and branch of the Methodist church—and he will stare at you as if you had lost your wits, or were talking in riddles. The idea is too absurd to be proposed even as a matter of inquiry. But why not? Why is not the Presbyterian church a part of the Methodist church; or *vice versa*, why is not the Methodist church a part of the Presbyterian? Let him answer who can. But there is no more absurdity—no more inconsistency with historic facts—no more violation to the common use of language and the common sense of men, in calling any one of these sects only a part of another, and identified with it, than there is in calling any one of them a part of the Church of Christ, and identified with it. The Presbyterian church is no more a part of the Christian Church properly so called, than it is of the Methodist, the Baptist, or the Congregational church. In the first century, our Lord and the Apostles introduced an organization which gathered the Christians out of the world into a body or society by themselves, and that was the Christian Church. In the sixteenth century, Calvin, and the early Presbyterians, introduced another, which gathered the Presbyterians from all other societies, and organizations, into one by themselves, and that was the Presbyterian church. In the eighteenth century, Wesley and the early Methodists, introduced another organization which gathered the Methodists in like manner together into a distinct and separate society or church. And so of all the rest. Now these separate movements, and organizations, and the churches which resulted from them, are no more one and identical with the origin of the Christian Church, and the Church itself, than they are with one another. And so as we have seen is the subject always regarded, and spoken of in the common use of language. So it is in the accounts which these sects give of themselves—as has been proved already by our quotations from their own writers.

We have no way, therefore, of escaping the conclusion, that whatever the Scriptures say of the Church at all—the necessity of being in its communion—the importance of its identity—the functions it has to perform—or the privileges of its members—they say of that visible Society which began its existence in the days of the Apostles, and must continue always and uninterruptedly until the end of the world.

We apply what the Scriptures say of the Church, to a Modern Body, on account of the Identity between them, and not for any mere similarity.
§ 66. Among the Sects already enumerated, we may find almost every variety of doctrine and organization. Some are, doubtless, much more nearly conformed to the Scripture model than others. And it is possible that one might find among them some that are preferable on this score to some that are undoubtedly branches of the Holy Catholic Church. This, however, is a point that we will not now discuss, since it is not because the Church is Episcopal or Presbyterian; because it worships with or without a Liturgy; nor for any other

peculiarity of doctrine or organization, that it is said to be the Church that our Lord "purchased with His own blood;" "gave Himself for;" "that He might sanctify and cleanse it, and present it to Himself without spot, or wrinkle, or any such thing." But it is on account of identity or sameness with the Church spoken of in the Scriptures, that we can apply these things to any modern body professing to be Christians.

The great point of our inquiry has been identity of origin. The same vine can never grow from several different roots. From separate fountains, flow separate and distinct streams. They may flow into one, but, until after their confluence, they are in no sense one and the same.

But there has been no such confluence of these sects into the Church. They have not become lost or merged in her communion. They are as distinct from it to-day, as they ever have been since their origin.

I have compared the Church to a vine, starting from one root, and throwing off branches in diverse directions, until it had reached every nation and land on the face of the earth.

We may also compare its history to a stream rolling on to the ocean. From some elevated point we may see its course through the lapse of ages. Mountains enclose it on both sides. Here a rock rises in rugged barrenness, there an island, covered with verdure and beauty, separate, for a time, its waters into several channels, each pursuing its circuitous course to a union with that from which it was separated. Perhaps the last that the eye can see will be deltas extending their dividing influence into the very bosom of the ocean. The separation between the East and the West in the eleventh century is one such division. The Reformation is another. These may prove islands in a stream yet to be reunited; or the river may empty itself by different mouths into Eternity. But whether separate channels flowing round rock and island, or separate mouths flowing into the same ocean, the stream is one and the same. Beyond the mountains flow others, that have started from other fountains, and flow in different channels. The geographer never confounds the one with the other. Their identity is never mistaken.

Such is the history of the Church, and so separate from it are the diverse sects we have named. They start from different fountains, flow in separate channels and have never been united with the Church in the same current of visible existence.

<small>We may, therefore, omit all Discussions relating to the Peculiarities of the Organization of the Church.</small> § 67. We may then dismiss all consideration of the peculiarities of the organization, doctrine and discipline of these sects, and not involve ourselves in the endless controversies which a discussion of these points would occasion. We may lay it down as a matter of certainty, that Christ has no Church, except that which he founded in His own blood. His Church became visibly established and known by that name in the days of the Apostles; and, by His own decree and revelation, it must ever continue successive and visible—spreading and expanding itself over the surface of the earth, with branches in each nation, articulating with the main body, and must continue thus to exist and spread, until it includes all nations,

and He Himself comes in His Second Advent, to separate the evil from the good, and terminate the present Dispensation of Mercy.

§ 68. The rise of sects is no new thing. It commenced before the Apostles had gone to their reward and their rest in Heaven. The Scriptures frequently allude to them.[1] During the few centuries immediately before the Reformation, they were not so numerous as they had been before; and most of those that had previously arisen, had become merely matters of history, having no longer an existence. Thus God had declared his judgment of them: "Every plant which my Heavenly Father hath not planted, shall be rooted up."[2]   *The Rise of Sects distinct from the Church no new thing.*

§ 69. In speaking of these Sects it must be distinctly understood that we are speaking of them as *societies* or *churches*, and not of the persons composing them, as individuals. Of their members individually, no one is more ready than I am to see and acknowledge whatever there is, in them, that is good and commendable. Their sincerity and their zeal I do not call in question. And though it is an undeniable fact, that their piety is of a different character from that which we find in the Church —a difference which has very generally led them to disparage the piety of churchmen—and even to deny its existence altogether; yet nothing that I have said must be understood to deny that their's is sincere, and may be accepted in the day of judgment. This is a point on which I wish to form no judgment—to express   *A Distinction between the Sects and their Members.*

---

[1] See John ii. 18, &c., iv. 1, 2. Jude 18.   [2] Matt. xv. 13.

no opinion, but rather yield myself up to that sentiment which thinketh no evil, believeth all things, hopeth all things, and never fails.

These Sects claim no communion with the Church. § 70. We have now tested these sects by the history of their origin. We may proceed to apply to them the other tests, indicated in our second chapter. It is manifest from what has been said, that none of these sects claim to be parts of those Branches of the Church from which their founders seceded. They have indeed thought that they *ought to be* admitted to the communion of the parent Church, and have their ministrations acknowledged by her to be valid. But none of them claim that, as a fact, they are admitted to such a communion, or that the validity of their ministrations has been so acknowledged. No one of them claims to be in communion with any church which has existed since the Apostles' days, or with any that is in communion with a Church that was founded by the Apostles.

I now proceed, therefore, to a more full consideration of the second test—namely, that the Church does not acknowledge them to be entitled to any such recognition.

§ 71. I have several times referred to the fact, that the Church refuses to allow the validity of the ministrations of these Sects, or to acknowledge them to be legitimate branches of the Church. *The Church refuses to acknowledge these Sects as parts of Her Communion.* Whatever misunderstandings and alienations there may be among the different parts of the Church, they are all agreed on this point.

§ 72. Now the Church has, from the very first,

steadily and uniformly refused to recognize Sects which have arisen within her bosom, as valid branches of the Church itself. There were scores of such sects before the conversion of CONSTANTINE: the period which is generally fixed upon by the sects as that at which the corruption and apostacy of the Church commenced. Even in the days of the Apostles, such sects arose. St. JUDE, and also St. JOHN, allude to them.[1]

The Church has always Refused to be Identified with Sects.

Before, therefore, the example of the Apostles and the light of inspiration had ceased to be its immediate guide, the Church refused to acknowledge sects that had thus been got up by seceders, in opposition to herself, not merely for holding errors—but also, and chiefly for being sects. St. Paul says of them, that they hold not "to the Head from which all the Body, by joints and bands, having nourishment ministered and knit together, increaseth with the increase of God."[2] By "*holding to the Head*" the Apostle means something more than professing to *believe in* Christ. Without that they would not be considered Christians: and with it, they could not be spoken of as "not holding to the Head," if nothing more was meant by the words than believing in Christ, or professing to receive Christianity as they themselves understood and interpreted it. The language refers to an outward unity—a visible connection with the Church "which is His Body" by "joints and bands," and they of whom the Apostle was speaking, were persons professing to be Christians without being in the Communion of the Church.

[1] Jude 19; 1 John ii. 18, 2.   [2] Collossians ii. 19.

From first to last, therefore, the Church has claimed and exercised the right to exclude from her communion, and from identity with herself, all that have arisen as our modern Sects have done.

The Right to be Exclusive, indispensible to the Preservation of the Distinct Existence of the Church. § 73. The right to be exclusive must belong to the Church. Without it, its distinct existence could not be preserved. For if the Church may not decide for herself what are the essentials of Christianity, and whom she will receive and be united with; and so, on the contrary, whom she will reject and not be united with, she must receive all that choose to take to themselves the office of Preacher, or organize themselves into a church, professing to receive Christianity *as they themselves understand it*, and to keep Christ's Commandments *as they themselves expound those commandments*.

A glance at the diversities of doctrine and opinion held by the different sects in our land, will show that there is hardly a doctrine or a practice that might not be thus introduced and prevail, instead of "the Faith once delivered to the Saints."

If the Church may not exclude any, but must receive all that choose to come as a part of herself—on their own terms, instead of their conforming to hers, she must receive their members to feed at her Tables, and their ministers to preach from her Pulpits —for unless she does this she excludes them; or, which is the same thing, declares that they are no part of herself.

The consequences of receiving them all, are easily foreseen. There would be such a variety and contradiction as would divert the attention of people from the devotional part of their services, and convert the seasons, which ought to be devoted to worship, into an intellectual gymnasium or a theological digladiation. The great mass, from hearing so many different doctrines, and so much contradiction in matters of faith, would become avowed and unblushing infidels; and the few that remained and professed to be believers, would be brought to the very lowest standard or quantum of faith that might be advocated by any class of preachers, or run wild in the licentiousness of fanaticism. Every new theory must be received and circulated through the whole Church. No matter by whom originated—no matter how wild—it would find followers and advocates. They organize themselves, constitute their leaders, preachers, and must be received as a legitimate Branch of the Church. And thus the Church must be open to all, and the preacher of each new sect, each wild fanaticism, or daring blasphemy, be allowed to hold forth in the pulpits and before the congregations of that Church which the Blessed Saviour purchased with His own blood, whereever and whenever they choose to present themselves for the work of their calling.

§ 74. It can hardly be necessary, therefore, to show from the Scriptures, that the Church has this right. It is implied in the very fact of its existence, and of the intention that it should continue to exist until the second coming of our Lord. But there are passages in which it is distinctly implied. Thus when our Lord directed the reference of the case of an offending brother to the Church, *The Right to be Exclusive proved from the Scriptures.*

after all proper efforts at a private reconciliation had failed, He implied the existence of this right. "But if he neglect to hear the Church, let him be unto thee as a heathen man and a publican."[1] A "heathen man," is of course one who is out of the Church, and a "publican" was one who was held in such an estimation by the Jews, that they would have no friendship or familiarity with him.

The Right to be Exclusive, indispensable to the Preservation of the Faith. § 75. A sacred trust was committed to the Church at its institution. In the language of St. Paul, it was made the Pillar and ground of the Truth,"[2] and its duty is to preserve "the faith once delivered to the saints."[3]

It can be hardly necessary to prove, that the value of the Church must depend upon its adhering to the Faith, and upholding the doctrines and principles of Christianity. Our Lord came into the world to provide a way for the salvation of men. That way is not the mere dictate of the conscience—the offspring of human reason. It is a direct revelation from God. And, as we learn from Revelation itself, the way of salvation which God has chosen, is not such as the unrenewed heart and mind of man will readily understand or approve. To the Jews it was a stumblingblock, and to the Greeks foolishness. "The natural man receiveth not the things of the Spirit of God, for they are foolishness unto him, neither can he know them, because they are spiritually discerned," and he is yet carnal.[4] And if any man will become a Chris-

---

[1] Matt. xviii. 17.   [2] 1 Tim. iii. 15.   [3] Jude 3.   [4] 1 Cor. ii. 11.

tian, he must take up his cross daily and deny himself.[1]

These things are sufficient to show that there will always be a tendency in human nature to corrupt the Gospel and subject it to its own control and modifications. Hence the Church was committed to an unceasing warfare against this corrupting tendency. Those who in their sincerity are ignorantly in error, as well as those who are wilfully perverse, will contend that their opinions are right, and that the Church is wrong. And the matter will come to the pass, that either the Church must yield or they will secede, and organize themselves into a church, claiming to be acknowledged as a Branch of the Church which our Lord instituted, and to have their ministrations acknowledged to be valid. If now, the Church is obliged to acknowledge these claims, she gains nothing by their being a different church. She sanctions their doctrines and doings—that is, acknowledges them to be true and good in one case as much as in the other. Thus a few Presbyterians, unless the Church may exclude them, or refuse communion with them in case they leave and become a church by themselves, may control the whole Church, and compel it to become Presbyterian. A few of the Presbyterians, by the same process, may compel the Church, with the rest of the Presbyterians, to become Congregationalists, and a few of these Congregationalists becoming Unitarians or Universalists, may compel the whole Church, Presbyterians, Congregationalists and all, to become

[1] Luke ix, 23.

Universalists, and acknowledge the doctrines and usages of that sect to be the true and uncorrupted Gospel of our Lord Jesus Christ.

And thus any handful of men, by a pertinacious adherence to what they may chance to think is right—or by persisting in what they know to be wrong, for the ruin of the Church, may compel all other members of the Church to yield their opinions—violate their own consciences, and adopt the opinions and preferences of the few, unless the Church has the right to interpret for herself the Scriptures and exclude those who do not conform to her interpretation of the divinely-appointed terms of communion. It is no matter so far as the point now before us is concerned, whether the Church is obliged to tolerate them, holding and inculcating their errors within her bosom, or to receive them to communion, and acknowledge them to be on an equal footing with herself after they have become organized into another body. In either case she is alike compelled to countenance their opinions, acknowledging that they are good and scriptural, and that whatever she has held different from them is either unimportant or erroneous.

The Right to Interpret its own Formularies claimed by every church and society whatever. § 76. Questions often arise between a society and one or more of its members, out of something that depends upon or involves a construction of their laws and regulations. And in all such cases, the society, though in some sense, and to some extent, a party to the controversy, claims and exercises the right to interpret and put an authoritative and final construction upon its own laws. In a Temperance Society—a

Literary Association—a Mason's Lodge, or an Odd-Fellow's Encampment, a question arises concerning the conduct of a member, whether certain acts alleged to have been performed by him, are violations of the principles and rules of the society or not. There may be differences of opinion on the subject, even among the members who are not implicated in the disputed points. Yet these societies never think of appealing to any other body than themselves, and their own judicatories. A question arises between a citizen and the commonwealth, whether he has broken its laws and incurred a penalty or not. The commonwealth decides the question by its Courts, or by its Legislature, and never for a moment thinks of referring the subject to any extraneous arbiter or judicature. A question arises between an individual State, or perhaps several of them, and the United States. Something of the kind did occur between South Carolina and the Union, in the well-remembered case of *Nullification*. The General Government—though a party to the controversy—decided the question itself, and would have enforced its own decision in the case, as it clearly intimated, by an appeal to arms—if the nullifying state had not submitted.

Instances involving the same principle occur almost daily in every religious body in our country. A member of the Presbyterian church, for instance, is represented to have committed some offence against the rules and regulations of the society. He thinks, perhaps, that his act is liable to no blame or censure. The matter is brought before the Session. It may be carried up to the Presbytery—and to the General

Assembly. But how high soever it be carried, and wherever it may be decided, the Presbyterian church claims the right and authority—as Session, Presbytery, General Assembly, or in some other capacity, by herself and her own judicatories,—to interpret her own Documents—decide upon the acts of her own members —and deal with them according to her own decisions. She never thinks of appealing to any judicature out of her own communion, or of allowing her formularies and laws to be made of none effect by the pertinacity of private interpretations. She puts her own interpretation upon the law, judges of the acts of her members, and they must submit—or be excluded from her communion. The excluded members may be in the right, and the church altogether wrong, in the case. Yet if she decides against them, and excludes them from her communion, they are no longer members of the Presbyterian church.

The same is true of every sect and church in our land. In some form they claim the right to exercise discipline over their members—to decide upon the terms of communion which they will adhere to and enforce. And if any number of their own members choose to depart from them, or organize on a different basis, they are forthwith regarded as a distinct body —another church.

The Bible itself is a document of the Church. It was written after the Church was instituted. It was written in the Church by members of the Church, for the Church, and is addressed to the Church and its members; and the right to interpret the Scriptures and every other revelation of the Divine Will—if there can be any other—is implied in the authority described in Matt. xviii. 15–17, where it is said that if one "neglects to hear the Church, let him be unto thee as a heathen man and a publican."

§ 77. In this there is implied no assumption of infallibility for the Church, but only the right which every religious sect, and every society of persons associated for any object, find it necessary to adopt and act upon in order to preserve their distinct existence. *The Right to be Exclusive implies no Infallibility.*

Although the Church has always had creeds and canons of her own composition, yet these have always been regarded by her as either brief and convenient statements of what was contained in the Scriptures, or such subordinate regulations as were necessary for the due performance of the divine functions entrusted to her, and which, therefore, she had a right to make. The Church has never claimed the right to make additions to the Faith or to decree anything contrary to the Scriptures. It is true, indeed, that the *Roman Branch* of the Church has advanced such claims. And in withholding the cup from her laity in the Sacrament of the Lord's Supper, she acknowledges that our Lord instituted the Sacrament *in both kinds*, and directed it to be so received.[1] And it may be said that Romanists generally hold that they have a right to decree, from time to time, new Articles of the Faith —which must be received on pain of damnation.

The Church of England, on the contrary, claims no such right or authority. She says that "Holy

---

[1] Council of Trent, Sess. xxi. Chap. i.

Scripture containeth all things necessary to salvation: so that whatsoever is not read therein, nor may be proved thereby, is not to be required of any man that it should be believed as an article of the Faith, or be thought requisite or necessary to salvation." "The creeds [the Nicene and the Apostles'] ought thoroughly to be received and believed, *for they may be proved by most certain warrant of Holy Scripture.*" "The Church hath power to decree rites and ceremonies, and authority in controversies of Faith; and yet *it is not lawful for the Church to ordain anything that is contrary to God's Word written*, neither may it so expound one place of Scripture that it be repugnant to another."[1]

Since, then, the Romish Branch of the Church claims the right to decree new articles of faith, and rites, and ceremonies, which are contrary to the Scripture—the rejection of these sects by her might be nothing to their disadvantage. Her rejection might be their commendation.

But when their ministrations are disowned by the Oriental Branches of the Church which have never fallen into the Romish corruptions, and never claimed the right to add to "the Faith once delivered to the saints," and by the Reformed Branches, which have returned for their Standard, to the Scriptures alone as understood by the Primitive Church, the case is materially different. A decision in which all these Branches of the Church—every body of Christians that can be identified with the Church spoken of in the Scriptures,

---

[1] Article vi., viii., and xx.

diverse and divided as they are on many important points—carries with it a weight of moral power that cannot well be disregarded.

§ 78. Now the Scripture contains the Gospel which the Church is to preach—and the terms of Communion which she is to adopt, and should enforce. We claim for the Church no right or authority to make laws of her own, except so far as shall be necessary for the performance of those functions which her Lord gave her to do. *The Church must have the Right to Interpret the Scriptures for Herself.*

But the Church must have the right to interpret the Scriptures for herself, to decide what are the instructions that have been given her. There is no extraneous judicature—no body having authority over her to which she is subordinate, and to which an appeal can be made.

§ 79. The right to be exclusive is claimed by every sect and church in our land. No denomination will open its pulpits indiscriminately to those that are recognized as ministers in other denominations. *The Right to be Exclusive claimed by all Sects and Societies.* They will receive none, in fact, who do not mainly agree in sentiment with themselves. If they should do otherwise, their creeds and standards would be disregarded and contradicted, and the denomination itself would lose its distinctive features. Hence they are all more or less exclusive. The Presbyterians would not receive to their Presbytery, or admit to preach in their pulpits, men who deny the Divinity of Christ, or the future punishment of the finally-impenitent. Universalists will not fellowship and harmonize with those who hold high Calvinistic notions of Election and Reprobation, or who deny the sacredness and binding obligation of the Marriage Covenant.

This is only what each sect and church in our land is doing. There is no one of them that is not seeking to extend its communion. They have applications from persons and societies of persons to be received into union with themselves.

This devolves upon them the necessity of ascertaining what are the opinions, the character, and the usages of the applicants. The Church examines into these matters, and accepts or rejects their application as it is found necessary.

Now the refusal to receive applicants is based on the same principle as the expulsion of unworthy members, or the refusal to be in communion with them if they organize themselves separately into a distinct church.

It is the right to decide for themselves what are their own terms of communion, and to exclude all that will not conform to them.

But suppose, for a moment, that any denomination—the Presbyterians for instance—were obliged to open their pulpits to all who call themselves Teachers of the Gospel; or all who are recognized as such by any Sect or denomination. It would be impossible to preserve the distinctive features of their system. To-day an *Armenian* would deny their view of Election—to-morrow a *Socinian* would deny the Atonement; soon a *Unitarian* would deny the Divinity of Christ; a *Universalist* the Future Punishment of the wicked; the *Quaker* would deny all ordinances and creeds;

Shem Zook would denounce the use of buttons on one's coat as Anti-Christian; *William Miller* would teach that the end of the world was even now at the doors; and *Joseph Smith* must be allowed to set forth the claims of his new revelation and " the church of the Latter Day Saints." And the actual creed of the church, whatever might be its name, would include all these views and as many more as any one might choose to present—that is, the Presbyterian church would teach them all.

Now certainly, what could not but happen in the case of the Presbyterians, would most inevitably be the result in the Church if it were not allowed to be exclusive and decide for itself against whom it must close its pulpits and whom it must reject from its Communion. There is not an Article of its Creed that would not be denied in the pulpits—quite as often perhaps as it would be affirmed. There is not a principle of its constitution that would not be held up to contempt and ridicule—not a canon or rule of its salutary Discipline that would not be continually trampled under foot—for there is not a point in all her doctrines or discipline that has not been denied and on account of which sects have been formed in opposition to the Church, because she would not allow them to persist in denying it within her communion. The Divinity of Christ—the Incarnation—Human Depravity—the possibility of forgiveness for sins after Baptism, were all denied by one and another Sect before the Papal Corruptions began to overspread the Church, and if the sects who advocated these errors had not been excluded and condemned by the Church, the Faith itself could not have been preserved within it. The Church must have yielded point after point, until she had descended to the dead level of infidelity and natural religion.

And it could not be otherwise now; the Faith would be denied, the Sacraments omitted, and the Church itself would melt away and become merged as an undistinguishable part of the unconverted world, if it were not allowed to keep up its own lines of demarkation.

The Church excludes only those who have erred in what She regards as Fundamentals. § 80. It is sometimes thought that all should be recognized and acknowledged by the Church, who hold to the fundamental articles of the Christian Faith. Suppose we admit the position. The question then arises, who is to decide what are the Fundamental and essential articles? If the Sects themselves— then none will be excluded, for none of them will admit themselves to be deficient in these points. Shall the sentiment of the majority prevail? The Church herself is always the majority. Even at this day she is more than ten to one against all the sects combined. And besides this, she has a past of nearly two thousand years to appeal to, and to learn from the ages before us, what have been held to be the essentials of the Christian Religion by those who are now glorified. And they of course, are always a majority against those living in this or any one age.

If the Church should draw a line excluding some of the sects and receiving others—those excluded would have the same ground of complaint that they now have, and could enforce their demand to be received by an appeal to the precedent set in the reception of their more highly favored brethren. For the common ground upon which they all stand, is sincerity in the reception of the Christian Religion, as they themselves understand it. Whereas, the ground on which the Church stands, is the fact that she was divinely instituted to keep and inculcate this sacred trust—the Christian Faith—whereby alone men can obtain the remission of their sins, and are made partakers of the kingdom of Heaven.

But the fact is, all these sects have violated and rejected some of the principles of the Christian Religion which the Church holds and always has held, to be fundamental. In this I refer not only to her view of the unity of organization and jurisdiction of the Church in each particular nation—but also to her view of the Sacraments, the Ministry and the Worship. But an investigation into these points would lead us aside from our plan and require more time and space than can be devoted to it. I refer to the fact only for the purpose of saying that the Church must draw the line where she has drawn it, or depart from what she has always held to be fundamental points in the sacred trust committed to her.

If, then, we allow the Church to have this right, the line must be drawn somewhere, so that all beyond it will be excluded. In excluding all as new sects which have been founded by persons that had forsaken or been expelled from her communion, established on a different basis, and in a country where they wage perpetual warfare against herself—she pursues a course that is perfectly consistent, and the only one that can secure her integrity and perpetuity—she is adhering to the fundamental principles laid down in the Scriptures.

The Recognition of these Sects by the Church, could not after all, make them Identical with Herself.

§ 81. But after all, it is unnecessary to insist upon this point. For if the Church should recognize these sects as legitimate Branches of the Church of Christ, and acknowledge the validity of their ministrations—they could not be identified with her so long as they continue their distinct and separate organizations with ministries and congregations of of their own, separate from hers. The sects themselves cannot be identified with her. Their origin is different. Their organization is different. Their history is different; and until their sectarian existence ceases, they must be distinct from the Church. When their organizations are dissolved, and they cease to be Presbyterians, Baptists, Lutherans, Methodists, &c., &c., their members, as individuals, may be received into the Church and identified with her existence. But until then, no recognition or acknowledgment by her can be of any advantage to their ecclesiastical position. She cannot acknowledge that they are herself, and that she is somebody else. She can neither change her own identity, nor the history and circumstances of their origin. These things are fixed beyond the possibility of recall in the inexorable past.

I trust now that it is perfectly evident that the Church has done only what she had a right to do, and has acted a consistent and uniform part through the whole period of her history, including now over eighteen centuries, and has taken the only course that could preserve her existence. At all events, there are none that can condemn the principles on which she has acted; since they have all found it necessary to adopt and act upon the same principles themselves. Without them, neither their existence, nor hers, could be preserved.

CHAPTER VI.

THE CHURCH OF ENGLAND SINCE THE REFORMATION.

We now recur to the Church of England in order to explain a few events in its history from the commencement of the Reformation in the reign of Henry VIII. to 1789, at which time the Branch of the English Church in America was fully established, and became complete in its organization and independent in its existence.

The English Church always a Distinct Branch of the Church of Christ. § 1. We have seen that the Church of Christ was established in England in the first century, that it continued perfectly independent of any foreign jurisdiction until after the Saxon invasion at the close of the sixth century—that from that time the Papal influence increased in England until its final rejection by the Church as a united body, in 1534, and that since that time, the Church of England, with those derived from it, constitutes the chief part of the third Great Division of the Catholic Church of Christ—to wit: the Reformed.

Henry VIII. opposed the Reformation in the last part of his Reign. § 2. Henry VIII. died in 1547, and was succeeded by his son, Edward VI., January 29. During the last ten years of Henry's reign, he had rather retarded than promoted the Reformation. The spirit which had been thus repressed burst forth with perhaps too much of impetuosity on the change in the sovereignty. The first reformed Liturgy was published May 4, 1549, and came into use the *Whitsunday* following.[1] The first Book of Homilies had been published in the July before. But before the end of 1551, the Prayer Book had been again revised and materially altered. This second Prayer Book of Edward VI. was brought into use from the Feast of *All Saints*, November 1, 1552. In the next year the *Articles* (now XXXIX., but then XLII. in number) were published.

§ 3. But it pleased Almighty God to put a stop to the rapid progress of this work by the death of Edward, who was succeeded by his half-sister Mary, July 6, 1553. Mary was the daughter of Catherine of Arragon, and a zealous Papist. She set about restoring Popery to its former position in the English Church, and thus occasioned the first of those events, which for our purpose, we need to consider. *The Accession of Mary, the Papist.*

§ 4. At the time of the rejection of the Papal Supremacy, the Church of England consisted of two Archbishoprics and nineteen Bishoprics—twenty-one in the whole.[2] Besides the immediate acts of the chief Pastors, or Bishops of these Sees, the ecclesiastical authority was exercised by *Legitimate Mode of Church action in England.*

---

[1] CARDWELL's *Two Liturgies of* EDWARD VI. *compared.* Pref. p. 13.

[2] CANTERBURY, *London, Winchester, Ely, Lincoln, Coventry and Litchfield, Salisbury, Bath and Wells, Exeter, Norwich, Carlisle, Worcester Hereford, Chichester, Rochester, St. David's, Landaff, Bangor,* St. *Asaph,* YORK, *Durham.*—COLLIER, vol. iv. p. 188.

Convocations and Synods as follows: There were two Convocations, one for the province of Canterbury, and one for that of York. These Convocations usually assembled separately, though they often transacted business in common. They consisted of two Houses each—the upper composed of the Bishops of the Province, and the lower of Priors, Deans, Archdeacons, Proctors, &c., &c.[1] The Convocation assembled only at the call of the king and transacted no business without his permission. The Synods, on the other hand, are councils of the Church assembled by the Archbishops, or by the general consent of the Bishops, and act independently of the state.

New Bishoprics founded. § 5. After the Reformation had been commenced, six new Bishoprics were erected during Henry VIII.'s reign, 1540–1542—*Chester, Oxford, Gloucester, Peterborough, Westminster* and *Bristol*. Westminster, however, was dissolved and united to London, in the Parliament which met January 23, and sat until April 15, 1552.[2] The *Bishopric* of Gloucester was suppressed the same year and added to Westminster.[3]

Durham was suppressed by the Parliament in March of the next year, [1553,] with the design of establishing two in its stead. But Edward dying soon after, this design does not seem to have been carried into effect.[4]

Hence, at the commencement of Edward's reign,

---

[1] Lathbury's *Hist of Convocation*, p. 99.
[2] Burnett's *Hist. Ref.* vol. ii. p. 302. N. Y. Ed. 1842.
[3] Burnett, vol. ii. p. 324.
[4] Burnett, vol. ii. p. 342. See also Collier, vol. v. p. 501, 502.

there were twenty-seven Bishoprics in the English Church. Westminster, Gloucester and Durham having been suppressed during his reign; there were only *twenty-four* when Mary came to the throne, July 6, 1553. In the August following she restored the See of Durham,[1] and it was confirmed by the act of Parliament in April of the next year, [1554.][2] I have not been able to find in any documents within my reach an account of the restoration of Gloucester, or the date. But I find in Burnett[3] a declaration, that on or before the 18th of March, [1554,] a *congé d' élire* was issued to the Dean and Chapter of Gloucester, among others, for the election of a Bishop, and Brooks was elected. He died in the year following, and the See was vacant when Elizabeth came to the throne. It has since been united to Bristol.

Ripon was erected in 1836, and Manchester, 1847, so that the whole present number is twenty-seven.

During the most of Edward's reign there were *twenty-seven* Bishoprics. At the commencement of Mary's reign, however, there were only *twenty-four*, and during her reign there were, for the most part, *twenty-six*.

My object in these statements has been to get at a definite fact whereby to determine what, in the estimation of the English Church, was at that time necessary to constitute an Ecclesiastical body, or Convocation, capable of acting in a legislative capacity, or

---

[1] BURNETT, vol. ii. p. 382.

[2] COLLIER, vol. vi. p. 71, and BURNETT, vol. ii. p. 434.

[3] BURNETT, vol. ii. p. 427. See also WORDSWORTH's *Eccl. Biog.*, 3d Ed., vol. ii. p. 361. n. 8 .

in such a way as to have its acts binding on the Church.

<small>No Changes in the Bishoprics, or in the Clergy made in Henry's Reign, in order to effect the Reformation.</small> § 6. During the reign of Henry VIII., no changes in the Clergy were made in order to effect the Reformation. Fisher of Rochester, however, refused to acknowledge the Supremacy of the King over all persons in his kingdom, claiming that supremacy for the Pope. He was accused of high treason, and beheaded June 22, 1535, aged seventy-seven.

<small>Changes in Edward's Reign.</small> § 7. In the reign of Edward VI., there were several deprivations for political and religious causes. October 1549, EDMUND BONNER, Bishop of London, was deprived of his see. In April of the next year, STEPHEN GARDINER, Bishop of Winchester, was also deprived. The cause in both cases was partly political, and partly ecclesiastical. There were also four other deprivations during this reign; DAY, of Chichester, HEATH, of Worcester, VOISY, of Exeter, and TUNSTAL, of Durham.[1]

I do not design to undertake the defence of all these things. I mention them only for their bearing upon the question of the identity of the English Church, through the period named above, that is, from 1534 to 1789.

None of these deprived Bishops continued to claim their Sees or to exercise the functions of their office after their deprivation, and their places were immediately filled by others. Six out of *twenty-seven* were a minority too small to affect the integrity of the

---

[1] COLLIER, vol. v. p. 425, 441, 500.

Episcopate, and no pretence is set up that the identity of the Church was lost, or that a division *in the Church* or a *secession from it*, was effected thereby.

§ 8. But on the accession of Mary, we find changes made that were of a different character. She recalled all of the Bishops named above, as having been deprived, except Voisy, who had died. Four Bishops were imprisoned—*Ridley* and *Latimer* in the tower, *Hooper* and *Coverdale* in the Fleet.[1] Soon afterwards *Holgate*, Archbishop of York, was sent to the Tower also.[2] In March, 1553-4, *four* Bishops, *Holgate*, of York, *Ferrar*, of St. David's, *Bird*, of Chester, *Bush* of Bristol,[3] were deprived for being *married*. In the same month *Taylor*, of Lincoln, *Hooper*, of Gloucester, and *Harley*, of Hereford, were deprived on the ground that they held their sees *only during good behavior*,[4] a condition which Mary pretended that they had forfeited.[5] Bishops *Poinet*, of Winchester, *Barlow*, of Bath and Wells, *Scorey*, of Chichester, and *Coverdale*, of Exeter, had been compelled to flee the country in order to save themselves. And besides these, *Cranmer*, Archbishop of Canterbury, had been attainted of high treason, for signing the instrument settling the crown upon Lady Jane Grey.[6]

Thus *thirteen* Bishops, viz:—Cranmer, Ridley, Hooper, Coverdale, Holgate, Ferrar, Bird, Bush, Taylor, Harley, Poinet, Barlow, and Scorey, a majority out of all that were in possession of sees when

---

[1] COLLIER, vol. vi. page 14.
[2] Ibid. page 23.
[3] Ibid. page 64, comp. 66.
[4] *Durante bene placito.*
[5] Ibid. page 65.
[6] Ibid. page 36.

Mary came to the throne, were deprived and put to silence by her on one pretence or another; this was not done, however, by any competent ecclesiastical authority. It was, therefore, as completely an act of persecution against the Church, as though it had been done by the Emperors of Pagan Rome, or the Authorities of the Mahometan Imposter. The places of these men were all filled by Mary with men who were violent papists. And besides these, as we have before seen, Durham was restored, and Tunstal, a papist also, restored to it.

Hence fourteen Bishops of her own choosing were put into possession of sees in England, to fill vacancies of her own creating, within a very short period after Mary came to the throne.

With a majority *thus* provided it is not at all wonderful that the Queen succeeded in making any changes in religion that she chose to make.

LATIMER had resigned his see during the reign of Henry VIII. He, with four other Bishops, CRANMER, RIDLEY, HOOPER, and TAYLOR, were burnt at the stake for their refusal to conform to papacy. From the list given by MAITLAND,[1] it appears that no less than *two hundred and seventy-seven* persons, including the four Bishops just named, suffered martyrdom for their religion during this reign.

§ 9. Of the Bishoprics, *six*, to wit: Canterbury, Hereford, Bangor, Gloucester, Salisbury, and Oxford, were vacant by death, on Elizabeth's accession, November 1558: *four* became

<small>Changes on the Accession of Elizabeth.</small>

---

[1] ESSAYS *on Subjects Connected with the Reformation in England.* pp. 576-582.

vacant by the death of the incumbent before the oath of supremacy was offered them, to wit: Rochester, Chichester, Norwich, and Bristol. *Fourteen* Bishops were deprived for not acknowledging the Queen's supremacy, and *one*, ANTHONY KITCHEN, of Llandaff, took the oath. Of the deprived Bishops, some of them, as Bonner, Gardiner, and Tunstal had, in Henry VIIIth's reign, acknowledged and maintained the very supremacy which they now refused, and for refusing which, they were deprived.

From the foregoing account it appears that only one of the Bishops in England that was in the exercise of Episcopal functions at the close of Mary's reign, continued to hold his office after the accession of Elizabeth. STANLY, of Sodor and Man, also retained his place.[1] But of the fourteen Bishops deprived, *three*, to wit: CHRISTOPHERSON, of Chichester, BOURNE, of Bath and Wells, and TUBERVILLE, of Exeter, at the least, held sees whose lawful Bishops had been driven out by violence, and consequently, after their return, they were the rightful incumbents of those sees. Hence the number that were ejected by the oath of supremacy is reduced to *eleven*. Thus *fourteen* sees, a majority out of the twenty-six, were at that time vacant in the course of nature, or filled with Bishops acknowledging the supremacy, and who would concur in restoring the Reformation; and this, too, without any ejection either violent or otherwise, on the part of Queen Elizabeth.

KITCHEN conformed. BARLOW, SCOREY, COVERDALE,

---

[1] BRAMHALL's *Vindication of the Protestant Bishop's Consecration.* Works, vol. iii. page 232, ed. 1844.

HODGKINS—besides some suffragan Bishops—returned from abroad and were put into a condition to resume their duties and jurisdiction. By these Bishops the vacant sees were filled up.

§ 10. The restoration of the Reformation seems to have been generally popular, as is to be inferred from the fact that only one hundred and eighty-nine out of about ten thousand (that is, less than one in fifty) of the Clergy refused compliance.[1]

The Clergy generally conform to the Reformation.

§ 11. Now, in the first place, the fourteen non-conforming Bishops did not draw off a party with them over whom they continued to exercise jurisdiction. They lived and died vacant Bishops—some in England, (eleven,) and the rest (three) went beyond seas.[2] And when, some ten years after, the Papal adherents seceded and formed a sect by themselves, these Bishops were not placed over them, nor did they set up any claims to be Bishops over any body, or any thing in England.

These Changes did not effect the Identity of the Church.

And here again I must say that I am not now aiming to justify all that was done by Elizabeth. The whole matter may be stated thus in the alternative. If the proceedings of Mary, in restoring popery, are held to be valid, then the proceedings of Elizabeth are much more so : for they were less the result of the exercise of secular and political authority. But if the proceedings of Elizabeth are not valid, on account of the secular authority used in bringing them about, then those of Mary are not valid for the same reason

---

[1] SHORT'S *Hist.* § 407. [2] COLLIER, vi. p. 251.

acting with an hundred-fold greater force, and popery was never lawfully established during her reign, and no authority of any kind, either secular or ecclesiastical, was required to abolish it on the accession of Elizabeth. In either case Protestantism was legally and validly established in the English Church in the first years of Elizabeth's reign.

The identity of the Church, therefore, was not affected by the occurrences of this period.

§ 12. In a very few years, perhaps as early as 1567, persons who had learned Presbyterianism during their residence abroad, in Mary's reign began to secede from the Church, hold meetings, and form a sect by themselves. *The Earliest Secessions from the English Church.*

1. The first Presbytery was organized at *Wandsworth*, in the county of Surrey, about four miles from London.[1] This occurred 1572. Other Presbyteries were soon organized in other parts of England: and thus commenced the Presbyterian Sect in England.

2. In 1569, Pope Pius V. issued a Bull calling upon all who regarded his authority to secede from the English Church, and form themselves into a Sect in subjection to him. This Sect was first governed by Jesuits and Missionary Priests. In 1593, an Arch-Priest was appointed over them, and in 1623, they were placed under *titular* Bishops.

3. In 1583, ROBERT BROWN organized a society or church, on Independent or Congregational principles—and thus began another Sect in England. They are, perhaps, best known as "*the Puritans.*"

[1] COLLIER, vi. p. 529.

Besides these, there was also a small Sect of Baptists or Anabaptists.

But all these sects put together, included only a very small part of the population of England. The great mass of the people still remained in the Church.

No one of these sects ever claimed to be "the Church of England," properly so called. But on the contrary, by their acts and by their admissions, they acknowledged themselves to be new Sects.

From the restoration of the Reformation at the accession of Elizabeth until the Rebellion of 1640, nothing further occurred that we need to notice in this place.

The Rebellion. § 13. I need not now enumerate the causes which contributed to the growth of Puritanism in England. In 1640, the Church entered upon a more energetic course than it had previously pursued, to prevent the spread of Popery, and other forms of error in England, which provoked a determined resistance from all against whom these efforts were directed. The calamities that overtook the Church, however, arose, to a very great extent, from her alliance with the State, the administration of which had become unpopular, and needed reformation.

Early in November, was assembled what is called the Long Parliament. They soon resolved themselves into a "Committee of religion," and this branched off into divers sub-committees, one of which was for providing "preaching ministers and for removing scandalous ones." On the 10th of March a bill was brought into the House of Commons and passed "that no Bishop should have any vote in Parliament." The bill, however, did not pass the Upper House.

On the 17th of July, the Commons undertook a measure for materially changing the form of Church-government, but finding it impossible to accomplish any of their plans while the Bishops retained their constitutional seats in Parliament, thirteen of the Bishops were impeached of high treason. The ground of their impeachment was, in fact, the fidelity with which they had done their duty according to the laws of the Church and of the Realm. This impeachment was found untenable, and dropped soon after it was made. The opposition to the Bishops increased, however; and soon after, they were prevented from going to attend in their places in the House of Lords by a mob throwing stones, &c. &c., at them. The mob was encouraged by the Commons. The Bishops protested against the validity of any laws that might be passed while they were thus deprived of their vote. They were immediately impeached of high treason for this protestation, and imprisoned in the Tower. Soon after, hostilities actually commenced against the king.

In May, 1643, the Commons (who were now the only branch of the Parliament that can be regarded as responsible for what was done) called the famous Westminster Assembly, for re-modeling their ecclesiastical affairs. An arrangement was made with the Scotch Covenanters, by which the Scotch were to assist the English against their king, and the English were to abolish Episcopacy and establish Presbyterianism in the English Church. In October, 1644, it was declared in Parliament, that Presbyterian ordinations should be held valid in the Church of England. The Ordinance for abolishing the Common Prayer and establishing the Presbyterian Directory was finally passed March 13th, 1645, and Episcopacy suppressed by the same authority the 9th of October following.[1] And it was made a crime to use the Common Prayer either in the Church or in their families, punishable with a fine of five pounds for the first offence, ten for the second, and one year's imprisonment for the third.[2]

The Church did not consent or conform to these Changes. § 14. Notwithstanding these laws, the Bishops and the great mass of the Clergy never complied. Many of them, as Sanderson, Hackett, Bull, Fell, Alliston and Dolben, continued to use the Book of Common Prayer or to repeat its contents without the Book.

This change it will be observed was made by an authority that was purely and exclusively secular—for the Bishops had been excluded from the House of Lords by the mob, and then by attainder; and the Westminster Assembly were only a committee to prepare matters for the Parliament to set forth and enforce by its own authority. We certainly cannot call the Parliament and its adherents *the Church of England*, as things then were, without doing violence to all our ideas of identity and all sense of propriety in the use of language.

The Restoration. § 15. We now pass over several years to the Restoration in 1660. On the 29th

---

[1] BEREN's *History Prayer Book*, p. 195. [2] COLLIER, vol. viii. p. 296.

of May in this year, Charles II. was recalled to the Throne of his ancestors. The Presbyterians had been defeated in their original intention by the Independents, and therefore readily joined with the Churchmen in desiring the Restoration. It is not improbable that they entertained the hope that Presbyterianism might be established in the Church—being a sort of middle ground between Episcopacy and the Independents, who were then the ruling party. But in this they were disappointed. The Restoration necessarily implied the nullification of all the laws and ordinances that had been passed since about 1643, when the constitutional requisites for the passage of a law had been disregarded. This restored the Bishops and the other Clergy who had been ejected by Parliament, to their old places again.

§ 16. *Nine* out of twenty-six Bishops lived to recover their sees at the Restoration, to wit: Juxon of London, Pierce, of Bath and Wells, Skinner, of Oxford, Warner, of Rochester, Roberts, of Bangor, Wren, of Ely, Duppa, of Salisbury, King, of Chichester, and Frewen, of Coventry and Litchfield. The other sees of course, had not been filled; for the object of the change was to do away with Episcopacy altogether. On the first Sunday in Advent, *six* new Bishops were consecrated for the following sees, Durham, St. David's, Peterborough, Llandaff, Carlisle and Chester. The remaining sees were filled soon after, and all things restored in the Church as before 1643. *The Filling up of the vacant Sees.*

§ 17. We have seen the character of the measures which Mary took to secure a majority in the Convo-

The Polity of the English Church never changed by any Competent Authority. cation that should be of her views. When she had done this, *and not before*, she became compunctious about using the *secular* authority for religious purposes, and resigned the *regale* into ecclesiastical hands. On the accession of Elizabeth, *six* sees were vacant, *four* became so before the oath of supremacy was tendered to them, *three* were lawfully in the hands of Protestant Bishops who returned from their exile, and *one* conformed—making *fourteen*, a majority, which were soon filled, without any violence to the laws of the land or the Church, with Bishops who were friends of the Reformation. Thus by an act of Providence, Elizabeth was saved the necessity of any violent or arbitrary ejection in order to secure a majority in the Church in favor of Protestantism. Providence had done the work before she had any occasion to do it herself. Even the three who held the sees from which the returning exiles had been unlawfully expelled, would not have been disturbed if they would have acknowledged the Queen's supremacy. She could have provided for the returning Bishops in some of the vacant Sees. The other eleven who occupied places for which there were no lawful claimants living, might also have retained their places notwithstanding their religious opinions, if they would have acknowledged her supremacy. But by holding that she herself, and her government, were rightfully subject to the Pope in temporal as well as in ecclesiastical affairs, their opinion was of the nature of treason, and was so regarded. And for this they were ejected.

But in the Rebellion, as it is called, the changes

were made without even the pretence of the concurrence of the Church, acting either in Convention or Synod—by any means produced. Neither Convention nor Synod were held—from the commencement of the long Parliament in the autumn of 1640, until the 8th of May 1661, after the Restoration.[1]

The Church of England, therefore, never consented to the change that was made in its Doctrines, Worship, and Polity during that period, and as soon as the state of the kingdom would permit, resumed her former position and went on as before. An effort was indeed made at the Savoy Conference to modify the Liturgy so as to retain some that were inclined to secede, but nothing of importance in this respect was accomplished.

§ 18. We now pass to the Revolution. On the 18th of May 1688, seven Bishops drew up a protest and petition against certain measures of King James II., for introducing Popery into his kingdom. This protest was afterward approved and signed by six other Bishops. The measure resulted in James' fleeing from the kingdom, and the call of William, Prince of Orange, to the Throne. On the accession of William, however, six of these Bishops—SANCROFT of Canterbury, TURNER of Ely, FRAMPTON of Gloucester, WHITE of Peterborough, and KENN of Bath and Wells, refused to acknowledge him as king while James was alive, and were ejected, with a large number of the Clergy, for their refusal. The Non-Jurors, as they were called, continued for some

The Revolution.

---

[1] LATHBURY's *History Convocation*, pp. 235-239,

time to maintain a separate communion. Boothe, the last of their Bishops, died 1805,[1] and the party became extinct soon after.

After the accession of William, an attempt was made to change the Doctrines and Worship of the Church materially. But, as Bishop Burnet confesses,[2] this was not done chiefly through fear of the advantage which the change would give the Non-Jurors in claiming to be the Church of England, and declaring the adherents to William to be seceders.

This fact is sufficient to determine the identity of the Church after the Revolution with that before it. The ejection of the Non-Jurors may have been unjustifiable, (that is a point not now under discussion,) but it did not change the identity of the Church.

From this period no change occurred that needs to be mentioned, until after the Protestant Episcopal Church in this country, having been founded by members of the English Church, became entirely independent of it, and therefore we need not pursue its history, for our present purpose, any further.

The English Branch competent to Extend the Church of Christ. § 19. The competency of the English Church to extend the communion of the visible Church of Christ by founding new branches, is, I suppose, sufficiently obvious from what has already been said. Being herself, by her perpetuated existence, unquestionably a branch of that Church, and having set up no standard of her own, which she would have interpreted to mean anything contrary to the Holy Scriptures and "the Faith

---

[1] LATHBURY's *Non-Jurors*, p. 412.
[2] *History of His Own Times*, p. 544, SMITH's edition, without date.

once delivered to the Saints," as held by the Church in its earliest and purest days, and having neither rejected nor lost anything that is essential to its integrity and jurisdiction, she can send forth her missionaries with the assurance that Her Lord will accept their work.

CHAPTER VII.

THE INTRODUCTION OF THE CHURCH INTO THE UNITED STATES OF AMERICA.

We come now to a most important stage in the progress of our investigation: the introduction of the Church into the United States.

As this continent was unoccupied by Christians until the sixteenth or seventeenth century, it will be in vain to look for, or expect any establishment of the Church here by the immediate Apostles and Disciples of our Lord. We are, therefore, compelled to look to the labors and efforts of missionaries and colonists of a later date; and all that we can reasonably ask is, that we may find that the Church was extended into this country in accordance with the fundamental principles of its extension and identity.

The First Settlement. § 1. The first settlement made by any Christian people within the portion of the continent which subsequently became the United States of America, was at Jamestown, in Virginia, May 13, A. D. 1607. Earlier attempts had been made, but they all came to nothing.

"As early as 1580, letters patent were granted by Queen Elizabeth to Sir HUMPHREY GILBERT, to go to America, and ' prosecute effectually, the full possession of those so ample and pleasant countries for the crown and people of England.'[1] His patent granted him 'free power and liberty to discover all such *Heathen Lands as were not actually possessed by any Christian Prince or people,*' and to establish his jurisdiction there, 'provided, always, that the statutes he devised should be, as near as conveniently might, agreeable to the laws and policy of England; and provided, also, that they be not against the true Christian Faith professed in the Church of England.'"[2]

"In consequence of some collision at sea with the Spanish, as it is supposed, this expedition came to no permanent result.

"Though Sir Humphrey had sacrificed the greatest part of his fortune in fitting out his first missionary expedition to this country, yet he was not discouraged by this failure. About five years after, he sold all that remained of his property, and obtained the assistance of other wealthy persons, and fitted out another expedition. He landed at Newfoundland, and after various reverses and misfortunes, was obliged to return. On his way home, he was shipwrecked. 'Gilbert was forced most unwillingly, to turn his course homeward. His own little barge was ill-suited for the violence of the open sea, but he would not forsake his comrades. On the voyage, the storms grew more outrageous, and he was pressed to come on board the larger vessel.' 'We are as near Heaven by sea as by land,' was the answer of the gallant man. But he could not save the crew he would not leave. That same night, as he

---

[1] WILBERFORCE's *Hist. of the American Church*, p. 9. [2] Ibid. p. 10.

led the way, his companions in the larger vessel saw the lights of his barque suddenly extinguished. She had sunk, with all on board.'"¹

"Soon afterward, Sir WALTER RALEIGH obtained a similar patent, and sent forth two vessels for the coast of Carolina. Six times did this man despatch expeditions on the same errand, till his fortune was expended in the attempt.

"In 1606, a new company applied for, and obtained, from James I., a charter for settling Virginia. Their expedition sailed on the 19th of December, and reached Cape Henry, in Virginia, April 26, 1607. They had with them the Rev. ROBERT HUNT, a Presbyter of the Church of England. On the 14th of May, the day after their arrival at Jamestown—the place of their settlement—they took possession of the territory, and Mr. Hunt administered the Holy Eucharist, according to the rites of the English Church, to the company.² Among the first buildings erected was a Church.

"Thus," says Dr. HAWKS,³ "Jamestown was the first permanent habitation of the English in America, and Virginia commenced its course of civilization with one of the most impressive solemnities of the Christian Church."

§ 2. A leading motive in all these efforts at the settlement of America, is declared to have been "*the honor of God, and compassion for the poor infidels (Indians,) captivated by the Devil*," it seeming probable that

A leading motive in this Settlement, was to extend the Church into this country.

---

¹ WILBERFORCE, as above. p. 16.   ² Ibid. p. 22.
³ *Narrative of events connected with the rise and progress of the Protestant Episcopal Church of Virginia*, p. 20.

God hath reserved these Gentiles to be reduced into Christian civility (civilization) by the English nation." And in the patent it is expressly ordered that the officers of the colony "should provide that the true Word and Service of God be preached, planted, and used, according to the rites and doctrines of the Church of England, not only in the said colonies, but also, as much as might be, among the savages bordering upon them;" and "that all persons should kindly treat the savage and heathen people in those parts, and use all proper means to draw them to the service and knowledge of God."[1]

§ 3. In order to show how completely the doctrine, discipline, and worship of the English Church were enforced, I will give an abstract of some of the laws adopted in the colony in the earliest periods of its existence, [1611] for the purpose of enforcing them. *(The Doctrines, Discipline, and Worship of the Church of England strictly Enforced.)*

The first commands that Daily Prayer, morning and evening, be observed.

No person could speak against the Holy Trinity—blaspheme the name of God—speak lightly of His Holy Word, or demean himself unworthily or disrespectfully unto any minister of the same, under severe penalties.

The sixth law ordains that "every man and woman, daily, twice a day, upon the first tolling of the bell, shall upon the working days, repair unto the Church to hear divine service." No man might break or profane the Sabbath.

---

[1] WILBERFORCE, pp. 9, 20, 21. See also HAWKS' *Narrative,* p. 19.

Ministers were obliged, in addition to the *daily* Service, to preach on Wednesday and on Sunday morning, and to catechize the children on the Sunday afternoon.

Every person on arriving in the colony must give an account of his or her faith to the minister, and submit to be instructed, if he or she were not sufficiently informed in what every Christian ought to know.[1]

With the policy or justice of these laws I am not now concerned. I cite them merely as proofs of the course that was taken to carry out the system of the English Church, and be identical with it.

In 1621-2, met the first Legislature in Virginia; and " among the first enactments were those which concerned the Church." " The general provisions " above recited, " were embodied in a statutory form," and provision was made by law for the support of the Clergy.[2]

Soon after this there is reason to believe that a small number of Puritans came to the colony; but their number was too inconsiderable to produce any change in the religion of the colony, and public worship continued to be conducted as it always had been, in conformity with the ritual of the Church of England.[3]

In 1628, Lord Baltimore, father to the Lord Baltimore who settled in Maryland, visited Virginia. The Legislative Assembly was in session, and as he was known to be a Papist, they required that he should take the oath of supremacy and allegiance, but he

---

[1] HAWKS' *Narrative*, pp. 25-27.   [2] HAWKS, p. 35.   [3] Ibid. p. 35.

refused. This act, whether right or wrong, in itself, shows, and is cited to show the strictness, with which the Virginia settlers adhered to the English Church.

In 1642, however, Puritan discontent had gone so far as to make application to the General Court of Massachusetts to send ministers of *that order* to Virginia, "that the inhabitants might be privileged *with the preaching and ordinances of Jesus Christ.*"[1]

It will be remembered that notwithstanding the Puritan insinuation, the preaching of the Gospel and the administration of Christian Ordinances according to the English Church, was established and abundantly provided for in Virginia. Dr. Hawks[2] remarks, "that it is possible, and indeed probable, that the application was *suggested* by some of those who had emigrated from New England two years before, and sought a home in the southern colonies."

Thus it appears that the Puritans were not content with having everything their own way in their own colony, but they must intermeddle with the more peaceable and harmonious affairs of another colony, and cause dissent and confusion there.

The historian, to whom we are already so much indebted, adds, "Up to the period of Harvey's arrival in 1629, there was no complaint. The colonists were content to remain in the bosom of that Church in which they had been reared; and there is ample evidence of a conscientious and general attachment to the faith which was established."[3]

The foregoing account has been given so much at

[1] HAWKS, p. 51. [2] p. 52. [3] p. 52.

length, for the purpose of showing what was the leading design of the first settlers in these States.

§ 4. The English Church continued to take charge of its children in the colonies—to make provision for their wants—and to gather in the wanderers and outcasts. They were under the Diocesan supervision of the Bishop of London.

<small>The Jurisdiction of the English Church continued until the Revolution, 1776.</small>

I need not go into a detail of the efforts that were made to introduce Episcopacy into this country, before the Revolution; nor enumerate the special acts of supervision and fostering care which were manifested by the mother Church. I will rather pass on to the organization of the Church after the Revolutionary War.

<small>The Church in the United States assumed an independent existence.</small>

§ 5. Independence was declared in 1776, and peace made by the acknowledgement of our separate national existence, in 1783. Up to that period this country was a part of the English dominions and dependencies. And when the connection with the mother country was severed, the Church which she had planted became independent also.

As early as August, 1782—that is, before the recognition of the national independence by England—a scheme was proposed for the organization of the "*Church of England people*" into an independent branch of the Church, by themselves. This scheme, however, was purely an individual proposal, and resulted in nothing. It is indeed doubtful, whether if it had been carried into effect, the religious association which would have been the result, would have been recognized by the Church of England, or any other branch of the Church of Christ, as a part of that Church. And it is certain that the author of this proposal—the venerable Bishop WHITE—afterwards repudiated some of the fundamental points which *were understood* to be combined in it.

§ 6. The first measure towards completing the organization of a Church in America identical with the English Church, was taken in Connecticut, in March 1783, when at a meeting of the Clergy of the State, the Rev. SAMUEL SEABURY, D. D. was elected Bishop for the Church in that State.

<small>The first steps towards an organization.</small>

I do not however dwell upon this fact at length, for two reasons: first it was only local in its character, and did not *profess* to aim at anything beyond the single Diocese of Connecticut: and secondly, because a single Diocese is not competent to an independent existence as a branch of the Church. There must be, at the least, "two or three" Bishops and Dioceses in order to enable them to perform *all* the functions requisite to their existence—the ordination of Bishops for instance.

But on the 13th of November, 1783, the REV. DR. WHITE, afterwards Bishop of Pennsylvania, having previously consulted with the other Clergy of that city, proposed for consideration, at a meeting of the vestry of his parish, the appointment of committees from the different city vestries, to confer with the Clergy on the subject of forming a representative body of the Churches in Pennsylvania.

These Committees met with the Clergy on March

29th, 1784. Another meeting was called for May in the same year, and a Committee was appointed to confer with the Churches in other states.

A few days afterwards a meeting, for another purpose, of several Clergymen from New-York, New-Jersey, and Pennsylvania, was held at New-Brunswick, New-Jersey. The proceedings of the Philadelphia meeting were communicated to them, and it was determined to call a fuller meeting in New-York, on the 5th of October following. At this convention there were delegates from *Massachusetts, Connecticut, New-York, New-Jersey, Pennsylvania, Delaware, Maryland,* and *Virginia.*

At the meeting in Philadelphia, March 1784, the following basis of a general organization was proposed. It was also brought to the notice of the meeting in New Brunswick, in the May following, and was adopted by the First General Convention that was duly called, viz: September 1785.[1]

"1. That the Episcopal Church is, and ought to be, independent of all foreign authority, ecclesiastical or civil.

"2. That it hath, and ought to have, in common with all other religious societies, full and exclusive powers to regulate the concerns of its own communion.

"3. That the doctrines of the Gospel be maintained as now professed by the Church of England, and uniformity of worship continued, as near as may be, to the Liturgy of the same Church.

---

[1] BIOREN's *Journals,* pp. 5, 6, and the Preface, by Bp. White.

"4. That the succession of the ministry be agreeable to the usage which requireth the three Orders, Bishops, Priests, and Deacons—that the rights and powers of the same, respectively, be ascertained, and that they be exercised according to reasonable laws, to be duly made.

"5. That to make Canons, or Laws, there be no other authority than that of a representative body of the Clergy and Laity, conjointly.

"6. That no powers be delegated to a General Ecclesiastical Government, except such as cannot conveniently be exercised by the Clergy and Laity in their respective congregations."

At the meeting in New-York, 1784, eight different States were represented, and it was agreed :—

"1. That there should be a General Convention of the Episcopal Church in the United States of America.

"3. That the said Church should maintain the doctrines of the Gospel, as now held by the Church of England, and adhere to the Liturgy of the said Church, as far as shall be consistent with the American Revolution and the constitutions of the several States."

There were also other resolutions, 2, 4, 5, and 6, providing for a General Convention, and its meeting, which was to be held in Philadelphia on the 27th of September following.

This may perhaps be regarded as the organization of the Church in this country. It took to itself the name, "Protestant Episcopal"—Protestant, to denote its freedom from Popery, and Episcopal, to denote its adherence to the Apostolic Ministry.

It may be well to notice, particularly, that this was not called, nor regarded as, the commencement of the Church in this country. The Clergy and Laity came together, only to provide for some deficiences in their organization. The Church had been founded here in 1607, by the Jamestown colonists. And now that a separation from the mother country had been effected, by the Revolutionary War, they came together to provide for those ministrations and elements of growth and edification for which, until that event, they had depended upon the mother Church, and the mother country.

It may be well, however, to show from the records of those times, that this was not regarded *by those who took part in the transactions*, as the origin or first establishment of the Church in this country. Thus, on the second day of the Convention, it was *Resolved*, that the testimonials produced from *the Churches* in the several States . . . . . are satisfactory.[1]

Here *the Church* is spoken of as an existing body, and as *one*, though distributed through many states; and that too, before any formal constitution had been adopted, a Liturgy provided, or the Episcopate obtained.

Again, the adoption of the Constitution of the Protestant Episcopal Church was not spoken of as the origin of that Church; the Preamble to the Constitution as reported by a Committee, reads—"Whereas, in the

[1] BIOREN, p. 5.

course of Divine Providence, the Protestant Episcopal Church in the United States of America, is become independent of all foreign authority," &c. It also spoke of meetings of Clerical and Lay Deputies of the said Church previously held.

These expressions are quoted to show that the men of those times did not consider the Church in this country as originating with themselves, but that they did consider that it had been in existence as a Church before their time.

The address to the English Archbishop and Bishops, is also worthy of being referred to for its bearing on several important points now before us. The Convention call themselves "the Clerical and Lay Deputies of the Protestant Episcopal Church in sundry of the United States of America." They say, "Our fathers, when they left the land of their nativity, *did not leave* the bosom of that Church over which your lordships now preside; but, as well from a veneration for Episcopal government, as from an attachment to the admirable services of our Liturgy, continued in willing connection with their Ecclesiastical Superiors in England, and were subjected to many inconveniences *rather than break the unity of the Church to which they belonged.*

"When it pleased the Supreme Ruler of the Universe, that this part of the British Empire should be free, sovereign and independent, it became the *most important* concern of the members of our communion *to provide for its continuance.*"[1]

[1] BIOREN, p. 12, 13.

The Organization Completed. § 7. The leading objects which claimed the attention of the Convention of 1785, were

(1) a more complete system of union and organization for the whole country (2)—the preparation of the Liturgy, and (3) the obtaining of the Episcopate.

The Constitution reported to that Convention was adopted, with some modification, on the 26th of June the next year, 1786.[1]

Before this time, however, the Rev. Dr. SAMUEL SEABURY had been consecrated Bishop of CONNECTICUT, at Aberdeen, in Scotland, on the 14th of November, 1784, by three Scotch Bishops. The reason of his being consecrated in Scotland, rather than in England, is to be found in the fact, that the English Bishops were restrained, by a law of Parliament, (not of the Church,) from consecrating any Bishops, without certain oaths which could be taken only by Englishmen.

The Convention of 1785, however, made application to England for the consecration of Bishops there. After a series of events, which need not here be recited in particular, an act of Parliament was obtained for the purpose, and the Rev. Dr. PROVOOST, of New-York, and the Rev. Dr. WHITE, of Pennsylvania, were consecrated, in the Lambeth Palace, February 4, 1787. And on the 19th of September, 1790, the Rev. Dr. JAMES MADISON was ordained Bishop for Virginia, at Lambeth, in England, by English Bishops.

The Church in America had now four Bishops—a

---

[1] BIOREN, pp. 22, 23, 24.

number, according to the uniform usages and principles of the Church, competent to perform all the functions requisite to an independent branch, or Provincial Church.

In 1789, the General Convention met for the first time with a full organization. The Bishops now constituted a separate house. A new Constitution was adopted, and the Prayer-Book, as revised, was set forth, to be used from and after the first day of October, 1790. The Ratification bears date, October 16, 1789.

§ 8. The settlement at Jamestown was the first that was made at all, by any Christian people, within the limits of what was the United States, when they became an independent nation. *The Settlement at Jamestown considered in relation to the General Principles of the Extension of the Church.*

In this there was an exact compliance with the terms and principles of the extension of the Church, of which we have already spoken.

1. The settlers were members of the Church, from the English Branch.

2. They came into a country (the English possessions of North America,) at that time unoccupied by any other branch of the Church,—

3. For the purpose of establishing here "the true Word and Service of God."

That all these conditions were fulfilled, is a matter of fact. The design of the settlers, however, was not exclusively religious. They did not come here for the *sole* purpose of converting the heathen. They claimed the territory for their own, and designed to found a colony, as well as a Church, which should be a part of the Church and the nation to which they belonged. This, however, cannot invalidate the missionary character of their undertaking.

Thus, in the most general view—considering this western continent as unoccupied country—we find that the commencement of these English missionaries was such as to identify their communion with the English Church, and was no violation of the rights or claims of any other branch of the Church.

<small>The Settlement within the English Dominions.</small> § 9. But there is still another light in which this matter ought to be placed. From its first discovery, some part of this continent was acknowledged to belong to England. Virginia, and Jamestown—the place of the first English settlement—were within those limits. This fact must be considered as giving the English Church a peculiar right and claim here. The territory was a part of the English dominions. Hence this country—as a part of the English Domain—was a part of England—as much so as though it had been within the Island that is called by that name. Hither Englishmen might come and settle, with all the rights and privileges of Englishmen, subject to the laws of England, and entitled to claim her protection. The right to bring their religion and the peculiarities of their worship with them, will not therefore be questioned. And as these colonies were a part of the English dominions, so also those members of the English Church, who came hither did not lose their membership, or transfer it to another communion, by their removal. They were a part of the English Church still.

It is, indeed, true that Royal Authority gave grants

to others of its subjects, who had forsaken the communion of the English Church, to come and settle on this continent also. But something more than King's patents, and Parliamentary grants, are necessary, to enable persons to found a branch of the Church of Christ. HE is the Sovereign of His Earthly Kingdom, and its Colonies must be founded by grants obtained from Him, and in conformity with His laws and institutions.

King Charles, or any other English King could confer ample authority for founding colonies that should be a part of his dominions and kingdom. But he had no such authority over the Kingdom of Christ.

Of course I am not denying the right of the English Puritans, and other seceders from the English Church, to come and settle in this country. So far as man, or human authority is concerned, their right was unquestionable. But although they had a right to settle here, and to have what religion they pleased, or none, if that had been their choice; still, however, the relation of their ecclesiastical institutions to the identity of the Church could not be changed by the peculiarities of their location. They were persons whose consciences had compelled them to leave the English Church, and they came here, not to establish the Church in which they had found that they could not live at home, but to extend the communion of that which they had themselves founded. It was, therefore, no more a part and branch of that which had always been known as the Church of England, when established in this country, than it was in that which they left in order to come here.

§ 10. *This Principle recognized and acted upon in all similar cases.* The principle on which these remarks are based is recognized and practised upon, every day, in this rapidly growing Republic. Emigrants are going from the States in which the religious institutions are established on a well-understood basis, into new territories. Some of them are of one religion, and some of another. They locate and form themselves into churches, as they choose. Those who were Presbyterians here, and organize on the Presbyterian platform there, are regarded as a part of the Presbyterian church still. So with every other denomination. It is not supposed, or held, that their ecclesiastical identity is changed by the change of location. If they adopt different views, and a different organization, then, of course, they will become a different church, or at least a part of a different one: but not otherwise.

So with the first settlers in this country. It was a part of the English dominions—and the settlers were Englishmen, going from one part of the English dominions to another; neither changing nor intending to change either their civil allegiance or their Church-communion and membership.

Until the colonies became a separate nation, by the Revolution, they were considered a part of the English Church. The others that came here were also considered as belonging to the same church, or communion, as that to which they belonged on the other side of the great waters, and sustained the same relation to the English Church here as they had sustained there.

With regard to the immigrants from other countries, they were of two classes: those which came to parts of this continent then belonging to England, and those who came to parts belonging to their native countries—as the Spanish, in Florida, and the Dutch, in New-York. The case of these last will be considered by and by. But those who came to settle in the English colonies became thereby subjects of the English crown, and therefore stand on the same footing in relation to the object now under consideration, as Englishmen themselves.

§ 11. Thus it appears that the Protestant Episcopal Church was founded in this country, then a part of the English dominions, by members—missionaries and colonists—from the Church of England, with the concurrence and approbation of that Church, and under its fostering care. *The Protestant Episcopal Church in the United States, and the Church of England in the same Communion.* That it is a branch of the English Church, is, therefore, a matter that admits of no doubt.

The fact, that the English Church consecrated for them the number of Bishops required by the universal practice of the Church, to constitute an independent Provincial Branch, is proof that they acknowledged the Protestant Episcopal Church in this country as a part of their own communion. Beside this, there has always been a free communion and good understanding between them. Until quite lately there has been, however, a law of the English Parliament excluding from the pulpits of the English Church all Clergymen who had not made certain declarations equivalent to an oath of allegiance to the English Government. This, of course, our Ministers had not done, and could not do. Therefore, they were excluded, by a Parliamentary regulation. This law was repealed in 1840. But the validity, and regularity of our ministrations have always been recognized and allowed by the English Church, and our Clergy (now that the *political* obstacle is removed) are received to preach in their pulpits, and to minister at their altars: and members going from the Church in this country are received to communion there, simply on a certificate of their having been admitted to communion here, and so, *vice versa,* they are received in this country.

These facts prove identity of communion between the two Churches.

Though hardly anything more can be necessary on the point of our unity and identity with the English Church, yet I will quote the declaration made by the House of Bishops, in this country, May 20, 1814:—

"It having been credibly stated to the House of Bishops, that, on questions in reference to property devised, before the Revolution, to congregations belonging to the Church of England, and to uses connected with that name, some doubts have been entertained in regard to the identity of the body to which the two names have been applied, the House think it expedient to make the declaration, and to request the concurrence of the House of Clerical and Lay Deputies therein, That the PROTESTANT EPISCOPAL CHURCH *in the United States of America is the same body heretofore known in these States by the name of the* CHURCH OF ENGLAND; the change of name, although not of religious principle, in doctrine, or in worship, or in discipline, being induced by a characteristic of the

Church of England, supposing the independence of Christian Churches under the different sovereignties to which, respectively, their allegiance in civil concerns belongs." This declaration was concurred in by the House of Clerical and Lay Deputies.[1]

§ 12. During the course of the preceding sections, I have often had occasion to designate Churches by the name of the country in which they are located—implying thereby some sort of a connection between the Churches and the States.   *The Nationality of Churches.*

The subject demands a few words of explanation; and we have now arrived at a point in our investigation, where a due consideration of that relation will be of material assistance.

By the nationality of Churches, I do not mean any recognition of the Church, *as a legal establishment* by the State. The idea that I wish to use is equally consistent with *all possible relations* between the Church and State. Whether, as in the Roman Empire in the second century, the State persecutes and opposes the Church; or whether, as in England, it supports it by law; or whether, as in this country, it leaves the Church to itself, neither opposing nor supporting it; or finally, whether, as in Scotland, it establishes a rival Sect—the doctrine which I wish to make use of, is equally consistent with that relation.

Where, as in the nations of the old continent, there is a Governing Class consisting of persons who are born to authority, live in its exercise, and leave it to their heirs as an heritage when they die—my opinion

---

[1] WHITE's *Memoirs*, pp. 356, 357. *Also,* BIOREN's *Journals of the General Convention,* vol. i. pp. 310, 311.

is, that they are bound, and must, if they will regard their own welfare, make the Religion of Christ a part of the law of their dominions.[1] This, of course, implies a support of the Church and its institutions.

But, in this country, where we have no such governing class, but only a number of citizens called for a time to execute the people's will in relation to certain matters of a more general concern, no such incorporation of Christianity, its doctrines and institutions, into the laws of the land, can well be made. The People, who are the government themselves, yield their support to religion in another way, and thus perform, without the intervention of the state authorities, what the nations differently constituted can perform only by a union of Church and State.

But the duty of "nations" and "kingdoms" toward the Church is not the subject which I wish now to present to the consideration of my readers. It is rather the fact, that the territorial limits of the jurisdiction of the Church are commensurate with those of the nation in which it is situated. This is what I mean by the nationality of Churches.

Scripture Reasons for such a Relation. § 13. There are several considerations derivable from Scripture which confirm this idea.

1. It is obvious that the Apostles, in locating the different and independent branches of the Church, had regard to the political divisions of the world, as has been already stated.

2. It is evident that the members of the Church, *as*

---

[1] Isaiah lx. 12.

Christians, owe some duties to the government that is over them, and to their governors, such as are incompatible with any allegiance or obedience to persons or governors out of the nation in which they live. Hence it has been held, by thoughtful Christians, that a belief in the Papal Supremacy by persons in nations that are politically independent of Rome, is inconsistent with due allegiance to the national sovereignty.

3. But again. In a Christian country, the government or administration must come into either concurrence or collision with the Church and her regulations in regard to some points. Even in this country, where there is the least possible amount of connection between Church and State—some points are assumed, and must of necessity be assumed, by the State. For instance, the officers employed in the administration must either keep or violate the Christian Sabbath. And the nation must have a law upon the subject. If that law regards the day as holy, then, in so far it adopts the doctrine of the Church: if not, then it may require, and in some cases it will require its citizens, if they are members of the Church, to violate their consciences by continuing in secular occupations which the laws have required regardless of the day. The laws of our country recognise this day, notwithstanding the many Jews, Seventh-Day Baptists and infidels, who differ from the Church in their religion on this point. Our Congress, also, adjourn for Christmas and the Holy Days connected therewith, notwithstanding the fact that neither Presbyterians, nor Baptists, nor Methodists—the most numerous denominations in our country—regard them as Holy Days at

all. On the subject of marriage and divorce, both the Church and the State must have laws which will be either concurrent or contradictory.

With regard to many of these things, the Scriptures have left the Church to make her own laws and arrangements for the mere circumstantials. If, now, the Church and the nation are co-extensive and conterminous, there will be no difficulty in securing an harmonious arrangement between them. But if there were parts of several different and independent Churches, or the whole of them within the limits of the same State, it would be impossible to adapt the laws so as to harmonize with them all.

<small>This Principle regarded in the Primitive Church.</small> § 14. When the Church was first planted, regard was had, as we have repeatedly seen, to the secular and political divisions of the earth, so as that there should never be two different Churches or ecclesiastical authorities in the same division. And in following down the history of the Church for several centuries, we find this rule to have been pretty carefully adhered to.

"This may be evidenced both from the rules and canons, and known practice of the Church; for when any provinces were divided in the State, then commonly followed a division in the Church also; and when any city was advanced to a greater dignity in the civil account it usually obtained a like promotion in the ecclesiastical. It was by this rule that the Bishop of Constantinople was advanced to Patriarchal power in the Church, who before was not so much as a Metropolitan, but subject to the Primate of Heraclea in Thrace: and this very reason is given by two general

Councils, which confirmed him in the possession of this newly acquired power. . . . . It sometimes happened that an ambitious spirit would petition the Emperor to grant him the honor and power of a Metropolitan in the Church, when yet the province to which he belonged had but one metropolis in the State; which was so contrary to the aforesaid rule of the Church that the Great Council of *Chalcedon*, made it deposition for any Bishop to attempt it. But, on the other hand, if the Emperor thought fit to divide a province into two, and erect a new metropolis in the second part, then the Church allowed the Bishop of the new metropolis to become Metropolitan in the Church also. . . . . The canons of the Church were made to favor this practice in the erection of new Bishoprics also; for the Council of Chalcedon has another canon which says, that if the Imperial power made any innovation in the precincts or parishes belonging to a city, then the Church precincts might be altered in conformity to the alterations that were made in the political and civil state, which canon is repeated and confirmed in the Council of TRULLO."

§ 15. I am aware that this rule is not one of necessity, and that history presents many exceptions to it. The rule, if strictly adhered to, would present serious difficulties in times of general commotion, when the boundaries of Empires and Kingdoms are subject to sudden and frequent changes. Still, however, the evils with which the present divided state of Christendom

The Principle not to be denied on account of the present abnormal state of the Church.

---

[1] BINGHAM's *Antiquities*, Book ix., c 1, § 7.

would embarrass the application of the principle, ought not to be urged against its soundness: for those divisions and their causes are themselves anomalies and evils which ought not to exist. We have no right, therefore, to expect the rules and principles of the Church to be such as to sanction and perpetuate them.

If, for instance, any part of Canada should become politically incorporated with the United States—the Church in that part would find no difficulty in coming into our General Convention, and becoming incorporated with the Protestant Episcopal Church in this country, for the reason that there is no material difference between us and them in matters of religion. But if we should acquire a part of Mexico, inhabited by a Church in the Roman Obedience—the incorporation would be more difficult, and probably in fact would not take place—so great is the difference between us and them. But yet this should be no objection to the rule laid down: for such a difference has no right to exist between any two branches of the Church. It is itself a wrong.

This Principle recognised and acted upon by all the Denominations in our Country.

§ 16. But the practical object of this discussion is to say—what the practice of all sects and denominations implies and presupposes, namely, that the Branch of the Church which has the right to existence and jurisdiction in any nation at all, has a right to jurisdiction in any and every part of it, and throughout the whole extent of its Domain.

I have aimed, in what I have said, to prove the nationality of Churches only so far as is requisite for this practical conclusion. And that, I suppose, I have proved. If not, who shall deny it? Surely no one without condemning himself. There is not a church or sect in this country, that would hesitate to extend itself into any village, town, or settlement, where it was desired, on the ground that some other church or denomination had a society established there. The thing was never heard of. Not a denomination doubts its right to extend its communion anywhere within our country. Now this right is what I mean by the *nationality* of an independent Branch of the Church. And this is the right that I claim for the Church of Christ.

Most of the larger denominations in our country, do not hesitate to identify themselves, by *name*, with the country. I believe that all of them that are any ways diffused throughout the country, or ever expect to be so diffused, do so. Thus we have "*The Associate Presbyterian Church of North America*," "*The Reformed Protestant Church of North America*," "*German Reformed Church in the United States*," "*The General Reformed Synod of the American Lutheran Church*," "*The Presbyterian Church of the United States of America*," *&c.*, *&c.* Thus in some way or other, every denomination recognises the nationality of their church, and claims the right to extend it into any town or settlement where it may be desired.

§ 17. The Papists do not so distinctly recognize this principle in some of its bearings, while in others, they are unbounded in their arrogance. They claim the right to *The Papal disregard of the Principle accounted for.*

extend their jurisdiction everywhere, regardless of others. But still they do not recognize the principle in its relation to the independency of the national Churches. They aim rather to destroy that independence and reduce them all into one consolidated Hierarchy, that the Papal domination may thereby be the more effectually established, or unrestrained in its exercise. And while on the one hand, the uncertainty and variations of the boundaries of the secular kingdoms have doubtless done much to uprear and support that consolidation, let us also admit that the consolidation itself has done much to preserve the nations from those hostile collisions which lead to dismemberment and overthrow.

The English and American Churches, have always acted with a conscious regard to this Principle.
§ 18. But the Church of England and our own, recognize and act upon this principle. Though we believe the Churches of the East to be ignorant and degraded, and those in the Roman Obedience to be corrupt and idolatrous, we make no effort to establish a purer Branch of the Church in their midst. I say this with a full knowledge of all that has been done. In every case, that might have the appearance of an exception, a caution has been observed, which, whether the course pursued be justifiable or not, has saved them from the violation of the letter of the rule laid down. Thus when the English Bishop LUSCOMBE resided at Paris, he claimed no jurisdiction over the citizens of France or the Netherlands, but only over Englishmen who were *temporarily* residing in those countries. The present Bishop of Gibraltar takes his name from a point of land be-

longing to the English, but he exercises jurisdiction over persons within territory belonging to the Greek Church. Yet it is only over the *Englishmen* who are residing there. So with Bishop Southgate, residing at Constantinople. He is an American Bishop, residing within the limits of the jurisdiction of the Patriarch of Constantinople. But he claims and exercises jurisdiction over no territory, but simply and only over American citizens residing there.

In the latter case, the object is purely missionary. —the improvement of the Church as it now exists, and has been in existence there, ever since St. Andrew first preached the Gospel to that people. But with regard to the two British Bishops mentioned above, the fact that occasioned the necessity of the anomaly is urged as its only justification, namely, that the Church in those places was so corrupt that the English Church could not recommend or willingly permit her members, to commune with it. For this reason, an English Chaplain is permitted by the English Church to hold services according to her Liturgy within the very walls of Rome itself. Yet in all these cases, she neither claims jurisdiction over, nor pretends to provide for any but her own children in their temporary wanderings from their home.

The same adherence to this principle is seen in our course toward Texas. While it was considered a part of Mexico, we took no measures to send missionaries there, or to establish a Church like our own. But so soon as it came to be regarded by our government as an independent nation, our missionaries, with a truly Apostolical zeal, and with the approbation and support of our Church, went thither to establish the Gospel in the newly erected Republic. And until the Annexation of Texas, they were regarded as *foreign Missions*. But now they are placed on the list of " Domestic Missions," and may become a Diocese and enter into the General Convention, whenever they choose to do so, and can comply with the Constitution and Canons of our Church.

<small>This Principle applied to the present Subject.</small> § 19. The application of this principle, which is thus seen to be established, no less by the Scriptures, than by the recognition and practice of all Churches and Sects, is serviceable to us in many ways.

1. In the first place, others settled in some places in the United States, as their limits were in 1783, before the Church of England had made a settlement in those particular places, as the Puritans in Massachusetts, the Dutch Reformed in New-York, the Quakers in Pennsylvania, &c., &c. Yet, inasmuch as these were but parts of the *country* in which the Church of England was established before those Sects, her claim would not be prejudiced or precluded by their settlements, even admitting them to be Branches of the Church of Christ.

The Roman Catholics settled in the State of Maryland before the members of the Church of England settled in that state, though not until twenty-six years after the English settlement in Virginia. This gave to the English Church-settlement priority of claim over the Romish.

But in regard to all these settlements, the Romish—the Congregational—the Dutch Reformed, &c., &c.,

it is to be observed that they were in what was then, or soon after became, territory belonging to the English Crown, and therefore within territory which the English Church had a right to occupy, before the Revolution of 1776; nay, was bound to occupy and provide for as soon as she could.

2. But again. Since the organization of our Government, we have acquired territory that was occupied before our acquisition of it, as for instance, Louisiana, Florida, and parts of Mexico. In these territories, Churches in the Roman Obedience had made a settlement, and though there was no independent or Provincial Church in any of those territories, yet the Roman exercise of jurisdiction was established there. Belonging as they did to Spain, to France, and to Mexico, nations in which the Churches are in the Roman Obedience, those Churches had a right to extend their communion within their borders.

But when those tracts of country became united to, and incorporated with, the United States, the Christians there ought to have come into the communion of the Protestant Episcopal Church—that being the Branch of Christ's Visible Church holding jurisdiction in this country. And if the Churches in the Roman Obedience had not departed from their original purity, and assumed an attitude of schismatic opposition to the rest of the Church, these members would undoubtedly have come into union with us. And their neglect or refusal has given us a right to regard as null and void, their jurisdiction, since their admission to the Union; and to extend our communion into the very places where their's was before established.

We do not become schismatics thereby. On the contrary, they are the schismatics for refusing communion and unity with those, with whom, by the Providence of God, and in accordance with the Scriptures, and the principles of the Catholic Church, they ought to be perfectly united.

I am aware that I may be asked if I should give the same advice in a reversal of the circumstances of the case. It is said to be a bad rule that will not work both ways.

But to this I say, in the first place, that the errors of the Romish Church have no right to exist at all; nor be encouraged anywhere, and therefore their existence is no valid objection to any rule or principle, whose operations would lead to evil results in consequence of the existence of those errors.

In the second place, I remark, that no case has yet occurred in which a portion of country in which a Reformed Branch of the Church had canonical jurisdiction, has been brought under the jurisdiction of a Papal country in temporal things. But if such a thing should happen, I could of course no more recommend the inhabitants of the conquered territory to conform to the peculiarities of Popery, than I could encourage or recommend those now living in Papal countries to conform to them. We must always obey God rather than man; and we are obeying man only, when we yield, even to those that have lawful authority over us, obedience in those things which they have no right to teach and command.

But finally, I may be permitted to avow my belief, that God in his Providence, will never permit any

Papal nation to extend its dominion over one in which a purer Branch of the Church exists. If we look at the Papal nations now existing, whether we consider the South American Republics on our own continent, or the kingdoms of the old world, France, Spain, Austria, Italy—we shall see but very little to encourage the belief that there are any of them likely to subjugate any of the Protestant nations. Where is there one that could for a moment cope with Great Britain or the United States? Alas! they are hardly able to sustain themselves, crumbling in fact with their own weight, and rent with internal feuds and commotions. In these things we can hardly fail to see the hand of Providence. "Verily there is a God that judgeth in the Earth."

§ 20. If, now, we can fix our attention upon the facts and principles that have been brought before our minds in the foregoing sections long enough to see their full force and bearing, I think we cannot fail to see, that it is as certain that the Protestant Episcopal Church in these United States, is the Church of Christ for the people of this Union, throughout its whole extent, and in all its parts, as if no ages of darkness and corruption had intervened between us and the Apostles, and no Sects had arisen claiming the Christian name. This communion, therefore, is the Church of Christ in and for the people of this nation— identical for all the purposes that immediately concern their eternal interests with that Church which is spoken of in the Scriptures. It is a branch of the

[margin: The Protestant Episcopal Church, therefore, the Church of Christ for the People of the United States.]

Original Vine duly articulating with the parent stalk and thereby connected with the root.

The only difficulty in identifying the Church, as I said at the outset, results from the lapse of ages, and the vicissitudes of fortune through which it has to be traced. In some histories it may be concealed by the overshadowing importance conceded to the secular concerns of the age. Passions, prejudices, and sinister designs, have also had their influence in diverting attention from the naked and controlling facts in each important epoch. My aim has been to bring these facts distinctly forward—shutting out from our view, for the time, all others, that these might be the more justly estimated in their bearing upon the main and all-involving conclusion. I do not mean to say that the Church has not in some ages been very corrupt, that it has not been, at times, greatly at fault in its treatment of its members. But my main points are to identify the Protestant Episcopal Church in these United States, as an outward and visible institution, with the Church of which we read so much in the Scriptures, and to show that it has not lost its character or importance in a spiritual point of view, by anything that has transpired in its past history.

Relations of the Protestant Episcopal Church to others. § 21. The Scotch Church, (not the Establishment, for that is a Presbyterian affair,) and the Irish Church, are in full and free communion with the Protestant Episcopal Church in the United States.

But neither of these Churches, nor any that are in communion with them, recognize as parts of the visible Church of Christ, any of the Sects enumerated in a preceding Chapter, or any others that have arisen since the Reformation. Neither of them recognize the validity of their baptisms—though individuals in their communion have so done. Neither of them receive the members of those denominations to communion by letter, or on certificate of membership, from them. And both the English Church and our own have laid down a condition that excludes their ministers from being received as ministers by us until they shall have been ordained anew, by our Bishops.

But this is not the attitude which these Churches have taken towards the other parts of the Visible Church. Between us and the Oriental Churches there is free communion and full recognition, notwithstanding some important differences in doctrine, discipline, and worship they remaining where they were at a period somewhat later than that which we have taken for our standard. We also receive both members and ministers of the Roman Communion to the same standing in ours, on a distinct renunciation of those points in which that communion differs from our standards, and a profession of agreement and conformity to ours. Thus we admit the Churches in the Roman Obedience to be true, though corrupt, Churches of Christ.

The Roman practice toward us has been variant. They use certain rites in Baptism, Confirmation, and Ordination, which are omitted by us, and to which some of their members attach a great importance. For this reason they have sometimes admitted the validity of our Baptisms and Ordinations, and at others denied it. Thus though they admit the validity of baptisms by *unordained* persons in their own communion, yet they usually regard as unbaptized those persons whom they can succeed in perverting from ours. The validity of our ordinations was admitted until some years after Elizabeth's accession to the throne of England. But latterly they have been almost uniformly denied by them.

In 1704, JOHN GORDON, Bishop of Galloway, in Scotland, apostatized to the Romish Communion. This brought the question of the validity of his ordination before the Romish See. Gordon had requested ordination in the Romish Communion, thereby denying the validity of that which he had before. The examination of the subject at that time, proves that it had not been previously regarded as a settled question. Clement XI. decided against the validity of Protestant ordinations; and since then, I believe, they have been generally regarded by the Romanists, as of no force or validity whatever.

It would be entirely foreign to my plan, to enter into a discussion of the grounds on which this decision of the Roman See is based, in this place. Many reasons are given for it by the Romanists: as is usually the case with those who are determined to do what they can find no one good reason for doing. If the Protestant ordinations were invalid in 1704, then they must have been so from the moment when the rejection of the Papal Supremacy took place, and ordinations began to be held without the Papal consent or approbation. But the validity of the Anglican ordinations was distinctly admitted by the Papists themselves, as we have seen, in the reign of Mary, and again in that of Elizabeth, her successor on the

Throne of England. It is true, indeed, that a Bull of excommunication was issued against Elizabeth, and all her subjects, who were in the communion of the English Church, by Pius V., in 1659. But, as has been said, the Pope had then neither in fact, nor by right, any authority in England, or over the English Church. Nor had any of the Bishops who were then in the exercise of the duties of the office—and whom he included in the pretended excommunication —been ordained under his supremacy—by his permission and approbation, or any pretence of having derived any authority from him. Of course, therefore, they were under no obligations to him; and his excommunication could have no effect upon them, (as is sometimes contended,) on the ground that they had derived their authority from the Pope and that he, that gave them their authority, could take it from them again.

Of course the Pope's adherents must maintain the validity of his Bull; and in consequence deny the validity of all ministrations within the English Church and its branches, after this pretended excommunication. They are consistent therefore in denying the validity of our ordinations. But the force of the Bull depends exclusively upon the divine right of the Papal Supremacy. If that, as we contend, and as I think I have abundantly proved, is a mere anti-Christian usurpation, then of course, Pius' Bull, and excommunication are of no force, and the whole ground for rejecting the validity of the English, Scotch and American Ordinations is shown to be untenable. It is, in fact, a mere expedient of malicious bigotry.

By many of the Roman Catholics, however, we are regarded merely as schismatics, whose ministerial acts are valid in themselves, and only voidable as an act of discipline by the higher authority to whom we are answerable. They claim to be that authority—with how much reason, may be seen from what has already been said. But, for the most part, an insane fury for the establishment of that most anti-Christian dogma, which lies at the foundation of the system they are now engrossed in propagating—the Papal Supremacy—has driven them to disregard and outrage all considerations, not only of charity and truth, but also of decency and decorum.

It may be thought by many that this is a reason why we should disclaim all alliance with them, and class ourselves, at once with the Protestant Sects. But this cannot be done. A sister may become a harlot, and her disgrace may change the nature and manifestations of our obligations to her; but she is our sister still. We cannot deny that the same mother bore, and the same father begat, both us and her. Others may be more worthy of our love, but neither this fact, nor any other, can change the relations which not ourselves, but the allotment of Providence, has formed between us.

Statistics of the Protestant Episcopal Church. § 22. The present statistics of the Protestant Episcopal Church, are:—28 organized Dioceses, 28 [1850] Bishops, in actual discharge of Episcopal functions in this country, two Missionary Bishops, 1566 clergymen, about 100,000 communicants, and a population of about 2,000,000.

In 1789, when the Church was organized, the whole number of Clergy was only about 180.

Each Diocese has a Convention consisting of its Bishop, the Clergy actually engaged in ministerial duty, and Delegates chosen by the people of the parishes. The chief Synodical Authority consists in the General Convention. This body holds its sessions once in three years, and is composed of all the Bishops, and four Clerical and four Lay Delegates from each Diocese.

§ 23. It may be expected, that I will not pass by without notice, a matter of so much importance in this connection, as the doctrinal character and teaching of that Body which we have identified as the Church of Christ for this country. *The Doctrinal Character of the Protestant Episcopal Church.*

It is obvious, that a consideration of this matter, does not come within my plan, and is not necessary to its completion. I will, however, make a few general statements on the subject.

§ 24. The first point that I shall mention in this connection, is the declaration in the VIth "Article of Religion," that "Holy Scripture containeth all things necessary to salvation: so that whatsoever is not read therein nor may be proved thereby, is not to be required of any that it should be believed as an article of the Faith, or be thought requisite or necessary to salvation." And by the VIIIth Article, the Church declares that the Apostles' and the Nicene Creeds are to be retained—"for they may be proved by most certain warrants of Holy Scripture." *The Protestant Episcopal Church recognises the Scriptures as the only Source and Standard of Divine Truth.*

I have, in fact, already, in the foregoing pages, repeatedly stated, that the Reformed Branches of the Church returned to the Scriptures as the only standard of Divine Truth—the only authority by which any thing can be proved to be obligatory upon man, as the commandment of God.

<small>The Church, however, claims the right to be her own Interpreter of the Scriptures.</small> § 25. While, however, the Church in this country acknowledges no other source of divine knowledge than the written Word of God, she claims, in all cases of doubtful interpretation or construction, the right to interpret and construe that Word for herself. And in doing this, she professes to be guided by the earliest and most prevalent construction.

In a preceding Chapter,[1] I have shown that the right to interpret the Scriptures for herself and for her members in all points included in their relations to her, is indispensable to her existence; and is only what is claimed and exercised by every sect and society of men. In other words, the Church claims to be above and superior to any one, or any part, of her members. Else she could not maintain her Faith or her Discipline—or continue her distinct existence.

The possession and exercise of this authority, I have justified from the Scriptures, as well as from the necessity of the case.

The inevitable inference is, that we are bound to look to the Church as in some sense and to some extent our teacher and guide, under God, in things pertaining to Religion.

[1] Chapter v.

This principle modifies our duty and our course to a considerable extent. The teaching of the Church becomes thereby an important item for our consideration in our investigation of truth. Hence, in practice, if we find the Church teaching, or holding any thing contrary to our view of the Scripture doctrines—we may not lightly dismiss the Church testimony. It is of more importance to us, than the opinion of any one man. Its doctrinal standards are the result of the wisdom and knowledge of the Scriptures possessed by a large number of men who have probably no superiors living in these respects. They have, moreover, stood the test of many hundred years of experience and discussion. And besides this, the authority necessary to the maintainance of its integrity and discipline, confers upon the doctrines of the Church, an importance that is not to be lightly esteemed.

We should never, therefore, dissent from the doctrines of the Church, except when, after a thorough and careful examination of the Scriptures, there is no doubt left of the irreconcilable contrariety between the two.

With regard to the Church in this country, then, we may be satisfied that she does not intend to teach, or to require us to believe, anything that is not according to the Scriptures, and contained in them or clearly deduced from them. This, of course, we ought to believe, and in all points which are not fundamental, it is a part of Christianity, to be willing to yield our preferences for the sake of unity, peace, and harmony.

CHAPTER VIII.

THE ROMISH CLAIM TO JURISDICTION IN THE UNITED STATES.

It is well known that there has long been a class of persons who advocate the Supremacy of the Bishop of Rome over all Christians and all Christendom. Persons holding these views have effected a settlement in the United States, organized a church, and claim for it the sole and exclusive right to the ecclesiastical jurisdiction of this country.

If this claim be well founded, it will greatly modify, if not entirely reverse, the conclusion arrived at in the last chapter, with regard to "*the Protestant Episcopal Church in the United States.*" If two messengers come unto us with contradictory messages, it is indeed barely possible that both came from God originally, but it is not possible that they can have been both designed to teach the same people. We cannot serve or obey two masters, or two different stewards of the same Master, whose instructions either do, or by possibility may, require different things.

The Romish claim presents for our consideration two questions, which, though not entirely distinct, cannot however be treated, in the present connections, as altogether one and the same. The one relates to the

CHAP. VIII.] ROMISH CLAIM TO JURISDICTION. 319

Papal Supremacy in general, and the other relates to the facts and circumstances connected with the settlement and organization of those in this country who advocate that Supremacy.

If the right to universal supremacy, as it is claimed for the Pope, be well founded, it follows, that no persons who reject that supremacy can be capable of exercising jurisdiction any where. But even if that claim be not well founded, it is possible (or at least, I am willing now to admit, for the sake of the argument, that it is possible) that those who advocate it may establish a Branch of the Church of Christ acknowledging that claim, and thus bind the consciences of all within the appropriate sphere of its jurisdiction to all of its own teachings, which are not plainly and undeniably contrary to God's Written Word. It may claim, in Christ's name, the support, the submission and obedience which He has authorized His Church to claim any where; and, consequently, this support, submission and obedience cannot be justly claimed *for the same people*, by any other Branch of the Church, or any other persons.

§ 1. Into the general and abstract claim of the Supremacy, I shall not now inquire any further than I have already done in the foregoing chapters. <small>The Supremacy in General.</small>

We have seen that it was unknown in the first centuries, and prohibited by the express law of the whole Church in Council assembled—that it was not recognized, and did not exist in England for the first five centuries, at least; that it was always regarded by the laws of England as a usurpation; the Church of England all the meanwhile being acknowledged to be a true and catholic branch of the Church of Christ.

There is nothing, therefore, in the general claim of the Supremacy which can give its advocates precedency of right in this country. Consequently our attention must be directed to the circumstances under which they settled here, and claim to have established their branch of the Church within these United States. And these facts and circumstances we must investigate in reference to the principles of Church identity, already laid down and applied to other Sects.

The time of the Settlement. § 2. I give the account of the first Romish settlement in what was the United States, when they first became a separate nation, in the language of a Roman Catholic writer, as follows:

"Lord Baltimore having obtained, from Charles I., the Charter of Maryland, hastened to carry into effect the plan of colonizing the new province, of which he appointed his brother, Leonard Calvert, to be Governor. This first body of emigrants, consisting of about two hundred gentlemen, of considerable rank and fortune, chiefly of the Roman Catholic persuasion, with a number of inferior adherents, sailed from England, under the command of Calvert, in November, 1632, and after a prosperous voyage, landed in Maryland, near the mouth of the river Potomac, in the beginning of the following year. The Governor, as soon as he landed, erected a Cross on the shore, and took possession of the country for our sovereign lord, the King of England. . . . . . On the 23d of March, 1634, the festival of the Annunciation of the ever-blessed Virgin, and, on St. Clement's Island, in the Potomac, the divine sacrifice of the Mass, was, for the first time, offered up to God in this portion of America."[1]

This, then, was the first settlement of Roman Catholics in the United States proper. St. Augustine, in East Florida, had been settled by the Spanish, in the Roman Communion, as early as 1564. Florida, however, was at that time a Spanish territory, and did not become a part of the United States until several years after the commencement of their independent existence as a nation. The Papists do not claim, that I am aware of, priority of canonical jurisdiction in the United States on account of this early settlement in Florida. We need not, therefore, give it any further attention in this place.

The author just quoted above continues:

"Between the years 1634 and 1687, Roman missionaries had already traversed that vast region lying between the heights of Montreal and Quebec and the mouth of the Mississippi, the greater portion of which is now known as the United States. Within thirteen years the wilderness of the Hurons was visited by sixty missionaries, chiefly Jesuits: one of their number, Claud Allowez, discovered the southern shores of Lake Superior."[2]

These missionary operations, however, were not earlier than the settlement of Maryland; and they present nothing that we need to take into special consideration in this connection.

---

[1] Prof. Walter's *Account of the Roman Catholic Church in the United States, in Rupp's Collection*, pp. 113–117.

[2] Walter, *ubi supra*, p. 119.

Hence it appears that this first settlement of the Roman Catholics was many years *subsequent* to the settlement of the English Church in the British Possessions of North America. The right of priority of canonical occupation, is, therefore, unquestionably with the Branch of the English Church.

Lord Baltimore and his party incapable of founding a Branch of the Church any where.

§ 3. Let us now turn our attention to the persons who founded this Romish Colony within the British possessions.

Since the Papists in this country refer to England for their origin, it may be well, before we proceed any farther, to notice briefly the origin of that Sect in England.

By the Bull of Pius V., February 23d, 1569, Queen Elizabeth was declared "a heretic and an encourager of heretics; those that adhere to her lie under the censure of an anathema, and are cut off from the Body of Christ." "We likewise," says the Bull, "declare the said Elizabeth deprived of the pretended right to the kingdom, and of all dominion, dignity, and privilege, whatever, and that all the nobility and subjects of the said realm, who have sworn to her in any manner whatever, are for ever absolved from any such oath, and from all obligations of fidelity and allegiance." "We likewise command all the nobility, subjects, and others above mentioned, that they do not presume to obey her orders, commands or laws, for the future."

In consequence of this Bull a few persons seceded from the English Church and formed a Sect by themselves in subjection to the Pope.

The Romish Sect in England was at first governed

by Jesuits and Missionary Priests, under the superintendence of Allen, a Roman Cardinal, who lived in Flanders, and founded the Colleges at Douay and Rheims. In 1593, George Blackwall was appointed Arch-Priest of the English Romanists, and this form of ecclesiastical government prevailed among them until 1623, when Dr. Bishop was ordained titular Bishop of Chalcedon, and sent from Rome to govern the Papists in England. Dr. Smith, the next Bishop of Chalcedon, was banished in 1629, and they were without a Bishop until the reign of James II.

Eleven of the Bishops who refused to acknowledge Elizabeth's supremacy, as we have before seen, remained and died in England. The last of them, Watson, of Lincoln, died in 1584. But the Romish seceders were never placed under their jurisdiction. Nor did they claim to be Bishops over them.. Not even this pretence to be the Church of England was set up for the Papists, by their most zealous defenders.

These titular Bishops, of whom we have spoken as placed over the Papists in England, were called Bishops *in partibus*, and *Vicars Apostolic*. " This is an officer," says Butler, " vested with Episcopal authority, by the Pope, over any Church which is in want of a Bishop, but which, *for some reason, cannot have one of its own.*" But if the Papists were a branch of the Church of Christ, having lawful jurisdiction in England, there was no reason why they could not have Bishops of their own. Butler was himself a Papist— his admission, therefore, is specially important, and is a confession that the English Papists were not a branch of the Church of Christ, competent to the performance of ecclesiastical functions. They were, therefore, mere intruders into a field which the Lord had committed to other laborers.

This is a most important fact. They were Papists, I admit, and in communion with the Churches in the Roman Obedience. But such was not the Church of England at that time. The Papal adherents in that country could be only a sect in opposition to the Church; and whatever sympathy, countenance, or support, they might have from the members of another branch of the Church in a different country, it could not benefit their situation in England. I will not, of course, deny that they might have gone to Rome, or France, or Spain, taken up their domicil there, and have been received into communion with that branch of the Church whose doctrine and discipline they seem to have preferred. But they could not be duly received into the Romish communion, and gain a right to jurisdiction *any where*, without first going into a country where some Church of the Romish Obedience had rightful jurisdiction, and taking up their domicil there, ceasing to be Englishmen altogether, and transferring their allegiance to some other national sovereignty.

As Englishmen, the English Church was the only one for them; and when they had rejected its jurisdiction they had rejected the Church of Christ altogether; they could not set up another jurisdiction within her midst, unless they could prove that she had become apostate.

The principle involved in such a step, is the fundamental one of Christianity itself. It is simply this:

whether we will obey God, by submitting to them that He has placed over us, or rejecting them, will place an object of our own choosing in their place, so that while pretending to obey God, we can follow the devices of our own heart, and exult in the triumph of our own unrestrained wilfulness.

The first settlers of Maryland, therefore, having rejected the jurisdiction and forsaken the communion of the only branch of the Church to which, as Englishmen, they could belong,—and having never sought or obtained reconciliation in any effectual way, with any other branch of the Church, they were incapable of founding a branch of that Church any where.

§ 4. Whatever right Lord Baltimore had to found a colony and a Church, was derived from King Charles; himself, a layman and member of the Church of England, and therefore he could give no authority to extend any other communion than that to which he belonged. *No jurisdiction could be gained for a Branch of the Church in the Romish Obedience, in the British Possessions.*

It has been said, and that too by a writer calling himself a Protestant,[1] "that a Romanist may reply, and that truly, that America was discovered by a member of the Romish communion—that the right to the country was derived from a Papal Bull," .... as a ground upon which to base the right to jurisdiction in this country by the Papists.

I do not design to enter upon any discussion of the accuracy of this statement of the two facts referred to. Let them pass for the present as true. It is undenia-

---

[1] CHURCH REVIEW, for Oct. 1849, p. 429.

ble that the British Crown did possess, and was universally acknowledged to possess, the sovereignty of the portions of this continent in which both the Baltimore and Virginia settlements were made, and at the time when they were made. Lord Baltimore himself came here under a grant obtained from the English Crown, and not under one obtained from the Pope.

Now there was nothing in the manner in which the English sovereign acquired the possession of this country, or in the tenure by which he held it, that obliged him to maintain, or even to tolerate, the Papal religion and worship within its boundaries. This I believe has never been pretended.

It is too manifest to be made the matter of remark, that King Charles could not give authority or permission to extend the communion of any Branch of the Church except that to which he himself belonged.

But let us look at the grant. "It professed to have in view 'a laudable zeal for extending the Christian Religion and the territories of the [British] Empire,'" and bestowed upon the proprietor "the patronage and advowsons of all churches, which, (with the increasing religion and worship of Christ) within the said region [granted to Lord Baltimore,] hereafter shall happen to be built, together with licence and faculty of erecting and founding churches, chapels, and places of worship, and of causing the same to be dedicated and consecrated *according to the ecclesiastical laws of our Kingdom of England.*" [1]

When we consider that "the Church of England"

---

[1] HAWKS' *Narrative of Events connected with the rise and progress of the Protestant Episcopal Church in Maryland,* pp. 21, 22.

was a part of "the ecclesiastical laws of our Kingdom of England," it must seem doubtful whether any churches for the Romish Worship could be built under this grant.

But it is hardly worth while to notice this point at length. Any claim that can be based upon it is too feeble to deserve much attention.

Whatever may be the proper authority of princes and kings in ecclesiastical affairs—or whether they properly have any or not—it is quite certain that that authority is no fundamental principle of Church extension. The King cannot so far set the laws of God and the Church at nought, as to give her enemies the right to oppress her and trample her under foot; or to come in and take her inheritance from her. He cannot erect any little knot of discontented subjects into a valid Branch of the Church of Christ, with all its solemn sanctions and mysterious spiritual agencies. All such churches would be founded on himself, and not on Christ.

§ 5. Lord Baltimore granted free toleration to all "professing to believe in Jesus Christ." On this basis things continued until the great Rebellion, 1640. Settlers of various views, in matters of religion, had been received into the colony. The Independents then gained the ascendancy, and repealed the laws of universal toleration, and proscribed entirely "Popery and Prelacy." But with the Restoration, 1660, Lord Baltimore regained his rights as owner of the colony, and for a season all things proceeded on the former plan. The mass of the population, however, had be- *The English Church established in Maryland in 1692.*

come Protestants. Accordingly, the accession of William and Mary to the English Throne, 1688, was followed, after some preparatory troubles, by the overthrow of Lord Baltimore's authority, and the substitution in his stead of a royal Governor.[1]

In 1675, the Church of England people made an effort to increase the efficiency and number of the ministrations according to the usage and doctrines of the English Church. In a short time the Protestants became by far the most numerous—thirty to one, as it is said[2]—and in 1692, we find them in the ascendancy in all the offices of State and places of trust. "It is not credible," says Dr. Hawks,[3] "that any very serious opposition was made to the change by a respectable part of the Protestant population—for tradition would, at least, have preserved some memory of the strife."

In 1692, met the first Legislative Assembly of Maryland, and the second act was "for the service of Almighty God, and the establishment of the Protestant Religion in the Province."[4]

This act provided, that the Church of England should have and enjoy all her rights and liberties and franchises, wholly inviolable, as they then were, or thereafter should be established by law; that the several counties should be laid out into Parishes; that the freeholders of each Parish should meet and appoint six vestrymen; that each person should be taxed, and the Vestries in the Parishes where there were no

---

[1] WILBERFORCE'S *Hist. of the American Church*, p. 88.
[2] HAWKS' *Maryland*, p. 59, on the authority of *Chalmers*.
[3] *Maryland*, p. 60.   [4] HAWKS, *ubi supra*, p. 71.

Churches should cause them to be built, and apply the remainder of the tax to the support of the clergy. Under this act the Province was divided into thirty-one Parishes, and it is said that there were then sixteen ministers of the Church of England in Maryland.[1]

I certainly am not disposed to ascribe much to the authority of the civil powers in ecclesiastical matters. But this "Reformation" in Maryland seems to have been made with but little or no opposition from any source, and the ecclesiastical authorities, such as they were, if, indeed, there were any, seem to have entirely acquiesced in it, if they did not in fact take the lead in bringing it about.

This act is worthy of notice; for Lord Baltimore's authority for establishing a Romish communion in Maryland, was from King Charles, and, of course, purely secular. If, therefore, Lord Baltimore's authority, acting as he did against the Church of which he ought to have been a member, and which had jurisdiction where he acted, was sufficient to give validity to his act, then much more the same authority, acting in 1692, in accordance with that Church, and for the purpose of establishing the very jurisdiction which he ought to have established, and which it had never consented to relinquish, was valid. In either view of Lord Baltimore's authority, therefore, the jurisdiction of the English Church was fully and rightfully established in Maryland, from 1692 downward.

§ 6. Immediately after this, Dr. THOMAS BRAY was

---

[1] *See* HAWKS, as above, pp. 71–72.

Dr. Bray appointed Superintendent. appointed Commissary by the Bishop of London, in his stead, "to redress what was amiss, and supply what was wanting in the Church" in Maryland, as far as a Presbyter could do so, and the Church of England continued to take direct charge of its colony in Maryland. In 1770, at a general meeting of the Clergy of Maryland, a petition was drawn up and addressed to the king—to the Archbishop of Canterbury, and to Lord Baltimore, praying for the establishment of an Episcopate in these colonies, but their prayer was not granted.[1]

Further support of the Church by the State. § 7. In the spring of 1779, after the Revolution, the Legislature of Maryland passed an act to establish select vestries, and vested in them, as trustees, all the property that belonged to their respective Parishes, while they were a part of the Church of England. And during the Revolutionary war the Legislature of the State actually took up the subject of organizing the Episcopal Church in that State. They were prevented from doing so by one of the clergy, the Rev. SAMUEL KEENE, on account of objections to the manner in which the thing was proposed to be done.[2]

Ecclesiastical movement towards an organization. § 8. In 1783, a number of clergy convened at the first commencement of Washington College, and the subject of an organization, the revision of the Liturgy, and the obtaining the Episcopate, was discussed.

In August of the same year, a Convention of the Clergy was held in furtherance of the same objects,

---

[1] HAWKS, *ubi supra*, p. 256.   [2] Ibid. pp. 290, 291.

and finally adjourned until the spring of 1784. In 1788, the Church in this State drew up and published a Code of Canons, and her first Bishop, the Rt. Rev. Dr. CLAGGETT, was consecrated September 13, 1792. Several previous efforts had been made to obtain the Episcopate without success.

§ 9. This brings us down to a most important epoch in the ecclesiastical history of Maryland. Up to the time of the Revolutionary war the Papists had no Church fully organized, as they understand its organization. They had nothing *in point of fact*, which even themselves could regard as a branch of the Church of Christ, and since they had, *as a matter of right*, no jurisdiction here, they could organize none afterwards. *[margin: The Romish Church had no right to jurisdiction up to the time of the Revolution.]*

We might, therefore, leave the subject here, but I prefer to consider their subsequent organization, to some extent, in relation to this matter.

§ 10. After the termination of the Revolutionary war, Maryland became a regularly organized Diocese, and was one of the first to move in the matter of an ecclesiastical union of "the Church-of-England people." This union was effected, as we have seen, in 1784, and the organization was completed before 1789, by the possession of the requisite number of Bishops, (four,) an established Liturgy or Worship, and settled Constitutions and Canons of Discipline. *[margin: Maryland became a Diocese in the Protestant Episcopal Church, before any Romish Organization was effected.]*

In 1789, some four or five years after "the Church-of-England people" had organized themselves into a Diocese in Maryland, and became a part of the Protestant Episcopal Church in the United States, Pius

VI., Bishop of Rome, erected Baltimore—the metropolis of Maryland—into a See for a Bishop in the Roman Obedience; and on the 7th of December, 1790, Dr. JOHN CARROL came to Baltimore as Diocesan.

§ 11. Carrol was a native of Maryland, where the English communion was regularly established before he was born. He was ordained Bishop in England, not by English Bishops, but by a Bishop who had no right to perform any ecclesiastical or ministerial functions whatever, in England. He came to establish the Romish communion where it could exist only by including those who ought to be in the English Church, and were like himself, either seceders or recusants from that Church. It was, therefore, an act of the most direct opposition to the Church of Christ, which was, at that time, lawfully and canonically established in Maryland.

The Nature of this Transaction.

Now such an interference with the lawful and scriptural ministrations of the Church, is opposition to Christ himself, and is what is called in St. John's Epistles, Antichrist. It comes in His name, under the pretence of His religion, but in opposition to those, who, according to His laws and institutions, are engaged in the same divine functions which the intruders come with a pretence of performing. His kingdom should be characterized by peace and charity. But such a proceeding brings, inevitably, contentions, animosities, strifes and divisions.

Carrol was himself, then, a recusant, ordained Bishop in contravention of the fundamental laws of the Church, come to a See erected by one whose claim to authority here was the most unfounded assumption, and within the limits of another branch of the Church, where he could have none for his flock except those that had rejected the communion to which they must belong, if they would be in obedience to Christ.

I might here leave my argument as completed, since, in fact, my plan requires me to consider only the priority of canonical occupation as the means of identifying the Branch of the Church of Christ for this country. I will, however, add another reason for regarding the claims of the Romanists to jurisdiction in the United States as invalid.

§ 12. They did not come here to found an independent branch of the Church on the simple basis of the Apostolic Faith. They came to extend a human theory of Roman aggrandizement. Their authority was based on the Papal Supremacy, and the doctrines which they came to teach, were, in part, additions to the original Revelation. *(The Romanists came to build upon another basis than that of Primitive Christianity and the Primitive Church.)*

This is a point to which I have already alluded several times. And I now give, as I have promised, the addition to the Creed made by Pius IV., which every minister in the Roman Communion is bound to teach, and every layman, consequently, bound to receive, as the Rule of his Faith.

After reciting the Nicene Creed, the Romish Creed proceeds with twelve articles, as follows:—

1. The Apostolic and ecclesiastical traditions, and other observances and constitutions of the Church, do I firmly admit and embrace.

2. Also the sacred Scripture, *according to the sense*

which our holy mother, the Church, hath holden and doth hold, (whose office it is to judge of the true sense and interpretation of Holy Scriptures,) do I admit; neither will I ever receive and expound it but according to the uniform consent of the Fathers.

3. I do also profess that there are truly and properly seven Sacraments of the new law, instituted by our Lord Jesus Christ, and necessary to the salvation of mankind, though all are not necessary for every man, viz: Baptism, Confirmation, the Eucharist, Penance, Extreme Unction, Orders, and Marriage; and that they confer grace; and that among these, Baptism, Confirmation, and Orders cannot be repeated without sacrilege. Also the received and approved rites of the [Roman] Catholic Church, used in the solemn administration of all the foresaid sacraments, I receive and admit.

4. I embrace and receive each and every thing that was defined and declared in the Holy Council of Trent, concerning original sin and justification.

5. I likewise confess that in the Mass is offered unto God a true, proper, and propitiatory sacrifice for the living and the dead, and that the most Holy Eucharist is truly, really, and substantively the Body and Blood, with the soul and divinity, of our Lord Jesus Christ; and that there is made a change of the whole substance of the bread into His Body, and of the whole substance of the wine into His Blood, which conversion the [Roman] Catholic Church calls Transubstantiation.

6. I confess, also, that under one kind only, all and

whole, Christ (totum atque integrum Christum) and the true Sacrament is received.

7. I do constantly hold that there is a Purgatory, and that the souls detained there are holpen by the suffrages of the faithful.

8. And likewise that the saints reigning with Christ are to be worshipped (venerandos) and prayed unto, and that they offer their prayers unto God for us, and that their relics are to be worshipped, (reliquias eorum venerandas.)

9. Most firmly do I assert that the images of Christ and of the Mother of God, always a Virgin, and of the other Saints, also, are to be possessed and retained, and that due honor and veneration is to be given to them.

10. Likewise, I affirm that the power of indulgences was left by Christ in the Church, and that their use is in the highest degree salutary to a Christian people.

11. I acknowledge that the Holy Catholic, Apostolic, and Roman Church is the mother and mistress of all Churches: and I vow and promise true obedience to the Bishop of Rome, who is the successor of St. Peter, (the prince of the Apostles,) and the Vicar of Jesus Christ.

12. I do also undoubtedly receive and profess all other things which have been handed down, defined, or declared, by the sacred canons and general councils, and especially by the most holy council of Trent; and at the same time, and equally, I also condemn, reject, and anathematize, all things contrary to the same, and whatever heresies have been condemned, rejected, and

anathematized by the Church. And I shall take care that this true Catholic Faith, (out of which no man can be saved,) and which I now willingly and truly hold, shall be held and confessed, whole and inviolate, most firmly, even to the last breath of life, God being my helper, and shall be held, taught and preached, as much as is in my power, to those that are under me, or over whom I may have charge, in my calling.

This I promise, vow and swear; so help me God, and these Holy Gospels."

After some declarations with regard to publishing this Creed, the Pope adds:

"It shall not be lawful, therefore, for any man to infringe this will and commandment, or by audacious boldness to contravene the same; which if any man presume to do, let him know that he shall incur the indignation of Almighty God, and of St. Peter and St. Paul, His Apostles."

<small>This constitutes a different Basis or foundation from that on which the Apostles built.</small> §13. This is the Doctrinal basis upon which the Romish Sect in this country is built. I shall not enter into a prolonged discussion of its contents. That is not necessary. It professes to teach something else, as equally binding upon the conscience, and equally necessary to salvation, as what is contained in the Scriptures. The chief motive, which lies at its foundation, is the building up of the colossal power of the Papal Supremacy—a power as fully anti-Christian as any that the world has ever seen.

This Creed is their Rule of Faith, which the clergy promise to hold and to teach to all over whom they may have charge. All their teaching, therefore, must be in accordance with this Creed.

It is readily admitted that any branch of the Church has a right to set forth definitions of the faith, articles of agreement, &c. Of such are the XXXIX Articles of the English Church, and its Catechism. And in such cases, the question is as to the conformity of the standards with the Scriptures, as interpreted by the Primitive Church. But the Creed of Pius IV. is not of this character. It professes to contain the essentials of the Faith of the Communion by which it is received. And it makes all of its articles—the Papal additions, as well as those derived from Scriptures—equally fundamental and equally necessary to salvation.

It is evident, therefore, that the Missionaries in the Roman Obedience came into this country, not with a design to extend the Communion of the Church of Christ as He established it—to inculcate simply the Faith once delivered to the saints—but to build upon a widely different foundation. Unlike the English, they make no pretence to adhere to the Scriptures, and the Creeds, Doctrines, and usages of the Church universal in its earliest age, when it was a united and uncorrupted body. But they came here to disseminate Popery, to inculcate what was peculiarly Romish.

Tried, then, by all the principles of Church extension and identity, the Romish Sect in this country is found wanting. It was established by those who were *not* then in the communion of the Church. They came to a country where the Church had been previously established, and their additions to the Creed and Faith once delivered to the Saints, were so great, and of such a nature, as to make the basis upon which they built diverse from that upon which the Church itself was at first established.

<small>Not necessary to regard the Churches in the Roman Obedience apostate.</small> § 14. It is sometimes said by way of excuse for disregarding the Romish claims, that the Roman Church is apostate. If by this it is meant that the Church has fallen into grievous errors, the assertion is readily admitted. But unless it has totally and wholly fallen from the Christian estate and condition, so that they have neither Baptism, Eucharist, nor any other divine ordinance that is valid and acceptable to God, then that which is designated by "*apostacy*," does not of itself void their jurisdiction.

I shall not assume that the Roman Churches are apostate to such an extent as is implied in this method of disposing of their claims.

A Church may be corrupt in itself without being apostate. But when it makes its own corruptions the stimulus to its missionary zeal, and goes forth to build on them as a foundation, the superstructure which it erects cannot be regarded as on the same basis with itself, nor deserve to be considered a part of the Church of Christ.

A proper regard to the plan with which I started prohibits me from entering into a comparison of the doctrinal character of the Papists and the Protestant Episcopalians. I am, therefore, limited to a consideration of what belongs to the ecclesiastical position of the two bodies.

My leading object in this chapter has not been to

present the corruptions and abuses of the Romish Church as a means of preventing people from entering its communion. There are many of its doctrines which it seems impossible to reconcile with the word of God. To these I could never consent or assent any where. But, besides these, there are many things in the Romish Communion different from what we have in ours, to which, though I do not like them, I should assent and conform without hesitation, if the Romish Sect in this country were the Church that has rightful jurisdiction here.

But I take no pleasure in exposing the faults and errors of others. It is always an unpleasant task, and exposes one to the danger of evil speaking and of uncharitable imputation. Hard names and abusive language are no part of my mode of argumentation. I have rather designed to show, *that whatever doctrines the Romish Sect may hold, no person can be in that communion in this country, and be in obedience to God* at the same time.

In the course of this argument, I have chosen not to assume that the Churches in the Roman Obedience are apostate. I have merely assumed that the adherents of the Papal Supremacy were schismatics in this country. But I hardly need remind my reader that schism does not, any more than any other sin, always, and necessarily, render those guilty of it, incapable of valid ministrations. Schism may be of two kinds. When, for instance, a minister intrudes himself into the cure of another, and performs ministerial functions without his consent, he is a schismatic in one sense of the word. In this case, the claim of the intruder may be disregarded with perfect impunity. But again. When one Church refuses communion with another, except on compliance with terms which it has no right or authority to demand—the party refusing is guilty of a schism in the Body of Christ. But this does not void its jurisdiction within its own proper territory. A man comes into my house without any legal right, and claims to dispose of my family and property. I have a perfect right to turn him out of doors. But if he stays at home and sets up a claim to my house, or whatever is in it, he is guilty of a breach of the peace as much as in the other case, but this gives me no right to go and turn him out of *his own.*

Still, however, the Romanists in this country cannot be regarded as occupying precisely the same relation to the identity of the Church as the other Sects that are to be found here. They have the Ministry of Christ in what the Church has always regarded as a valid, though not a regular succession. They are owned by and identified with a part of the Church. Hence their ministrations must be regarded as *per se* valid. This, however, is very far from putting them on an equality with the Protestant branch of the Church in this country.

<small>The Inference from the foregoing Arguments.</small> § 15. The facts and principles of this, and the foregoing chapters, establish, I think, as clearly as facts and principles can ever prove anything, the right of the Protestant Episcopal Church to jurisdiction in these United States, and throughout the whole of their domain; and prove that that Church is the Branch of the Original Vine which has reached these distant shores in this distant age—

here to blossom and to bear fruit to her Divine Lord and Master.

A particular Branch of the Church may become apostate. This is admitted. But, as we have seen, there is nothing alleged to prove that our Branch of the Church is apostate which has not been embraced, and was not held by the whole Church throughout all of its Branches in the first centuries of its existence. We cannot, therefore, regard the objection as valid against us without involving them all—the whole Church of Christ—in the same condemnation, which would be a manifest contradiction to the Scriptures. It would show that the divine purpose had failed, the Omniscient Foresight had erred in its predictions, and the Arm of Omnipotent Power had not been able to defend His Church against the gates of Hell.

§ 16. We have also seen that the Protestant Episcopal Church is established in this country in conformity with, and in exact fulfillment of, all the conditions and principles of the extension of the visible communion of Christ's Church, which are contained in the Scriptures, as interpreted by the Church itself. Whatever, therefore, the Scriptures say of the Church, is *for us in the United States* to be understood of and applied to the Protestant Episcopal Church in the United States, in so far as it can be applied to, or fulfilled in, any particular branch of the Church. All, therefore, of the obligations to belong to the Church, all of the items and considerations which go to make up the importance of its identity, meet and have their end, for us, in that ecclesiastical organization. In that communion we may preserve

[margin: The Duty of all Christians to be in its Communion.]

the unity of the Spirit in the bond of peace[1]—we receive whomsoever Christ sends[2]—we obey them that have the rule over us[3]—we are with those to whom He promised His perpetual presence always, even unto the end of the world.[4]

But on the other hand, if we enter the Romish Communion, we are rejecting those whom the Holy Ghost has made overseers or Bishops over *us*;[5] and we incur all the guilt described in the Scriptures as inseparable from divisions, heresy, and schism. Doubtless there are degrees of that guilt depending upon the circumstances of each case, the means and opportunities of the individual for knowing better what is his duty. With a full knowledge of the case, or the means for such a knowledge before us, and within our reach, it is doubtless direct apostacy and secession from Christ. We are rejecting those whom Christ has appointed to rule over us in His name, and are yielding our support and obedience to those that have set themselves up in opposition to Him. They are, therefore, Antichrist, in the proper and legitimate sense of the word. They are carrying on an opposition to Him— to what He has ordained—to those whom He has sent.

[1] Eph. iv. 3. [2] John xii. 20. [3] Heb. xiii. 17.
[4] Matt. xxviii. 20. [5] Acts xx. 28.

CHAPTER IX.

THE IDENTITY OF SPIRIT.

I MIGHT now regard my plan as completed. But "it is the development of a true life in an organic body (which must, therefore, have historical existence) that identifies the Church. No identification of the Church can be satisfactory or conclusive, that does not take into preminent consideration both modes of examination. The historical existence of the body without the life, no more identifies the Church, than identifying a *corpse* identifies the *man*."[1]

Every organized society may be regarded as having a certain spirit of its own; not merely what the French call an "*esprit du corp*," but a state of mind and feelings produced by their association and the pursuit of the common object which they have in view. We see this among the Masons—among the Presbyterians—among the members of a Temperance Society, and indeed, among every society or association of men. There is a feeling of interest in the affairs and history of the society, and in each of its members—a zeal and promptness in denying unfounded calumnies, and in apologising for undeniable faults and mistakes; a

---

[1] *Church Review*, Oct. 1849, p. 428.

sympathy of feeling and a general similarity in character and in the state of mind and heart among all the members.

This holds true with much greater force in the Church, for that is a society designed for special spiritual purposes, and a supernatural agency has been promised to all its members—to make them to be all "of one heart and one mind"—to renew and transform them into a likeness with our Blessed Lord. The identity of spirit, therefore, must be an object that can be easily distinguished and traced by its outward forms and manifestations.

<small>This state of Heart and Mind produced, in the Church, by the Holy Ghost.</small> § 1. St. PAUL says: "There is one Body, and one Spirit, even as ye are called in one hope of your calling; one Lord, one Faith, one Baptism, one God and Father of all."[1]

It is quite probable that when St. Paul says "there is one Spirit," he refers by these words to the third Person of the Blessed Trinity, the Holy Ghost. There is one Body—the Church; and one Spirit—the Holy Ghost. He is in the Church, and the Church would be apostate without Him. And the difference in their spiritual condition—between Christians and those who are not—is the fruit and operation of the Holy Ghost in and upon their hearts.

<small>This implies a renewal of our Nature.</small> § 2. The existence of genuine piety, which may be considered as the spirit of the Church—being the effect and influence of the Holy Ghost, does most unquestionably imply the

---

[1] Eph. iv. 5, 6.

renewal of the heart; and without such a change in man it cannot exist.

§ 3. We may refer to a variety of mani- *There are many Tests.* festations, or tests of the identity of spirit— and to their existence in various ages and branches of the Church as proofs of identity in them all. Observance of the moral precepts—the duties of good citizenship, and of good neighborhood—meekness, humility, quietness, temperance, sobriety and truth— may all be regarded as fruits of the Spirit; and hence these things, or at least a tendency to them, and an approval of them, must be found in all the Branches of the Church.

I shall at present, however, refer to only a few tests, of the identity of spirit, as being not only satisfactory, but the most convenient of application.

§ 4. If we look at the present condition *Our treatment of the Faults and Corruptions of the Church.* of the various branches which we have identified as being parts of the one Catholic Church, or at its past history, we shall doubtless find much to excite emotions of one kind or another, according to the spirit by which we ourselves are actuated. We shall see much zeal and suffering for the cause of Christ. We shall see also much ignorance—much corruption—much superstition— much depravity—much, in short, to love and admire —much to censure and condemn, as well as much to pity and bewail.

All this we may admit as matter of fact and of history. And it will excite various emotions in different classes of individuals, according to the spirit by which they are actuated. Now, the Sects will undoubtedly be

15*

inclined to represent the corruptions in the Church to have began at as early a period as possible—perhaps to exaggerate them, and at least, to speak of them in as strong language of condemnation as the subject will bear. This is a part of their justification for their existence as Sects.

On the other hand, a Churchman—one who recognizes in himself a member of that same Church in which these corruptions are represented to have prevailed, will be disposed to extenuate, and as far as truth and candor will allow, to draw the veil of charity —" for charity covereth a multitude of sins "—over their errors and faults. He will feel towards the reputation of the Church as a Puritan in this country does towards the history of the English Non-conformists—as the Presbyterians do towards that of Calvin, and the Presbyterians on the Continent of Europe—as the Masons of the present day do towards the past history of their institution.

§ 5. Now, as a general thing, the Sects *This Test applied.* which we have enumerated in a foregoing chapter, as a matter of fact, do consider the Church to have become corrupt at a very early age—much earlier than the members of the Protestant Episcopal Church in this country, or the members of the Church in any other country, will admit that it became corrupted in any important point. The members of these Sects also represent the extent and influence of those corruptions as much greater than any branch of the Church has admitted.

Undoubtedly there is an extreme on both sides to which we may run. I do not now undertake to say that the Church-people in this country have not gone to one extreme; nor that the Sects on the other hand have gone to the other. I only refer to the fact that they tend in different directions and *towards* opposite extremes.

No special proof of this assertion, I presume, will be demanded or expected. The matter is obvious to all men. The Sects universally reproach the Episcopalians with making tradition—which is but the testimony, opinions, and usages of the Church—a joint Rule of Faith with the Scriptures—of looking with a blind reverence to the past, instead of sympathizing with the improvements of the age. It is thought that we do not condemn and reject the errors of Rome and the Oriental Churches with sufficient decision, and we are accused of inclining towards them.

If we look behind these outward acts to the motives from which alone they can proceed, we shall find, in one case, a partiality for the Church, and in the other, a disposition to disparage it; though those who are actuated by the last named motive, may be unconscious to themselves of any such feeling. But without it, most certainly they would not be disposed to exaggerate the faults of the Church.

§ 6. None of the Sects, I believe, have any Holy Days for the commemoration of the Apostles and Martyrs, by whose blood, no less than their lives, the infant Church was nurtured and made strong. *[margin: Regard to the Early Liturgies, Canons, &c.]* They pay but little regard to the decisions and Canons of the early Councils—to the early Liturgies and Creeds. Many of them know nothing at all of these things, and do not appear to care anything about them. The sufferings of the early Martyrs and Confessors interest them less, and apparently excite less sympathy in their minds, than the labors, privations, and persecutions of the founders and early fathers of their own Sects.

Diversity between Churchmen and Sectarians in this Respect.
§ 7. I refer to this obvious difference between the Protestant Episcopal Church on the one hand, and the Protestant Sects on the other—a difference which, so far from being denied by any body, is a matter of boast on both sides, and a matter with which each in turn reproaches the other, as proving that they are actuated by a different spirit in this particular. And, without going into the question of right and wrong in the case, I say that the difference shows where the *Church-spirit* or the spirit of the Church is. The Protestant Episcopalians may go only to the just and the justifiable extent of brotherly love in this matter, or they may have gone to the extreme, and be justly censurable for the abuse of that sentiment. But which view soever be taken of this peculiarity of the Churchmen in this country, in either case it shows where the sentiment exists, and where it does not.

This Sentiment of Partiality for the Church, Scriptural.
§ 8. I have said that there will be a sympathy and sentiment of brotherly love among the members of the Church as a consequence of their common experience, common hopes, and common interests. The cultivation of this sentiment is also represented as a duty. "Let brotherly love continue."[1] And our Saviour has made

---

[1] Heb. xiii. 1: Rom. xii. 10; 1 Thess. iv. 2: 2 Pet. i. 7.

it a test whereby we may know who are His disciples: "By this shall all men know that ye are My disciples, if ye have love one to another."[1]

§ 9. This sentiment, however, will not extend merely to the members of our own parish, nation, or age; but it will embrace the whole fellowship of the Church—the whole family of Christ. *Brotherly love includes all the Members of the Church of Christ.* Those whom He has received throughout the past ages of the Church, and in the different nations where it exists, are our brethren. Or if not, the fault is in *our* position, and not in theirs. The time has now gone by when *they* could be unchurched. If, therefore, *we* are in the Church, they are our brethren in Christ, and the sentiment of brotherly love, if it be genuine, will extend towards them, and we shall cultivate it if we discharge the whole of our duty. We are not left to select for ourselves who shall be our brethren in our spiritual, any more than in our natural, relations. And we must have sufficient self-denial to receive and acknowledge whomsoever Christ has received into the fellowship of His Church, however different our tastes and preferences might have made the selection if the making of it had been left to ourselves.

I refer then to this sentiment which is manifested towards what is known and acknowledged to have been the Church of Christ in ages past, as proof of identity of spirit between the Protestant Episcopal Church in the United States, and the Church of the Fathers, the Apostles, and Martyrs.

---

[1] John xiii. 35.

§ 10. It will be understood that I am not pointing out the course that ought to be taken; or suggesting a direction in which we may go, without going to a vicious extreme, or amiss from the right way. Doubtless we should not deny that errors and corruptions have prevailed in the Church. Nor should our sympathy for those whom we must acknowledge to be brethren, lead us to imitate their faults. But even if this sentiment leads, or has led to this abuse, its existence is none the less on that account an evidence of the main point of our present subject—the identity of spirit manifested in what may be called a partiality for the Church—in all of its affairs and its history—a disposition to extenuate, rather than to condemn—to throw the veil of charity over faults, rather than expose them to the scoffs and sneers of the infidel and the profane—to treat them, in short, as we do the faults of our brethren in the flesh—faults which are too obvious to be denied, and yet too painful to be spoken of when it can be avoided.

Even the Abuse of this Sentiment proves its Existence.

Now there is no doubt which of these two opposite courses the Protestant Episcopalians in this country take. There is no more doubt which of the two the Protestant Sects take. And the adherents to the Roman See are, in fact, fast taking sides with the Sects in this matter. Their avowal of the doctrine of Development, including a right on their part to decree new articles of Faith, and to depart from the doctrines and usages of the Fathers—is a manifestation of the same sentiment as that by which the Sects are actuated, though in a different form. And so far as it extends it shows that the spirit of sectarianism and not the spirit of the Church, is prevailing among the Romanists.

§ 11. Unquestionably there are positive Institutions and outward tests in Christianity; and without them one great object of our call to the Christian state is lost. A leading design in the introduction of Christianity to the world was, that men, by the observance of these Institutions and tests on earth, should habituate themselves to self-denial and self-control, and to the continued yielding up of their wills, so that they may do the will of Another, and acquire, by religious discipline and experience in this state of their being, with the help of the Holy Ghost, that holy, and, to us, second nature which may fit them for the society and employments of the souls of the just made perfect.

The Estimation in which the Divine Institutions are held, another Test.

Hence the training which carefully observes the outward and positive Institutions, is a part of religion as essential in itself considered, as the inward experience of renewal and peace.

And these outward Institutions are a better test of our conversion, and the genuineness of our piety than the inward emotions: since they bring us at once and directly into connection with what God has ordained *for us*. Hence they are the test whether *we* will obey Him or not.

When a man changes his opinions and course of life with sobriety and emotion, he may be said to be converted. But not every conversion is *turning to the Lord*. Each sect and each impostor calls the embracing of his or their peculiar views "conversion." Hence we hear of converts to *Millerism*, to *Mormonism*, to *Popery*, and sometimes even to *Mahometanism*. All such changes are attended with much emotion, and are regarded by those who are the subjects of them, no less than by those to whom they are converted, as a light and joy from above—the fruit of the Holy Spirit. And if we appeal to the consciousness of the individuals themselves as the test, we shall be in danger of finding what may be regarded as the best evidence only there, where the fanaticism is the most unmingled and unrelenting in its hold upon its victim.

There must, therefore, be some objective test; and surely there can be nothing better than the regard paid to the Word and Institutions of God. One may be converted to the peculiarities of a Sect, and show no more regard for what is really divine than he did before—and the inward confidence which his experience has inspired may be a perfect shield against the truth itself.

It is a little remarkable, perhaps, that the Scriptures do not contain the word "*piety*" at all; but righteousness is described as "walking in all the statutes and ordinances of the Lord blameless."[1]

The Church itself is indeed a divine institution. But it includes within itself, and for the observance and regard of its members, several others—the Scriptures, the Ministry, the Lord's Prayer, Baptism, the Lord's Supper, &c.

I do not mean to discuss at length, in this place,

---

[1] Luke i. 6.

the nature, design, or importance of these sacred institutions. I refer only to the sentiment manifested toward them by different classes of individuals for the purpose of identifying the spirit.

To make my investigation complete I ought to refer to the past, and show that the Church has always, in all ages, been characterized by a high regard to these institutions. But we have neither time nor space to go into a discussion of that kind. I will, therefore, merely say—that those who have been found to be Sects by the outward indications of history, now, and in all ages past, accuse and have accused Churchmen of superstition and formality on account of the high estimation in which they hold these Institutions. These charges against the Protestant Episcopalians in this country have doubtless been heard by all persons.

§ 12. It is the well-known tendency of love to magnify—if that be possible—the importance of its object, and, at any rate, to exaggerate rather than disparage whatever is connected with, or has proceeded from it. *These Institutions intimately connected with our Lord Himself.*

Now, there is no doubt that our Lord did institute a ministry—that He gave His disciples, at their request, a Prayer—a Form of Prayer—that He instituted the Sacrament of Baptism to be received by all who should be converted to Him—and in which He also Himself, was declared from Heaven to be the Son of God—and the Sacrament of His Last Supper—by which His People are to show forth His death until His coming again. Most intimately, and most unquestionably, therefore, are these things connected with Him. And they were instituted by that Spirit which produces the unity and identity of spirit in the Church.

How, then, will genuine piety dispose us to regard these Institutions? I speak not now of erroneous views concerning them: nor of the superstitions of the past and present ages which have exalted the inventions of man, and the cunning devices of the designing into an estimation of equal importance with those Institutions which God has most certainly ordained. But is it not the tendency of genuine piety, of pure and unfeigned love, to place too high an estimation upon what God has ordained—if that be possible—rather than to disparage it? There may be extremes on both sides, and the best of sentiments may be abused. Yet the abuse shows the existence of the sentiment. The *abuse* of the sentiment now in question, is manifested in an *over* estimate of these Institutions. Its *absence*, on the contrary, is manifested by holding them in a light estimation and in a disposition to omit or neglect their observance altogether, as unimportant.

Now the Church has always held them to be means of grace, and ordinances whose observance is conducive to salvation. The Sects, on the contrary, generally regard this view of them as a dangerous superstition.

No danger of Reverencing the Divine Institutions too much. § 13. If we love Him who founded the Church and gave to it its Institutions, we cannot fail to venerate and esteem them very highly in love for His sake. If there were any doubt or reason to distrust their connection with Him, it might indeed, be superstition to bestow upon them the regard with which piety embraces them when they are ascertained to be genuine. The feelings of piety and love and gratitude and self-devotion, awakened in the renewed heart by the consideration of what the Saviour has done for us, flow out toward these Institutions, in which He comes nigh unto us and is present with our souls.

It rests upon the undoubted word of God that many will fail to enter into His Heavenly rest on account of their unbelief. But there is neither caution nor warning in all the Holy Scriptures against esteeming too highly, or loving with too ardent a zeal, anything which our Lord has instituted or commanded. There is no intimation that such a thing is possible. The Lord loved the Church and gave Himself for it: our highest glory is to be like Him.

§ 14. Again. The Church has always shown a preference for worship with a stated Liturgy, and such was the mode of worship in which our Saviour Himself engaged while He was here in the flesh. *(The Regard for Liturgical Worship a Characteristic of the Piety of the Church.)* It is equally certain and equally admitted that the Church has always been disposed to regard Baptism as a saving ordinance —that it has always manifested a disposition to a frequent administration and reception of the Lord's Supper, and that Daily Prayer in the Sanctuary, Morning and Evening, has been felt to be both a privilege and a duty. Through all the vicissitudes of the Church's history and throughout all its branches —amidst all the diversities in other matters—we find an identity of spirit manifested in these respects.

Whether we look at the centuries when the Disciples of the Lord had to creep stealthily before the light of day should facilitate their detection, to dens and caverns in the earth there to chant their praise to Christ, their God, and renew their vows, and refresh their souls in the Commemoration of the Last Supper, or whether we consider the oppressed remnants of the Greek Church, scarcely permitted by their Mahometan oppressors to meet in the most obscure and unpretending hovel, made a Sanctuary indeed by the presence of their God with them, or whether we look to the magnificent Cathedral and splendid pageantry of the more prosperous branches of the Church in the West, or, in fine, to the chaste simplicity and subduing grandeur of the reformed Ritual—throughout the whole from first to last, and in all the parts, and amidst all other diversities, we find a unity and identity of spirit manifested toward those acts of piety and faith. Combined with superstitions as it sometimes has been—and shining forth, as it sometimes does, from amidst errors and corruptions, perversities and abuses, that make us weep for the dishonor done to the Christian name—yet as tested by its regard for these institutions, an identity of spirit throughout the whole history of the Church is too conspicuous to be mistaken even by the most careless reader.

The Sects, on the contrary, very generally prefer worship with an extemporaneous prayer. It is thought that a stated Liturgy is a great hindrance to the manifestations of the spirit among them. Their piety is better promoted without than with a stated Form of Common Prayer.

THE IDENTITY OF SPIRIT.

§ 15. Another point intimately con- *The Church's regard for the Anniversaries of the important Events in our Lord's life.* nected with this subject, and indeed forming a part of it, is derived from the regard which the Church has always paid to certain days on which the most important events of our Lord's life occurred—His Birth, His Epiphany, His Death, His Resurrection, His Ascension, and the coming of the Holy Ghost. Let it be admitted that there is an uncertainty with regard to the day on which some of them occurs. Yet there is no such uncertainty with regard to the others—the Death, the Resurrection, the Ascension, and the coming of the Holy Ghost. Most of the Sects however pay no regard to those days. The day on which the Blessed Lord died to save their souls from the bitter pains of eternal death, comes in the annual round of earthly affairs; they apparently take no pains to identify it; they feel no interest in observing it with appropriate commemorations; they go about their work or their pleasures as if they were no part of the race for which He died. And if perchance they meet with one whose heart is too full of the sad recollections with which the day is associated to "eat any pleasant bread," or to pursue his ordinary vocations in the world, they regard his feelings as superstitious. On these days *their* piety—the spirit that is in them—does not incline them to lay aside all else, to forget all temporal concerns and indulge the feelings that the event of which they are the anniversaries, inspires in the heart of every devout son of the Church.

§ 16. It is not, however, because the Sects are opposed to commemorations on general principles, for

The Sects also keep Holy Days of their own. they all have some events in their history which they commemorate—some founders and fathers to whom they look back with veneration. There have been some strange manifestations of this kind. Thus the same people who ordered Christmas to be kept as a *fast*, a day of mourning, can commemorate the "Landing of the Pilgrims" with an anniversary festival. And in general, the Sects show a disposition to impress upon the minds of their members the importance of the principal events and persons in their history, by commemorations, festivities, and rejoicings, just as the Church attempts to impress upon the minds of her members the great events in the history of her origin—the Birth, the Death, the Resurrection, and the Ascension of Her Lord, and the coming of the Holy Ghost.

The whole Church cannot be charged with Superstition and Formality. § 17. It is hardly worth the while to attempt here a vindication of the Church against the charge which is brought against it, of superstition and formality in these respects. The fault of superstition, like that of idolatry, consists not in the excess of affection—but in a mistake in regard to its object. It is idolatry to bestow upon that which is not God the honor and glory due to Him. It is superstition to bestow upon human devices and the inventions of men, relics and institutions not mentioned in the Scriptures, the regard which genuine piety would bestow upon those institutions which have unquestionably proceeded from the Lord Himself. Doubtless there has been much of both, superstition and idolatry, in the Christian as well as the Jewish Church. But the spirit which has always and everywhere been manifested in the Christian Church in all of the ages and parts, of which we know anything, cannot be regarded either as superstition or idolatry. The Comforter, which is the HOLY SPIRIT, was promised to be sent *to the Church and to abide with it forever.*[1] This promise must have been fulfilled: for it proceeded from Him " whose word shall not return to Him void, but shall accomplish that whereunto He sends it." That, therefore, which has always been held in the Church "*always, everywhere, and by all,*" cannot be contrary to the unity of the spirit, but must have proceeded from the Spirit of God Himself.

§ 18. Now, as there has always been a unity of spirit in the Church, wherever the Church itself has existed—notwithstanding all the corruptions that have prevailed within its pale, and all the misfortunes that have oppressed and disturbed its functions—so among the Sects there is perhaps in one sense a unity of spirit diverse from that in the Church, yet for the most part there is an almost endless variety of manifestations of spirit among them. *The Spirit of the Sects diverse from that of the Church.*

§ 19. They have, each of them, a distinct standard or test of piety of their own. I need not enter into protracted specifications. Every one has observed the difference between the character of the piety of the Methodists and the Presbyterians for instance: a difference which it would not be easy to characterise in *They each of them, have a spirit, and a Standard of Piety of their own.*

[1] John xiv. 16.

words, but which no person of common sagacity could fail to observe on being acquainted with the religious experience of two individuals belonging to those Sects respectively. But to look at cases which are still more marked. The piety of a Shaker—a Second Advent Believer—a Latter Day Saint—manifests itself in very different ways from that of a Presbyterian, a Lutheran, a Moravian, or a Methodist. And within these Sects themselves, it is also judged by different standards and tests. A Methodist whose piety did not manifest itself by groans and responses in the time of prayer—a Shaker that could not dance, " moving about with extraordinary transport, singing and making a perfect charm "—a Second Advent Believer who did not think that " the time of the end was near " and " the judge at the door," or a Latter Day Saint who did not acknowledge the inspiration of Joseph Smith, and the genuineness of the engraved Tables which he claims to have discovered—would hardly be regarded by those Sects respectively as possessed of genuine piety.

Thus each Sect has a spirit of its own, and yet different from that of the Church: a kind of piety peculiar to itself which can be identified as well as the visible existence of the sect, and which makes up a part of its identity.

§ 20. So it is in the Church. There is something in the spirit of the devout and intelligent Churchman which science may fail to analyse and words may be insufficient to describe, but which enables us to distinguish him as soon as we become acquainted with him, and

The Spirit of Churchmen easily distinguished.

wherever we may meet him. There is something in the books of devotion and edification which have been written by Churchmen—aside from all the peculiarities of doctrine—by which we can recognize at once the identity of the Spirit. The more eminent and distinguished the members of the different ages and parts of the Church which we take for illustrations, the more conspicuous does this identity of spirit become—the more do they have in common with each other, and the less of the peculiarities of their age and nation. The writings of the early Fathers could be used from our Pulpits without presenting any contradiction either in doctrine or in spirit to what is contained in our Liturgy. And the works of Fenelon and A'Kempis, though distinguished members of the Romish Communion, are prized as devotional guides by all who have sought a practical acquaintance with works of that kind.

§ 21. I will not here undertake to account for this difference between the Church and the Sects in their regard for the outward Institutions and Ordinances of religion and in their tests of the genuineness of conversion and piety. *The Significancy of this difference between the Church and the Sects.*

But it is difficult to understand why any persons should disparage institutions and means of grace which they do not doubt that they possess. If they were conscious of being without them, or in a condition to have only the form without the validity and spiritual grace, we should expect them to believe and teach either as a cause or as a result of their position, that they are of no essential importance.

16

Again: there is always an advantage, in a sectarian point of view, in making the test of piety, something inward and subjective—for in that case, persons are committed to nothing that is permanent and unchangeable—but they can always adapt themselves to the inclinations of men and change from time to time to suit the spirit of the age.

The Protestant Episcopal Church identical in Spirit with the Church of Christ. § 22. Such differences are there between the spirit that is in the Sects and that which is in the Church. So different is the piety of the two different classes of persons. In all this we doubt not their sincerity, or their good intentions. And I have introduced the subject for no purpose of pointing an argument, or of drawing an unfavorable conclusion against them. I have spoken of it for the purpose of showing that that body, which I have historically identified as the branch of the Church of Christ in this country, claims to manifest, and is accused of manifesting, that sentiment toward the Church—even in regard to its undeniable faults and corruptions—which both nature and Revelation teach us to expect, if there really exists the identity between them which we have traced out; and that its sympathies are with the Church, as tested by its most important Institutions and its most characteristic Observances. And by this train of thought it must appear, as I think—taking the claims of the Protestant Episcopal Church and the accusations of those opposed to it (concurring as they do in this point) as the premises from which our conclusion is drawn—that there is an identity of spirit as well as of body clearly traced between the branch of the Church in this country and the original Vine.

IX.]   THE IDENTITY OF SPIRIT.   363

§ 23. Now this identity of spirit—that which has been held always, everywhere, and by all in the Church—is the fruit of the Spirit of God in the Church. And whatever any particular Church has more than this is peculiar to itself, and therefore, not catholic; and whatever any one may have that is contrary to it, is opposed to Christ. *This Identity produced by the Holy Ghost in the Church.*

§ 25. I think that I have now shown, that if one wishes to perform all the duties commanded in the Scriptures, to enjoy the unity of the Spirit in the bonds of peace, and to have the satisfaction of knowing that he is a co-worker together with God in the work of human salvation, or to give himself up in a life of devotion to Him who gave Himself for the world; this may be done without fear of mistake or failure, by any of the inhabitants of this Republic, in what is here called the Protestant Episcopal Church. I have pointed out a communion in which my fellow-travellers to eternity may find rest for their souls, with every assurance of the blessings of the Spirit and the enjoyment of the favor of God, which the nature of the case permits us to have. I could easily refer to experience, which attests the existence and reality of all that our course of investigation may have led us to expect. The joy and hope and peace of those who have drunk into her Spirit, are too deep and tranquil to attract the observation of the heedless and the noisy. But her " heavenly ways, sweet communions, and solemn vows " are being daily more and more appreciated and sought after; and wanderers, weary of the turmoil and burthen of the world, or *The Testimony of Experience.*

sick of the strifes, the instability, and the ever varying changes of sectarianism, are returning for a home, and for rest, in her bosom.

It is ascertained that out of *fifteen hundred* clergy in the Protestant Episcopal Church in this country, over *three hundred*, or about *one-fifth* have been ministers in some of the other denominations. One of them thus writes of his change:—

"My answer to the Dissenter is, who, but a Churchman, that has tasted the great delights of the sanctuary, can appreciate the Church's excellence? My vindication to the Churchman, is, who but the soul that has been 'tossed up and down like a locust' upon 'the winds of doctrine' and the sea of Sects, can understand the mazes, the dangers, the under-currents, and the disasters of sectarianism? Sectarians, you know nothing of the Church's blessings! Churchmen, you know nothing of Sectarianism's mischiefs!"

CHAPTER X.

THE MORAL DESIGN OF THE CHURCH, AND THE EFFECTS OF SECTARIANISM.

THERE is, perhaps, but little in the moral design of the Church which will help us to identify it; but there is much in that design which will tend to increase very much our estimate of the importance of identifying it. Therefore I devote a few pages to this subject.

§ 1. In my introductory chapter I have spoken of the importance of the identity of the Church as manifested by several very plain and obvious considerations, arising chiefly out of our duties and obligations to the Church. I shall now refer chiefly to the benefits which the Church was designed to bestow upon us. And in selecting them, I shall make no mention of those which have no direct relation to the main subject in hand—the identity of the Church. Most or all the benefits of the Church, which in the common sectarian view, are presented to our minds, do by no means imply its identity. They may result from *any* church—any mere human or voluntary association of men for the purposes of worship, instruction, mutual edification and helpfulness,

Only those points noticed which imply identity.

as well as from the Church which our Blessed Lord founded in His own blood. There is always strength in associations. If the members are united and harmonious, the strength of their influences both upon themselves and upon others, increases much faster by the increase of their numbers, than the numerical proportion. A society of one thousand members is far more than ten times as strong as one with only a hundred. There is an increase of wisdom in counsel—an increase of moral power in forming the characters of the members to a uniformity with one another and with their ideal—and a vast increase in the impression which they make upon others.

But of these things I shall not speak here, because they result from the very nature of an association of men, and not from any peculiarity of its origin.

§ 2. The first element in the moral design of the Church that I shall remark upon, is its relation to Divine Truth.

The Church the Pillar and Ground of the Truth. This element is very clearly indicated by St. Paul when writing to Timothy. He calls the Church "the Pillar and Ground of the Truth."

The Church instituted before the Scriptures were written. § 3. By recurring to its history it will be seen that the Church was instituted *before* the Scriptures of Divine Truth were written. We first read of the Church as already in existence on, or immediately after the day of Pentecost, in the common computation A. D., 33. But no portion of the New Testament Scriptures were

---

[1] 1 Tim. 3, 15.

written until several years after that date. And when they were written it was in the Church and by its members; and they were committed to the Church for use and for transmission.

§ 4. The whole value of the Scriptures to us depends upon our having them as they came from the pen of inspiration. If any part has been lost the loss is irreparable. If anything has been added to them, or anything changed in their contents, it becomes unsafe to rely upon what we have, as the word of God. Before, therefore, we can make any use of the Scriptures which we now have, as an authority for doctrine or for duty, we must identify them with those that were at first given by the inspiration of God. *The value of the Scriptures depends upon their genuineness.*

§ 5. We may learn from external testimony and from heathen writers, enough to prove that such a person as our Lord lived in Judea at the time designated in the Scriptures—that He taught a new religion and founded a Church, and that *some* Scriptures containing His doctrines were written by his disciples. But no copies of the Scriptures then written, have been preserved by the Heathen. They are not mentioned by name, enumerated, described, or quoted by heathen writers, so as that we can compare the Scriptures which we now have, with what was then written. Depending upon this source then, we are but little, if any better off, than as though we did not know that a Bible had ever been written—for we have no means of ascertaining that what we have came from our Lord or His Apostles. *The Church the only proof of their identity and genuineness.* *The Heathen have preserved no copies of the Scriptures.*

Nor shall we fare much better if we turn from the heathen to the Christian Sects. By their very position, the Sects were incapacitated from being competent witnesses to the genuineness and identity of the Scriptures. For not only their doctrines, but the very step which they had taken, and which brought them into existence as Sects, were condemned by the Scriptures. This they knew and felt. Hence they would be strongly tempted to corrupt the Scriptures, in order that they might bear no testimony against them.

The Early Sects corrupted the Scriptures. And this is not a mere conjecture of what they might do, and would be likely to do. But it is known that they actually did do it. Many spurious works were produced and circulated among the early sects as the works of the Apostles. Some of the genuine works were interpolated and badly corrupted; and others rejected altogether. So that if we were left to depend upon them we could no where find a pure and unadulterated copy of the Scriptures.

On the contrary, all the genuine productions of the Apostles would be received and carefully preserved by the Church. Their chief desire was to know the truth and the whole truth. They had no temptations to corrupt the writings of the Apostles. Those writings were constantly used in their daily and weekly worship. They were freely and fully quoted in the writings of the Fathers of the Church whose works have come down to us. And it is said, that if the Bible, as a distinct book, were now entirely lost, it could be restored by collecting the quotations made from it in the early Fathers of the Church, and putting them together in a volume. Of course, therefore, by comparing the Bible we now have with what we find there quoted, we can ascertain whether the Bible is precisely the same as it was then: in other words, we can identify our Bible with that of the early Church, and so with that which the inspired Prophets, Evangelists, and Apostles wrote.

Strike out of existence, then, the testimony of the Church and its members, and leave the inquirer to what he can find out of its pale alone, among heathen writers and outside sects, and it is very doubtful whether he could find a copy of the Scriptures anywhere in existence at all. He certainly could have no satisfactory proof that he was in possession of *all* that had been written for the guidance and instruction of man, by the inspiration of God. He could not know that what he had, is the work of the Apostles and others to whom it is attributed. He could not know but that what we have, has been so grossly corrupted as to be totally unlike what it was when it came from the pen that was guided by inspiration. On the contrary, knowing as we do how the early sects, the Ebionites, the Gnostics, the Montanists, &c., &c., corrupted the Scriptures, we could not doubt that, if we had only what is derived to us through such sources, that which we might possess would have been so much corrupted as to be no safe guide to practice—no sure ground of hope. But in the Church the Scriptures were first received. By it they have been kept, reverenced and used. In the early Fathers they were fully and freely quoted, and by

16*

this means the WORD OF GOD has been kept for us, and we *know* that what we have is the WORD OF GOD.

§ 6. But the value of this testimony depends upon the identity of the Church. If, instead of the testimony of the Church, we took that of the Ebionites, we should have a corrupt copy of St. Matthew's Gospel, as our only account of our Lord's life, and none of the writings of St. Paul. If we took that of the Gnostics, we should be without the best proofs of the Divinity of Christ. So with each of the Sects. Did we rely upon their testimony alone, we should have a copy of the Scriptures modified and altered to accommodate and inculcate their errors, instead of the truth as it is in Jesus. But the Church has had neither motives, disposition, nor opportunity to corrupt them. And more than this, we know from history that the Sects did corrupt the copies which they received, and that the Church did not.

§ 7. But this is not all—these early Fathers, by whose writings we are able to identify the Scriptures, contain such doctrinal statements and discussions as enable us to see how Christianity was then understood. "The faith once delivered to the saints" was explained to them in all of the Churches founded by the Apostles—that is, in Churches scattered over nearly the whole of the then known world—before they had received the Scriptures at all, and in many cases before any part of them was written. Some formularies, or confessions of faith—"*forms of sound words*"[1] existed and

[1] 2 Tim. i. 13.

were in use as bonds of union and baptismal confessions from the very commencement of those Churches. Perhaps no one of these can now be found precisely as it then existed, yet divers of them we do find in all the Churches founded by the Apostles. They are quoted, discussed, and explained, *as of authority*, in all the earlier writers from Alexandria and Carthage to Byzantium, and from Jerusalem and Antioch to Lyons in the west. We have also the early Canons of Discipline and the Liturgies of their Worship. We have the writings of CLEMENT, whose name was in the book of life,[1] of IGNATIUS, the friend and companion of St. Peter, of POLYCARP, the disciple of St. John, of TERTULLIAN, of IRENÆUS, of JUSTIN MARTYR, of CLEMENT of Alexandria, of CYPRIAN, and of EUSEBIUS, who wrote a history of the Church from its foundation to his days, A. D. 325.

Now from these writings we can ascertain how Christianity was understood, what the Scriptures were thought to contain, and how their contents were explained, as well as we can learn from the writings of Calvin and Beza, and the early Presbyterians, how Christianity was understood by them.

Thus we have an independent testimony, an extraneous witness to the faith once delivered to the saints, coming down to us in the Church from the very age in which the Scriptures were written. It is of course imperfect, but yet sufficient to enable us to identify the Faith as well as the Scriptures. All the salient points and leading doctrines of Christianity

---

[1] Phil. iv. 3.

are stated with sufficient distinctness. And these writings show that the same system was delivered everywhere: and on all these great and leading points there is a perfect harmony and agreement. They speak of the Faith as a historic thing, which had once been delivered to them, which they must keep and hand down to others; and not as something which they had invented, or adopted by agreement and compact among themselves, nor yet as something that each individual had been left to discover for himself by his own investigations and the exercise of his private judgment.

<small>The early mode of settling questions of interpretation.</small> And in all the earlier writers, when a question arose concerning any doctrine, or a dispute with the heretics called forth a defence of the truth, the appeal was not as now, to philology, to hermeneutics, to reason and to logic, but to the doctrine, or mode of explaining a doctrine or passage of Scripture which had been preserved in those Churches that had been founded by the Apostles in person, and received an explanation of Christianity from their own living lips.

<small>TERTULLIAN quoted as a specimen.</small> As a specimen of this kind of reasoning, take the following from TERTULLIAN's *Prescription against Heretics*.[1] "On this principle, therefore, we shape our rule, that if the Lord Jesus Christ sent the Apostles to preach, no others ought to be received as preachers than those whom Christ appointed.... Now what they did preach, that is, what Christ did reveal unto them, I will here also rule, must be proved *in no other way* than by those same

---

[1] § xxi. I quote the Oxford Translation of 1842.

Churches which the Apostles themselves founded; *themselves, I say, by preaching to them by the living voice, as afterwards by Epistles.* If these things be so, it becometh forthwith manifest, that all doctrine, which agreeth with these Apostolic Churches, the wombs and originals of the Faith, must be accounted true, as without doubt containing that which the Churches have received from the Apostles, the Apostles from Christ, and Christ from God; and that all other doctrine must be judged at once to be false, which soweth things contrary to the truth of the Churches, and of the Apostles, and of Christ, and of God. It remaineth, therefore, that we show whether this our doctrine, the rule of which we have above declared, be derived from the tradition of the Apostles, and from this very fact, whether the other doctrines come of falsehood. *We have communion with the Apostolic Churches because we have no doctrine differing from them.* THIS IS EVIDENCE OF TRUTH."

The reasons for this rule, as Tertullian says, are various. In the first place, the Heretics do not receive the entire and uncorrupted Scriptures. But secondly, the Scriptures were never given *to them:* they have no right to the use of them: and without the Scriptures we prove that they have no right to the Scriptures as an authority for what they do: and finally, by putting a meaning upon them different from that which they were intended to have, they confound and mislead the simple and unlearned, and make the Gospel itself to convey, only at best, an uncertain sound, and people will not know what to believe.

There is a pregnant text to this point in St. Paul's second Epistle to the Thessalonians:[1] "Therefore, brethren, stand fast, and hold the traditions which ye have been taught, *whether by word, or our epistle.*"

The Authority of St. Paul. When this was written the Thessalonians had no part of the Scriptures except St. Paul's first Epistle to them. They had, however, "the Faith," and were directed to hold that fast even as it had been taught to them orally—"by the living voice," as Tertullian says. Other passages of similar import might be quoted from the New Testament.

But I do not design to dwell on this part of my subject. Different men will of course attach very different measures of importance to this kind of testimony or authority. But call its value what we may, either a controlling and ultimate authority, from which there may be no appeal—or nothing; or place it anywhere between those extremes as we please, *the fact itself,* that we can thus learn from the early records of the Church what was received as Christianity, admits of no denial.

It may be difficult to say precisely to what degree of minuteness we might descend in specifying the points of Christian Doctrine, which can thus be proved from the early Fathers to have been delivered to the Church by the Apostles. This much we may say, at least, that man is in a fallen and depraved condition by nature, and needs forgiveness—renewal; that in the unity of the Godhead there are three dis-

---

[1] 2 Thess. ii. 15.

tinct Persons, the Second of whom was incarnate of the Virgin Mary, suffered as an atonement for us; and that the Third, was sent to sanctify the hearts of them that believe; that thus salvation was freely offered to all men, and all are capable, by the divine grace, of receiving it; that sin and depravity are washed away in Baptism; that the spiritual effects of Christ's incarnation are conveyed to us in the Sacrament of the Lord's Supper; that a Ministry was established to have charge and oversight of the believers; that respect, obedience and support are due unto them for Christ's sake; that there should be a resurrection from the dead, and a final judgment according to the deeds done in the body.

§ 8. It is true, indeed, that in these early writings we find nothing on many of the points that now agitate the world with controversies, because those points do not appear to have been thought of or suggested for discussion by any body. But most unquestionably all that is necessary to salvation, *all that has come from God*, was then known; for we can have nothing that was not given to the Christians of that age and has not come down to us through them. And on all the points named above, and a great many more, there is the most perfect harmony and uniformity of teaching in all parts of the early Church—in those that were the most remote and disconnected from each other, as well as in those that were adjacent and more immediately affiliated.

The early Church unanimous on all the great points of Christianity.

It is then undoubtedly certain that we are indebted to the Church for the preservation of the Scriptures whole and uncorrupted, and that we must depend upon the Church, and upon that wholly and exclusively, for our certainty that what we have is the Scripture, *as it was* "given by the inspiration of God,"[1] the source and fountain of Divine Truth. We are indebted to the Church for the preservation of that which "containeth all things necessary to salvation." And we learn from the Church too, what are the great facts and doctrines which it was understood to contain, and was explained to contain by those who wrote it.

§ 9. Was there no moral design in this? Does not this chain of facts give force and significancy to such passages of Scripture as these. "The Church of the Living God, the Pillar and Ground of the Truth?" "Hold fast the form of sound words which thou hast learned?" "Stand fast and hold the traditions which ye have been taught, whether by word or our Epistles?" "If he neglect to hear the Church let him be unto thee as an heathen man and publican?"

The authority of the Church based upon its moral design. The authority of the Church in matters of faith is based upon this element of its moral design. The necessity for it is seen in the diversities and distractions that prevail in Christendom.

§ 10. It is true there are some that call themselves Christians, who, in our day, reject a part of the Scriptures: and the Papists have added to the Old Testament Canon what we call the Apocrypha. Still, however, the main disagreement is not as to the

---

[1] 2 Tim. v. 16.

genuineness and identity of the Scriptures, but it is in the mode of interpreting them. And the phenomena of the present day teach us that some Rule of Faith or interpretation is as necessary, not only to uniformity, but even to a reception of the saving truths of the gospel, as is a preliminary agreement as to what is to be received as the WORD OF GOD, and the ultimate authority in all matters of faith. Which is the most perilous? to deny that the Epistle to the Hebrews which we have is the work of St. Paul, or any other inspired man, or to deny that the Scriptures teach that Jesus Christ is the Son of God, consubstantial with the Father? Which is the worst, to deny that good works are necessary to salvation according to the Scriptures, or to declare the Epistle of St. James an Epistle of Straw, and a lie against the Holy Ghost? Is it worse to reject the Book of Revelations, than to deny that the Bible teaches the future punishment of the wicked? Which may the best be added to the Scriptures—the writings of Swedenborg, or the theory of Calvin, as an interpretation of them? Why is the reception of the book of Mormon any worse than the modern Irvingite theory of restoring the Apostolate and miraculous gifts of the Spirit to the Church? The practice of the early sects was to reject the portions of Scripture which were understood to contain doctrines which they would not receive—that of the Moderns, is the more subtle course of denying that those Scriptures contain the doctrines. And thus the licentiousness of private judgment has filled the

Some authority necessary to secure the right interpretation of the Scriptures.

world with as many errors almost as there are varieties in the human mind.

I will not here pause to say that all these contradictory doctrines cannot be true or safe. It is more to my present purpose to say that they involve a rejection of the Church, which is the Pillar and Ground of the Truth, and the necessity of regarding those who do thus reject it "as heathen men and publicans,"—even when the awful sanction "whatsoever ye shall bind on earth shall be bound in heaven" hangs over us.

If, then, it is true that no other church can certify us of the genuineness and identy of those Scriptures which were at first given by the inspiration of God, and are profitable for doctrine, for reproof, for correction, for instruction in righteousness; it is no less true, that no other has preserved to us, or could preserve to us, that interpretation which was at first put upon them, and which, if we would be guided into the truth, we must now believe. If there is now a doubt about the Divinity of Christ, the freedom of salvation for all men, the remission of sins in Baptism, the necessity of good works to salvation, the future punishment of the finally impenitent, the threefold order of the ministry, the necessity of communion in the Church established by our Lord and His Apostles; there was certainly no doubt or uncertainty on these points, "while," in the language of Tertullian, "all were Apostolic, because all were one." These things without the Scriptures can be proved to have been taught by the Apostles "by word," even before the Scriptures themselves were written. And it deserves to be considered by him who would receive and hold "the Faith once delivered to the Saints" whole and undefiled, whether, and if so, when, and on what grounds, the command to stand fast and hold the traditions which ye have been taught, whether by word or by our epistle,¹ has been abrogated.

§ 11. We ought to be a little more definite on this point. I am constructing no argument for traditions, outside the Scriptures in general, but only for those which are clearly seen and known to have come from the Apostolic age. *What traditions are of value.*

The Christian world, if such an expression may be used, may be divided into three portions in relation to this point. 1. The Protestant Sects, who hold to the Scriptures as interpreted by themselves, and each one for himself. 2. The Reformed Churches, who hold to the Scriptures as they were interpreted and understood when first written and received ; and 3. The Churches in the Romish obedience, who hold to the doctrine of Development.

At the time of the Reformation the conservative or Papal party claimed that their religion was the old, and that the Protestant was the new one. On the part of the Church of England this point was stoutly denied, and issue joined with the Papists. But it was then found that so many copies of the early writings had been corrupted, and that there were so many forgeries current as the genuine works of the Fathers among the Romanists, that the first preliminary step,

---
¹ 2 Thess. ii. 13.

and one of indispensable necessity, was to identify the works of the Fathers, to distinguish between the genuine and the spurious, and to purge out all interpolations, and to restore all the designed or accidental omissions to those parts that were undoubtedly genuine. After many years of labor and of controversy this has been done, and both parties are now pretty nearly agreed as to the identity and genuineness of the works of the Fathers to which we may appeal. And what has been the result? The Romanists have abandoned the controversy, and admitting that most of their peculiar doctrines are new and modern, they have set up as a totally new ground of defence, the position that they have a right to make additions to the Primitive Faith, or in other words, to develop and declare from time to time new doctrines, which had not been received and acknowledged before.

Hence no objection to the view which has now been presented of this function of the Church can arise from the corruptions and darkness of the middle ages, or from the present position and claims of the Romish Church. The field is clear, and we can look above the fogs and mists of intervening centuries, take up the writings of the early Fathers just as they left them, and see through them what Christianity was understood to be when it was first committed to Holy Scripture, and "written for our learning."

Grounds upon which the early interpretations are considered valuable. § 12. We claim no value for this early interpretation, on the ground that the men of that age were wiser and holier than the men of this, nor on the ground that they had any special authority binding upon us.

But it is simply on the ground that their mode of interpretation, their view of Christianity, their Creeds, in short, must have been given on the same authority, and by the same persons, and in most cases earlier in point of time, than the writing of the Scriptures. So that in the language of the profound and cautious THORNDIKE,[1] "it remains that we affirm, whatsoever the whole Church from the beginning, hath received and practiced for the Rule of Faith and manners, all that to be evidently true, by the same reason for which we believe the very Scriptures: [to be the word of God] and therefore, that the meaning of them is necessarily to be confined within those bounds, so that nothing must be admitted for the truth of these which contradicteth the same," ["the Rule of Faith and manners."]

If then the testimony of the Church, (and we have seen that we have nothing else to rely upon,) is sufficient to satisfy us that the Scriptures which we now have are the WORD OF GOD, ought it not to be held sufficient to satisfy us that those doctrines which were then, with equal unanimity, plainness, and force, declared to be their true interpretation and meaning, are the doctrines which we ought also to receive? If it satisfies us that Sts. Matthew, Mark, Luke, and John wrote the Gospels under their name, ought it not to satisfy us that they teach that the Son of God is a proper object of religious worship? If it satisfies us that the Acts of the Apostles contains a true and reliable account of the doings and sayings of the Apos-

---

[1] *Principles of the Christian Truth.* B. 1. chap. vi. § 1.

tles, as far as it goes, ought it not to satisfy us that they teach us that Baptism washes away sins? If it satisfies us that St. Paul wrote the Epistles, which bear his name, ought it not to satisfy us that they teach that the Ministry of any completely organized Church consists of three orders, Deacons, Presbyters—and in Timothy and Titus, some one officer at their head—call him Bishop, or what you will?

But be this as it may, the fact cannot be denied, and it is nowhere denied, in practice, however much it may be in theory—that what men regard as the Church, is acknowledged to have authority over its members in matters of faith. No member is allowed to contradict anything that is held to be fundamental by any religious society or church, and yet retain his membership. The right of discipline and excommunication is claimed and exercised by all.

Now in the Church this right becomes one of fearful responsibility and import, for it declares the excluded member to have denied the Faith, whereof alone cometh salvation—it cuts him off from the means of grace, the fellowship of Christ, and unless he repents and is restored, from the hope of salvation. And it is as sure as the Revealed Word of God itself, that what is thus done on earth will be ratified in heaven, unless the Church in so doing has exceeded her authority, and made that to be a term or condition of communion, which is not clearly laid down in the Scriptures as of essential and fundamental importance.

Hence the Church, as a whole, comes to us, and each branch respectively, should come to each individual in its portion of the earth's inhabitants, with the Scriptures as the Word of God and the Revelation of His Will: and with its Creed or catechism containing a brief summary statement of what the Scripture teaches that he ought to believe and do, with fuller explanations of the same truths, in her Canons, her Liturgies, her Offices, and in the Homilies and Sermons of her Preachers. And this each one is authorized and bound to receive as the true meaning and intent of the Scriptures, until he is qualified to look beyond these elementary forms and teachings to the Bible itself, and to the teachings of the Catholic Church while it was undivided, and all of its different branches spake and taught the same thing. And if his branch of the Church brings him no other Creed than that of the Apostles, or that which was agreed in by the whole Church, and no teaching but what is in accordance with that Creed, and the teaching of the Church in its earliest days, I confess I cannot see how the guilt or the danger of him who rejects any fundamental portion of that teaching, can be less than that of him who rejects a certain portion of the Word of God, because it teaches what he thinks ought not to be found there, and could not if it came from God.

Now I say only that it was manifestly the design of the Church that it should be such a teacher, such a "Pillar and Ground of the truth" to men.

§ 13. But no sect, no other Church than that which Christ founded, can perform this function. No other can have the like security to the identity and genuineness of the Scriptures. No other could have had the right inter-

No mere Sect can perform this function of the Church.

pretation of the Scriptures, for then they would not have left the Church; and no other, therefore, can bring to us the message which Christ would have us receive, or has any authority to pretend to do it. Here is a function which it is necessary for man that something should perform for him. It is a function that can be performed by no other society than that which our Lord and His Apostles founded, and it is clear from the Scriptures that the Church was designed to perform that function.

In what I have said on this subject, I have not been considering or setting forth *the authority which the Church may have to bind all her members to the reception of her interpretations of Christianity;* but rather THE SECURITY WHICH SHE WAS DESIGNED TO AFFORD, THAT WE HAVE THE SCRIPTURES AS THEY CAME FROM THE PEN OF THOSE WHO WROTE AS THEY WERE MOVED BY THE HOLY GHOST, AND THE TRUE SENSE OF THEM, OR THE TRUTH AS IT IS IN JESUS.

§ 14. Let us now pass to the consideration of another element of the moral design of the Church as connected with its identity.

The Church designed to be a channel of grace. The Church itself, through its Ministry and Sacraments, was designed to be a channel or means of grace.

In discussing this subject, so far as our present purpose is concerned, I shall not need to enter much upon points that are purely theological, and I design to do so as little as possible.

It is evident from the records, and admitted, I believe, on all hands, that the Church was to be gathered, and extended, and perpetuated by the Preaching of the Word, and the Baptism of those who should be prepared for membership. Baptism was to be the dividing line—the distinguishing mark, between those who had been admitted as members of the Church, and those who had not. If, now, Baptism is a means of grace, and designed to convey spiritual blessings, then those blessings depend upon, and flow from the identity of the Church. They imply its identity, because the blessings of Baptism as a Sacrament, be they what they may, were promised to that Baptism, and that only which was to be administered to those about to be admitted, and who were thereby admitted to His Church.

I put the statement into this form on purpose to avoid the question of the validity of lay Baptism. I do not design to affirm or assume that ministerial authority is essential to Baptism. But I affirm as a part of my argument, that whatever is said in the Scriptures of Baptism at all, is said of that Baptism which was to be administered for the purpose of joining members to the Church. *Only the Baptism of the Church spoken of in the Scriptures.* No other is spoken of, or, so far as we can see, thought of, when Baptism as an institution to be observed and administered by the disciples of Christ, was the subject of remark. The Scriptures were not speaking of what might be done by others, or of the form of Christian rites that might be used for other purposes than that for which it was originally designed. If, therefore, persons design to institute a new church, and borrow their rites and ceremonies, and even their doctrines and form of organization from the Scriptures, we cannot attribute to these

17

things the same spiritual efficacy as when they are used for the purpose for which they were originally designed. To say that the outward form of Baptism, when used to admit members into the Presbyterian church, the Methodist church, or any other "voluntary association of men for religious purposes," is attended by the same spiritual results, as when it is used to admit members into the Church of Christ for which it was designed, is to commit the same logical error as would be committed by applying what the Scriptures say of the house and worship of that God who is over all, blessed for ever, to any of the idols which misguided men may have chosen to be "their god."

The Identity of Baptism depends upon the identity of the purpose for which it is used.

I am not here offering the Romish doctrine, that the intention of the minister is essential to the efficacy of the Sacraments. I am not speaking of his intention, or what he may intend at all, in reference to particular cases, as does the Romish dogma. Their doctrine is, that unless the Priest designs to convey the efficacy of the Sacrament, no effect is produced. But I am speaking of the totally different case of the use of Baptism, to admit members into other churches than that which our Lord founded. And I say, that to expect the efficacy of His Baptism to follow in such cases, is as absurd as to expect the blessings that follow from a sincere worship to the true God, will be bestowed upon one who pays the same worship at the shrine of some idol of his own choosing.

§ 15. With these remarks we will pass to a

consideration of what the Scriptures say of the design and efficacy of Christian Baptism. *The design and efficacy of Baptism.*

I. 1. "He that believeth and is baptized shall be saved."[1]

2. "Go ye, therefore, teach all nations, baptizing them, &c."[2]

From these texts I infer simply that Baptism is a positive institution, which all are commanded to observe as the first step of their discipleship.

II. 1. "Repent and be baptized, every one of you, in the name of Jesus Christ, *for the remission of sins.*"[3]

2. "Arise, and be baptized, and *wash away thy sins.*"[4]

3. "Christ also loved the Church and gave Himself for it; that He might *sanctify and cleanse* it with the washing of water, by the word."[5]

Taking these passages together, they prove two things concerning Baptism. 1. That it *sanctifies*, that is, sets apart from the world and consecrates to God, (for I am not disposed to put any higher sense on the word as used here, and there is no lower one to be used,) and 2. That it washes away sins. The expressions are "*for the remission of sins,*" "*wash away thy sins,*" and "*cleanse,*" all implying the same result, the cleansing the soul from the stain and guilt of sin.

III. 1. "Verily, verily, I say unto thee, except a

---

[1] Mark xvi. 16. [2] Matt. xxviii. 19. [3] Acts ii. 38.
[4] Acts xxii. 16. [5] Eph. v. 25, 26.

man *be born of water and the spirit*,¹ he cannot enter the kingdom of God."²

2. "According to His mercy He saved us, by *the washing of regeneration, and renewing of the Holy Ghost.*"³

3. "Eight souls were saved by water, the like figure whereunto even *Baptism doth also now save us*. . . . . . by the resurrection of Jesus Christ."⁴

From these passages we can infer no less than that in Baptism we "*are born again,*" receive "*the washing of regeneration,*" and are put into a state of salvation. By "doth now save us," I think we can understand no less than to put into a state of salvation, and I certainly would not cite it as proving anything more.

IV. 1. "So many of us as were *baptized into Jesus Christ*, were baptized into His death."⁵

2. "For as many of you as have been *baptized into Christ* have put on Christ."⁶

I shall not undertake to develop the full meaning of these expressions, "baptized into Christ." I shall rather pass them with the remark that they must be understood to indicate some close and intimate union with Christ to be effected by Baptism. Perhaps their meaning is only more fully explained by the following passage from Colossians.⁷

"And ye are complete in Him, which is the head of all principality and power; in whom also ye are

---

[1] The "*of*" in our version in this place is inserted without anything in the original to require it.

[2] John iii. 5.   [3] Titus iii. 5.   [4] 1 Pet. iii. 20, 21.
[5] Rom. vi. 3.   [6] Gal. iii. 27.   [7] Col. ii. 10–12.

circumcised *with the circumcision made without hands*, in putting off the body of the sins of the flesh by the circumcision of Christ; *buried with him in Baptism*, wherein also (that is in Baptism) ye are risen with Him through the faith of the operation of God, who hath raised Him from the dead."

Now in this passage, obscure as it is in many respects, it is manifest that the baptized Colossians, " the saints and faithful brethren in Christ which are at Colosse," though uncircumcised in the flesh, had obtained "through the faith" all that circumcision effected or prefigured—the "putting off the body of the sins of the flesh," and moreover, a hope in the resurrection, (" ye are risen," is the expression,) by the circumcision and the Resurrection of Christ, *in consequence of their having been " baptized into Him."*

It is impossible to say that the Sacrament of Baptism is not the thing here intended, for the water itself and its use, are spoken of, *in terminis*, as the very things by which the result is accomplished— " sanctify and cleanse with the washing of water,"— " the washing of regeneration"—" saved by water, the like figure whereunto even Baptism doth now save us "—" born of the water and the Spirit."

As I have already said, I do not design to enter into particulars or theological distinctions and qualifications. I cite these passages only for the purpose of proving that some very great and very important spiritual effect is dependent upon the Baptism which our Lord instituted as the Sacrament of initiation to His Church; and that whatever that effect may be, it is dependent upon the identity of the Baptism administered with that which was instituted by our Lord, and of which these things are said in the Scriptures. And the identity of that Baptism, as I have shown, depends upon the identity of its design, as well as upon the identity of outward form; and finally, the identity of design implies the identity of the Church.

The Eucharist bears a like relation to the moral design of the Church.
§ 16. Substantially the same things may be said of the other Sacrament, the LORD'S SUPPER, in its relation to the identity of the Church. Its observance was commanded to the members of His Church, and its whole efficacy must depend upon its being in His Church. If some one should undertake to use it in connection with Mahometanism, with the Platonic Philosophy, or with a refined Pantheism, which regards Christianity as only one of many original revelations of the Infinite in the finite, nobody would be so absurd and senseless as to suppose that it would be attended with the same blessed spiritual effects that are promised to it in the Church.

The design of the Lord's Supper.
§ 17. Let us look at these effects.

I. "Do this in remembrance of Me."[1]

From this we infer that the observance of this Sacrament in the Church is a commanded duty.

II. "For as often as ye eat this bread, and drink this cup, ye do shew the Lord's death till 'He come.'"[2]

The effect of the observance of the Sacrament here spoken of, is perhaps exerted upon the world of un-

---

[1] Luke xxii. 19: 1 Cor. xi. 24.   [2] 1 Cor. xi. 26.

believers, rather than upon those engaged in its observance themselves.

III. "The cup of blessing which we bless, is it not the communion of the Blood of Christ? The bread which we break, is it not the communion of the Body of Christ?"[1]

The word here translated "communion," κοινωνία, sometimes means communication, or that which communicates. Such, I apprehend, must be its signification in the passage before us. For communion, in the proper sense of the word, implies two living conscious personal agents, between whom the communion, fellowship or intercourse takes place. But in this case the κοινωνία, is between believers on the one part, and the Body and Blood of Christ—not Christ Himself—on the other, which is not a conscious personal agent, and therefore the κοινωνία must be a communication or impartation of the Body or Blood of Christ to the worthy recipients.

I shall not undertake to analyze this, which is manifestly figurative language, and to say precisely what it does mean, in plain didactic terms. For our present purpose it is sufficient to leave it as we find it, and say, that in any reasonable view of it, it must imply the impartation of *some* great spiritual benefit to those who worthily receive the Lord's Supper.

The passages already extracted refer to the Lord's Supper so unambiguously, that there has never been any diversity of opinion, so far as I know, as to their

---

[1] 1 Cor. x. 16.

application. The next passage that I quote has not been so universally applied to the Lord's Supper. I shall, however, quote it, as believing that it was intended to refer to that subject.

IV. "And Jesus said unto them, I am the Bread of life: I am the Living Bread which came down from heaven: if any man eat this Bread he shall live for ever: and the Bread which I will give is My flesh, which I give for the life of the world. Except ye eat the flesh of the Son of Man and drink His blood, ye have no life in you. Whoso eateth My flesh and drinketh My blood hath eternal life; and I will raise him up at the last day. He that eateth My flesh and drinketh My blood, dwelleth in Me and I in him."[1]

I lay no special stress upon this passage in this place, not only because of the doubt entertained with regard to its application to the Lord's Supper by some persons, but chiefly because, if it does refer to that Sacrament, it does not in my estimation imply anything more than is implied in the passage just quoted from Corinthians, which does unquestionably refer to the reception of the Lord's Supper.

It is therefore undeniable that this Sacrament is the medium or channel of important spiritual graces and influences. And these graces and influences are spoken of as depending upon the reception of the outward elements of bread and wine.

§ 18. But when the Scriptures are speaking of these beneficial results of the right reception of these visible symbols, they are speaking of their admin-

[1] John vi. 35–56.

istration to the members of the Church and within its pale. No other use of these emblems or symbols is spoken of, or appears to have entered the thoughts of the inspired writers, or of our Lord Himself. This, then, is the implied condition of the efficacy of the Sacrament,—its administration and reception in the Church; and its administration and reception in the Church imply the identity of the Church. It is true that there is no express declaration that it shall be without efficacy if it is administered out of the Church. But that is not necessary. Its blessings are a special gift and grant; and in the making of such gifts and grants it is necessary that the persons for whom they are made should be named or indicated. But it is not necessary to name or indicate all others to whom they are not made, except so far as that is done by naming or indicating those to whom they are made. If I make a donation to half a dozen persons indicated by myself, it is not necessary that I say that I do not do the same for others not named. That follows of course. So with our Saviour's promises. When He says He will give to certain persons a blessing, or will give it on certain conditions, we have no right to infer, and it would be most hazardous to infer that He will give it to any others, or on any other condition.

The benefits of the Lord's Supper can be received only in the Church.

§ 19. I will close this part of my subject with the consideration of one more text.

Forgiveness of sins in the Church.

Eight days after the Resurrection our Lord appeared to His Apostles and said unto them :—

"Whose soever sins ye remit they are remitted

unto them; and whose soever sins ye retain they are retained."[1]

I do not design to enter upon any inquiry into the powers of Absolution here conferred upon the Apostles. I am not disposed to understand the words as implying any judicial power of that kind. For all present purposes we need not suppose that the words convey anything more than the authority to preach that gospel which bringeth salvation, and for the administration of those sacraments which are so important a part of the means of salvation as we have just shown them to be.

The question for us is, to whom does this apply, or how far does its meaning extend.

If we recur to the context we shall see, that in all probability, St. Thomas was not present when these words were addressed to the other ten. St. Matthias and St. Paul were not Apostles then, and of course were no part of those to whom the words were addressed.

We must therefore extend the application of their meaning to persons who were not then present; for St. Paul was not one whit behind the very chiefest of the Apostles.

I apprehend that it was designed for all the Ministry of the Church—all whomsoever Christ shall send to preach the Gospel and administer the Sacraments. And this I infer, not only from the nature of the apparent meaning of the text itself, but also from the inference that will immediately follow from a restric-

[1] John xx. 23.

tion of it within any narrower limits. The grant of authority is both inclusive and exclusive. It confers remission on those on whom they confer it, and withholds it from those from whom they withhold it. But it makes no provision for others, nor for forgiveness beyond the limits of their ministrations, or after they should be dead, or as a class, cease to exist. If then the commission or authority does not extend to the whole Ministry of the Church to the end of the world, then the time either has come or may come when the grant will cease and be inoperative. In that case the *promise* of forgiveness is at an end, which of course is an event that will not occur until the end of the world and the second advent.

It is true that this adds but very little, if anything, to what we have deduced from the other considerations just referred to. But it connects the promise of forgiveness most intimately with the identity of the Church. It promises forgiveness to those that shall receive it at the hands of those whom I have here supposed to be the whole Ministry of the Church. But there it stops—there is no promise beyond or further than that. *This power implies the identity of the Church.*

Now these items show most conclusively that there is an important moral design in the Church in relation to the forgiveness of sins, and the renovation and salvation of souls. It is the channel of those blessings which God has promised to confer upon mankind.

§ 20. It cannot fairly be said by way of derogating from the importance of these elements of the moral design of the Church, that all these blessings are elsewhere pro- *These conditions of salvation do not derogate from the importance of Faith.*

mised, with no mention of such conditions, but simply on the ground of faith.

To this I reply in the first place, that faith on the part of the recipients is the essential condition of the blessings which are said to be conferred or bestowed in the Sacraments. The only exception is perhaps, that of baptism of infants. But secondly, and chiefly; the conditions on which God has promised His blessings can never be inconsistent with one another. And if He sometimes speaks of one where no mention is made of the rest, we are by no means to infer that they are not important or essential. We are to collect *all* the conditions that He has anywhere prescribed, acknowledging each to be as important as He Himself has represented it to be, and we shall then doubtless find that they all harmonize and easily fall into their appropriate places in the system, if we take the right view of them. Thus the merits and atonement of Christ are the only and sole ground of human salvation: faith and repentance on the part of man is the indispensable condition of his receiving the benefits of that atonement; those benefits are conveyed to the soul in the Sacraments, and we must bring forth the fruits of good works and obedience as the condition of our final acceptance at the day of judgment. Hence, there is no inconsistency in speaking of any one of these conditions as alone, and by itself, necessary to salvation, as the Scriptures have done. The mistake is when we *infer* from this mode of speaking that the means or condition thus spoken of as essential, is the *only one* that is to be so regarded. I apprehend that we are not authorized to institute or draw any comparison that designs to form a rule of belief or practice, between these several conditions. The disposition to disregard or omit anything in the divine law because we have concluded that it is not essential, is one of the most alarming and dangerous that man can well exhibit.

I think we may therefore say, that the Church was designed to be the chief agent in bringing to mankind " the truth as it is in Jesus," and that in its Sacraments and Ministry are the ordinary channels of forgiving and renewing grace.

But this is not all that man needs; nor all of the moral result that the Church was designed to accomplish.

§ 21. In looking at mankind at large, the first and most obvious fact, in a moral point of view that strikes the observer, who is acquainted with the contents of the Scriptures, is that of disobedience. On examination, every sin is found to contain this as the chief element of its guilt. The evils which result, in the ordinary course of consequences, great as they sometimes are, are nothing compared with the fact that the authority of the Supreme Governor, upon Whom all things depend, and for all things, is rejected, despised, and trampled under foot. A shock is thus sent throughout the universe—the effect is felt by every created thing. *Disobedience characteristic of man.*

If we recur to the first sin committed on earth, the transgression in Eden, we shall see that its whole guilt consisted apparently in its being an act of disobedience. So far as we know or can see it had no natural consequences of evil. But it was the exaltation of human pride, the aspiration of human ambition, the disposition to trust in human reason, to the disparagement of the revealed will or imposed commandments of God.

§ 22. And if we look at the dispensations of God to man, we shall derive a lesson of equal importance in relation to our present subject. We have alluded to this part of God's dealing with man in a previous chapter,[1] and shall not need to repeat here what was said there. From these considerations it is evident that OBEDIENCE is the cardinal point of our earthly probation, as including all the rest. Each of the prominent relations in life has its precept of obedience. Children are commanded to obey their parents, servants their masters, wives their husbands, citizens and subjects their rulers and governors, and Christians their pastors. Thus the law of obedience is made to run through all the gradations of society. And from the highest Archangel around the Eternal Throne, through each descending link in the scale of being, Angel, Seraphim, Cherubim, Apostles, Prophets, Bishops, Priests, and Deacons, down to the humblest individual that waits at the altar, or serves as a doorkeeper in the House of the Lord, there must be order and subordination; and the duty of obedience from each one to those that are over him in the scale of the Divine appointments, is essential to the stability and harmony of the whole.

The restoration of obedience a moral design of the Church.

§ 23. Now this obedience implies government and governors in the immediate exercise of authority over us.

Obedience implies governors.

[1] Chap. II.

EFFECTS OF SECTARIANISM.

The Scriptures, unaccompanied by any interpretation, or interpreted by each individual's private judgment, cannot accomplish the result. For in the first place, but only a very small part of the human race are able, or ever have been able to read and acquire sufficient familarity with the contents of the Scriptures to be able to know what they teach and require. The mass of Christians in the world cannot read at all. And a still greater number have no sufficient amount of leisure to make themselves familiar with all that is contained in the Holy Bible.

§ 24. But again, the endless diversities in the religious opinions that prevail in the community, show beyond question that without something having authority to intervene between the Scriptures and the private judgment of the individual, there is no possibility of bringing men into obedience to any one uniform rule, such as that which is contained in the Scriptures must be, unless they give an uncertain sound and contradict themselves. *[margin: Obedience implies some objective rule of interpretation.]* The diversities do not affect mere doctrines alone, but they affect the practice of our religion also; and the practices which are alleged to have been derived from the Word of God, are as diverse as the doctrines themselves. Some baptize their children; others consider it popery to do so. Some think the frequent observance of the Holy Communion good and edifying; and others pronounce it a mere superstition and formality. Some believe that the restitution of what has been wrongfully taken is necessary to the obtaining God's favor when one repents; others hardly ever think of the thing. Some believe that the tithe, at least, of their income is God's due for the support of His religion; others are thankful that they can enjoy all the advantages of religion and have it cost them nothing. Some think that a daily service is edifying and no more than is due to the mercy and goodness of God; others think that once in a week is often enough to spend their time in the public worship of God.

Now all these views cannot be right. They cannot all be inculcated in the Word of God or derived from it. And most undeniably it is best for each individual to know what is the view that is presented in the Scriptures, and to follow it.

<small>Obedience connected with the Unity of the Church.</small> § 25. But again, the idea that men may violate the unity of the Church, separate from its communion, and form a church of their own for every opinion which they may honestly and conscientiously hold, is a death-blow to all obedience.

If man were not depraved and corrupt in his nature, it is most certain that he could not honestly and sincerely entertain any view or opinion that is not in harmony with the truth. But it is one of the proofs, as well as one of the worst evils of our fallen condition, that we do sometimes love error rather than truth, and can most honestly and most conscientiously believe that which is not true and righteous.

No fact is more certain, or of a more fundamental importance, than that we need something to go behind even our convictions of right and truth, and bring these very convictions into harmony with that which is really the right and the truth. Undoubtedly "there is a way that seemeth right unto a man, but the end thereof are the ways of death."¹ We are not for a moment to suppose that all those who are wandering in the ways of error and unrighteousness are conscious of insincerity and hypocrisy. It is difficult to say whether such an opinion would imply most of uncharitableness, or of a total ignorance of human nature. No, those who are in error often give the most evidence of sincerity and good intentions. The Prophet speaks of the idolater thus: "a deceived heart hath turned him aside, that he cannot deliver his soul nor say, 'is there not a lie in my right hand?'"² Surely he has not duly estimated the fearful import and consequences of the fall of man, who has not seen that it has so deranged his moral and spiritual faculties, as to make necessary some guide and authority out of himself, to reduce great truths to definite and positive statements, great principles to practical precepts, and to speak with dogmatic and commanding authority. We see the necessity for this in the education and government of children. We see it in schools. We see it in our legislatures, and in our courts of civil as well as criminal judicature.

§ 26. If now man may throw off the regimen or government that God has placed over him, whenever he conscientiously differs from it, there is an end to all government and to all obedience; that is not obedience properly speaking, which conforms, *because* the thing required coincides with the private judgment of him who is to

<small>Obedience implies the acknowledgment of authority.</small>

---

¹ Prov. xiv. 12. ² Isa. xliv. 20.

do it. It is only when private judgment is yielded up to an authority duly placed over us, that our act becomes one of obedience, and shows any measure of subjection to the Divine Will. To give alms to a poor person, because his distress excites our compassion, may be indeed a commendable act, but no one would think of calling it an act of obedience. It becomes obedience only when we do it *because* God has commanded "be ye merciful because I am also merciful."

§ 27. Another essential element of obedience is, that it be rendered to the proper authority. Ultimately, it should terminate in God and in His Truth. Obedience to parents and to civil magistrates is right, because God has required it. But obedience to one who has usurped the authority which God has given to another, is rebellion against Him. When the people desired a king to rule over them instead of the corrupt and wicked sons of Samuel—who, nevertheless, were over them as judges, according to the established law of God, God said unto Samuel, "they have not rejected thee, *but they have rejected Me that I should not reign over them.*"[1]

The identity of the Church implied in its design to promote obedience to God. Here then we *see* the connection of our subject with the identity of the Church. We have seen that man needs an authority, and God gave such an authority to His Church. It, therefore, is the institution which He has appointed for the moral purpose of promoting obedience. We must be brought into a state of obedience

---

[1] 1 Sam. viii. 7.

before we can be admitted to the final kingdom and glory of God. The Church is the agent which He has appointed to accomplish this work, and the Bible is the Rule which He has given the Church whereby to be guided in doing it.

But if we may reject this authority and government for every scruple of conscience, every conscientious opinion, we may at any time escape the test proposed. We are under no obedience so long as we may make a matter of conscience of any opinion we entertain, or of any preference we may cherish, and set up a church or authority, that shall direct and govern according to our own opinions and wishes. In that case, the government or church becomes but the reflection of the volitions of our own will.

§ 28. And here is the broad difference between the Church and all forms of Sectarianism. The one represents unto us the authority and will of God, and the other but reflects our own. Hence there are as many sects as there are classes of opinion and preferences—and a form of error adapted to the weakness and peculiar susceptibilities of each individual, that so he may find something that he will like better, and on the whole prefer, to that which he ought, for his soul's health, to receive. Is not this the meaning of that saying of St Paul, "For there must also be heresies among you, *that they which are approved may be made manifest among you.*"[1] In our country Popery appeals to the imagination, to the love of pomp and show, and of arbitrary

<small>The Church promotes obedience: the Sects do not.</small>

---

[1] 1 Cor. xi. 19.

rule. Presbyterianism appeals to that element which has always inclined men to fatalism, and a comfortable conviction concerning oneself, combined with a belief that the character and fate of others was foreordained and cannot be helped. Methodism appeals to that species of excitement and enthusiasm which regards "the fervor of the animal sensibilities"[1] as religion. And so of all the forms of error around us. They make the command "deny thyself, take up thy cross daily," to be of none effect. They exhibit to each individual some form of religion which he may embrace without this painful and humiliating duty. If he does not find religion what he wants it, he may turn reformer and present it to the world in any form that he may choose.

Sectarianism cannot produce general obedience. § 29. Now it is but an insane folly to suppose that such a system can bring men "in the unity of the Faith and of the knowledge of the Son of God, unto a perfect man, unto the measure of the stature of the fulness of Christ." No: we need something to meet us in God's name at every step and turn in our lives, and with authority to give us His precepts and directions, until we are trained and *habituated* to that perfect resignation of our own wills, that perfect humility and self-renunciation, that perfect OBEDIENCE, which is the distinguishing characteristic of the angels in heaven, and was the crowning glory and charm in the life and character of our blessed Lord on earth.

Hence it is necessary to have the representatives

---

[1] I use the words of BISHOP WHITE.

of the Divine authority always present in the form of a living and personal agent. And not only so, but even the human infirmities and imperfections of the minister may be turned to our advantage. The perfect subjugation of every thought and wish to the law of Christ, can be more surely and speedily effected when the path through which He calls us to walk is attended with trials and hardships which it grieves our unsanctified natures to bear.

§ 30. But if all this self-renunciation and voluntary humiliation and submission be rendered to that which we have put in the place of God—some idol set up in our hearts—or some government which we have erected in the wilfulness of our unsubdued heart, and put into the place of that which God has placed over us; then we do indeed take up a cross, but it is not the cross of Christ; and we make a sacrifice, but it is not upon the Altar of the true and only God; and we obey, but our obedience is not rendered to Him whose right it is to reign on earth as in heaven. *True obedience must be rendered to the authority of God only.*

§ 31. The Church, considered in this light, is undoubtedly an object of faith. It is so regarded in all the early Creeds, and in all the forms of them that I remember to have seen. ARCHDEACON MANNING, in his invaluable little work, "*The Unity of the Church,*" has collected the testimony of the ancient Creeds and Fathers to the antiquity of this article in all the branches of the Church that were founded by the Apostles. He says, as the result of his inquiry, "It is evident that a belief in the unity of the Church forms an article in *The Church an object of faith.*

every Baptismal Creed of every Church, both in the East and in the West. I am not aware of any Baptismal Creed extant in which this article is not to be read." [1]

" All the early forms recite the article," says Manning, " in some one of these three forms.

" 1. ' One Catholic and Apostolic Church,' as the Constantinapolitan or Nicene : the Creed recited by Epiphanius and the Alexandrian, which adds, μόνην, ' one only.'

" 2. ' The Holy Catholic Church,' as the Apostles' Creed, the Spanish, the Gallican, the forms in the Roman Ordinal, and the Apostolical Constitutions, and one of the Aquillian Creeds.

" 3. ' The Holy Church,' as the Roman, two of the Aquillian Creeds, the Ancient Eastern, the Creed of Marcellus, the Creeds of Ravenna, Turin, the African, one of the Gallican, and the Form in the Sacramentary of Gelasius." [2]

The Archdeacon was quoting these passages to prove that a belief in *the Unity* of the Church was considered an essential part of the Christian Faith in the Primitive Church. The point for which I now refer to them, is somewhat different, though not the less clearly and certainly proved by his authorities—viz : that " the Church " *was universally regarded as an object of Faith.*

And this results from the necessity of the case.

We have seen that the identity of the Church, that is, the Church itself, is intimately connected with

---

[1] N. Y. Ed., 1844, p. 23.   [2] MANNING, *ubi supra*, pp. 25, 26.

the highest interests of man. We present evidence of that identity. Our evidence is addressed to the understanding and to the conscience for the purpose of inducing an exercise of belief, and leading us to put our trust in that which we allege to be the Church in this country, for all the purposes for which the Church itself was designed.

It is in this way that every institution and gift of God comes to us. The Bible comes to us in the same way. We take up a book, and on looking into its contents, we find it claiming to be a revelation from God. We look into its history. We find from external circumstances that such a revelation was once made, and under circumstances similar, or precisely the same, as those referred to in the book itself. We trace the history of the book then written, down to our own day, until we identify the copy in our hands with the original. We examine the circumstances of its transmission, and find that it cannot have been changed from what it was when first given. We receive it as the WORD OF GOD. Then it is an object of Faith—Faith based and exercised on testimony.

Our Lord Himself was an object of Faith. He had been foretold by Prophets, and was attended by miracles. These were the evidences of His Messiahship. But it was not what is called demonstration in the strictest sense of the term. It did not produce *irresistible* conviction. Many who had read the Prophets and saw the miracles, did not believe, but conspired to crucify Him as a blasphemer and a malefactor.

So with the Scriptures. Notwithstanding the

force and satisfactoriness of the testimony, there are many infidels and unbelievers in the world—many who pay no regard to their momentous truths and awful warnings.

Hence it is evident that there must be, on the part of man, that moral element which we call Faith—a disposition, or at least, a willingness to believe—to make him feel satisfied with the evidence, and to induce him, on the strength of it, to receive the Scriptures as the Word of God, or Jesus Christ as his Lord and Saviour.

I will not here inquire how far this faith is to be regarded as the gift of God, and how far it is to be considered a voluntary exercise of the faculties of which each individual is capable, and for which he is responsible. But its existence cannot be denied, without shutting our eyes to the fact that there is unbelief even among those who profess to have freely weighed the evidence.

<small>To deny the sufficiency of the evidence is to impeach God.</small> § 32. Nor can we deny that the evidence in these cases, or in any other in which God requires us to believe anything, or has attached any importance to our believing or doing anything, is sufficient to throw the responsibility upon us, and make unbelief itself a sin. There is such a thing as insufficient evidence; and in all such cases unbelief implies no moral fault, no guilt on the part of him who withholds his assent. But in all the cases mentioned, the Messiah, the Bible, the Church, anything in regard to which God has given us any commandment, or made any requisition upon us—the amount of evidence is just what God Himself has seen

fit to give us. To say then that He has not given us evidence enough to produce conviction—unless we ourselves willfully and wickedly interpose some obstacle, set up some idol in our hearts, or put the stumbling block of our iniquity before our faces—is either to accuse Him of injustice or to impeach His omniscience. It implies, either that He did not know what evidence would be sufficient, or that He has required us to believe under circumstances, when the best, the wisest, and the healthiest exercise of the faculties He has given us would be unbelief.

§ 33. Now all this is as applicable to the Church as to the Scriptures, or to the Messiah.

This is as applicable to the identity of the Church as to the Scriptures or to the Lord Himself.

It is an institution concerning which, as we have seen, God has given us commandments, and made requisitions upon us, and with which He has connected many and precious promises. It must be admitted, therefore, that He has given us the means and opportunities of doing what He thus requires; and among these, first and foremost, is sufficient evidence of the identity of that Church with which these commands, requisitions, and promises are connected.

If the evidence is not in itself sufficient, it is the fault of Him whose province it was to furnish the evidence. It implies that God did not know what would be sufficient, or could not furnish it, or finally, that He was so unjust, to say nothing of His love and mercy, as not to do what He could, and what He knew to be just and necessary.

Hence the Church must be an object of faith. It

18

has always been so, and such it always must be. We can have no direct intuition, no direct supernatural communication of the fact. Even in the days of our Lord and the Apostles, when miracles were wrought and supernatural gifts conferred, the Church was an object of faith. If Christ was the Son of God, if the Apostles were truly such, if the miracles were genuine, there was indeed no room to doubt that the society and fellowship of the Disciples was the Church and kingdom of God. But these premisses, each of them, were objects that tried the faith of the people of that age.

The points which try our faith are different indeed from theirs, but that does not alter the main condition, viz.; that the reception of the Church is with us as it was with them, and was with them as it is with us—an act of faith. With this moral element, men are satisfied with the evidence, without it they would not be convinced with any amount that does not take from them their moral freedom.

Opposition to the Church leads to Infidelity. § 34. Now from this we may proceed to another remark, which indeed follows from the foregoing, namely, that the rejection of the Church tends to infidelity.

As a general thing, the identity of the Protestant Episcopal Church with the Church of Christ is not denied. None of the Protestant Sects deny that we are a true and living branch of the Church of Christ in the fullest sense of the word. And although they claim the same for themselves, yet they do not claim that they are any of them, continuous branches of that visble Church which was instituted by our Lord in the days of His sojourn on earth.

Hence, in opposing the Church and advocating their own as *positive visible institutions*, they are seeking to persuade people to adopt, instead of the Church which God instituted, a voluntary association of their own, which is confessedly of human origin.

I need not therefore go into an investigation of the character of the objections that are made against the Church in détail, to show that they all tend towards infidelity. For, be they what they may, so long as it is not denied that our branch of the Church, is a branch of the Church of God, or maintained that these Sects originated with the Apostles, and have continued down from their days, the leading design and the main influence of all objections against the Church, and all arguments in favor of any Sect, are to persuade men to prefer the device or institution of man to the institution and commandment of God.

And this is the essence of infidelity. Men, or a society of them absolutely without religion, is not the object of any of those who oppose revealed religion. They all have some system of their own, which, under some name or another, they are seeking to introduce. They may call it "philosophy," "enlightened reason," "common sense," or "nature," or whatever they prefer. But always they propose some substitute for that religion which they oppose. They always aim to substitute something else for the Revelations and the Institutions of God. Hence they deny the obligation of what came from Him, and the superiority of its excellency.

The reasoning of those who under the pretence of religion oppose the Church, does not deny the fact of its historic identity. Nor does it claim a like identity with the Church of Christ for any of the Protestant Sects. But it finds fault with the Church, with its doctrines, with its discipline, with its worship, with its piety, with what they are pleased to call its restraints upon the moral freedom of man. It aims to show, that in all these respects and in many others, some one or more of these Sects, which are confessedly of human origin, is far preferable, if not better in point of intrinsic worth.

Now we will not deny but that the Church, like everything else committed to human keeping and administration, may err and become corrupt. But yet it is the Divine Institution; Christ is still its head, and its members are in communion with Him, if they are true and faithful to the privileges which their membership in it gives them.

To affirm, therefore, that any other Church or institution, designed for the same general purpose, can be as good as that which God has instituted, is to deny His wisdom, His veracity, His power. And, since these are fundamental and essential attributes, to deny them, is in fact to deny that He is God.

I am indeed far from charging all those who reject and oppose the Church, with the design of favoring infidelity. But there can be no denying that men's exertions often tend to and produce results which they neither foresaw nor desired. How far their sincerity and good intentions may be an excuse in the day of judgment for the evil that has resulted from their doctrines, is not a question for us to decide.

But, so long as our identity with the Church of Christ—that is, the fact that we are a part of His Church—is not denied, all inducements and arguments which are held out to lead people to join something else instead of this branch of the Church, involves the essence of infidelity, and tends to produce actual and avowed infidelity. If the institutions of God may be inferior to those which man has originated in one particular, why not in all? If His will may be set aside in order to follow our own in one point, why not altogether? No answer can be given to these questions which will arrest the onward current of downward tendencies thus commenced, until all reverence for things sacred is gone, and faith itself has disappeared in the abounding unbelief.

I might refer to the historic developments of those Sects which have been set up in opposition to the Church. Their course has always and almost proverbially been downward. It is a most full and complete commentary on the doctrine of St. Paul—"the Church of the Living God, the Pillar and Ground of the Truth."

§ 35. But again, since the Church is an institution of God, and one in its nature including so many other institutions and commands of His—the true and healthy development of man's religious nature can be found only in the Church. *The Church necessary to true piety.*

The religious sentiment is perhaps the most deep-rooted and ineradicable of any in the human constitution. It is certainly one of the most easy to be perverted. Its worst perversion is seen perhaps in the profane blasphemy of God's holy name and attributes that is so prevalent. Another form is seen in that idolary which bestows upon created objects and blocks of wood and stone, the adoration due to God alone. But superstition and fanaticism are undoubtedly perversions of this sentiment, and deformities in the manner of its development and manifestations. Perhaps we may say that superstition results from the accumulation of forms and ceremonies in religion which God has not ordained, and fanaticism from the opposite extreme of turning the attention inwardly upon one's own feelings and convictions, to the disparagement or neglect of outward duties and the institutions which God has ordained.

Now, the revelation of God was designed to guide the religious sentiment, and to produce its healthy development into piety, meekness, humility, holiness, and love. Consequently, when that revelation is departed from in any important particular,—whether it be in the accumulated forms of the Papal system, or in the excitements and machinery of the revival system—some perversion of the religious sentiment must be the inevitable result.

Of the correctness of this conclusion we need no other proof than that which is to be derived from the undeniable facts admitted and claimed by the two classes of persons referred to.

The Papists admit that they have made additions to the original system of faith and worship as it came from God, and claim that they have a right to do so.

Now without discussing the right to make these additions, we will content ourselves for the present with the remark, that if their piety were like that of our Lord and the Apostles—that is, pure and genuine, they would have no *disposition or desire* to change or modify, by adding to or taking from the faith and worship, the forms and doctrines, which they introduced, and with which their souls were satisfied.

The position which the Protestant Sects take is different in form though demonstrative of the same fact in reference to our present train of remark.

They all contend that the Church at a very early age became corrupt, and at length apostate. In other words, it appears that the idea of religion which prevailed in the early ages of the Church, was very unlike that which the Sects now entertain, and that at length it became totally unlike it, not in degree only, but also in kind. Now when we call this difference an apostacy, we apply to it a name which indicates our opinion concerning it, rather than the fact itself. The fact itself is the utter contrariety between the religious character of those Sects and that of the Church before the Reformation. Now without saying that this fact, in itself considered, may as well prove their own apostacy as that the Church was then apostate, we may safely say that there must be something wrong in the faith and in the religious feelings of those who can regard that Church, with which the Holy Spirit was promised to abide for ever; which St. Paul declared to be the Pillar and Ground of the Truth; and with which our blessed Lord promised His presence always, even unto the end of the world, and against which He said that the gates of hell should never prevail—as being apostate. The Divine promises are our guarantee that it had not become apostate; and the opinion of those who so regard it shows that their own religious feelings and condition are so different from it that they cannot be wholly right themselves.

I need not refer then to the instances of extravagant superstition on the one side and of fanaticism on the other, as proof that the truest religion must be in the Church, and in connection with "the Faith once delivered to the Saints." The position is too obviously true to require proof. Let a man depart from the right ways of the Lord on either side, either to the right hand or to the left, and a peversion of his own religious feelings and of his opinions on subjects connected with religion, is the inevitable result. The mind is enslaved to superstition or bewildered with fanaticism. You may see people worshipping a cross or a relic as though it were their Saviour; or, in the extravagance of their fanaticism, claiming a sinless perfection of life, or a freedom with the ineffable Majesty of heaven, that strikes modesty and humility with silent horror.

It is not improbable but that the great lesson which we of this age have to learn, is that the adversaries of Christianity against which we have most to be on our guard, are those who attack, disparage and undermine the positive institutions of our religion under the pretence of Christianity itself. They sap the very foundations of the Heavenly City, while they profess to be building its walls and strengthening its fortresses. They teach men to be irreverent and indocile, while they profess to be bringing them to Christ; and yet if they are brought there without the most self-abasing and reverential humility, and the most childlike docility, it can be only to hear the withering repulse, "Depart from me, I know you not whence you are."

Perhaps I cannot better conclude this work, than by some reflections upon the effects of the present divided state of Christendom.

I trust that we may now say, with the concurrence of all persons in our statement, that the day has gone by when it is regarded as a blessing that there are so many different Churches and Sects, so that each may find a view of religion that will suit himself.

The foregoing remarks will show that such a view is based upon a principle utterly subversive of all the good effects of Christianity upon man. It loses sight of the fact, that man needs to be converted to Christ, and that, until he is converted, he cannot be expected heartily to approve of all that He has taught. But if we start with the idea that men are to have such a view of Christianity as they like, and consequently that there may be many churches, each of which are equally good—the choice between them being purely a matter of personal preference with individuals—we are reversing the fundamental fact, that man should be converted to Christ and Christianity, and not Christianity itself undergo the change, and be converted to man.

§ 36. Let it then be understood, as a most fundamental point, that Christianity *Christianity cannot be changed.*

cannot be changed without ceasing to be the Religion of Christ—the way to the favor of God, and to the salvation of the human soul.

The Origin of Sects an attempt to change Christianity.
§ 37. The origin of every Sect is an attempt to adapt Christianity to the wants of the times, or the preferences of men. It is, therefore, an act of violence upon the original system. And in this attempt men are very likely to lose sight of the ultimate aim of the Religion, and settle down into some subordinate or heterogeneous one. Thus the inculcation of a certain view of some particular doctrine, or the promotion of certain moral or political reforms, has not unfrequently occasioned the origin of a new Sect. This object is first identified in the thoughts of its founders with Christianity, and then substituted for it. Such is the history of the rise, progress, and final result, of Sects in general.

Sectarianism throws Difficulties in the way of discovering the Truth.
§ 38. It is obvious that the presentation of so many creeds and theories, as the Gospel of Christ, can have no other effect than a confusion and bewildering of those who would be sincere inquirers after the truth. The subject is now so complicated that no one, whose mind and time is occupied with any important secular business—a condition in which the vast majority of people must always of necessity be placed—can make himself master of the whole, and see his way clearly through its labyrinthian windings.

Sectarianism diminishes the number of Professing Christians.
§ 39. The consequence is, that these divisions and diversities of religion serve as a pretext to the *natural* disinclination to the restraints and obligations of the Gospel, for

the neglect of the subject altogether. It is a fact which cannot have escaped the notice of any observer, that the greatest part of the people in our land are not professing Christians at all. They join in the observance of Christian ordinances no where. I think, beyond a question, that there never has been an age, or a nation since the introduction of Christianity to the world, where—after it had been fairly introduced—there was so large a portion of the people living in utter disregard of its requirements, as there is now, and in this country. Or to put the same thought into another form: assuming that a public profession of religion and the observance of its ordinances are required as conditions of salvation, there probably never was a people, that bore the Christian name, of whom so small a portion only are, to all human appearances, entitled to the hope of salvation. All this, I say, is true, on the most enlarged and liberal principles. The assertion is made without regarding schism and heresy as sins which can at all endanger the souls of those involved in them.

It is a solemn and melancholy fact, that in this nation, the most enlightened and liberal on the face of the earth—where freedom of thought and the right of private judgment are encouraged as they are no where else—where humanity is left to the most unrestrained liberty of development and progress—the number of souls that can be regarded as within the covenanted conditions of salvation, is less than in any other portion of the Christianized world. Yet the fact is undeniably so.

§ 40. There may be many causes for the irreligion

Several of our age and nation. Thus the amount of
causes for the attention that is paid to intellectual culture,
Irreligion of
the American and the cultivation of the sciences, by
People. occupying the mind and attention, may be
the reason why many are so thoughtless of religion.
Again, the opening of the road to wealth and to power
to all men, by abolishing all hereditary estates, titles,
and offices, has given an impulse to ambition—in those
who possess aggrandizements to retain them, and in
those who have them not to acquire them—that absorbs the energies of a large number of persons, to
whom religion would be only a hindrance in the accomplishment of their wishes. I admit that almost
all the circumstances of our outward condition conspire against spirituality. So unstable is everything,
that men are engrossed with an unceasing effort either
to get or to keep worldly advantages.

§ 41. But these are not the chief causes.
Sectarianism the chief Doubtless they add vigor to the natural inclination to say to the gospel invitations, "I
pray thee have me excused;" "when I have a more
convenient season I will call for thee." But the chief
cause of this state of things, so saddening to the heart
of him who wishes well to the souls of men, is the
prevalence of sectarianism.

§ 42. In considering this subject, a vast
Divers effects of Sectarianism stated. field opens before the mind. Sectarianism
cripples and thwarts all our attempts to
convert the heathen; it produces unbounded infidelity
at home; the disconnection of religion from our means
and systems of educating the young; and a very low

standard of attainment among those of maturer years who profess to be believers.

§ 43. The English nation, by adopting the policy of extending the Church wherever they extend their civil dominion, have indeed made rapid strides in the missionary work, within the last few centuries. It is now computed that Queen Victoria is the sovereign of about one-seventh part of the whole population of the globe. And wherever she goes she carries the religion of Christ with her. *Its effects on Missions.*

But besides her efforts, very little, comparatively, has been accomplished, when we consider the vast amount of men and money that have been expended in the cause. Scarcely could one denomination make a beginning in any place, before some one or more of the others would send their missionaries there also. They carry with them the sectarian feelings by which they were actuated at home. Each claims to show the true way of life, yet each has a different way. To the heathen, accustomed as they are to the idea of many gods, each having a worship peculiar to himself, and only one, the diversity between the different denominations is as great, and in fact, is the same as if each denomination preached a different religion, and were believers in as many different gods. And when this difficulty is overcome, how often have the devotees of blind superstition, and the worshippers of false gods, said to the emissaries of the Cross—"agree among yourselves what the religion of Christ is, and then we will give our attention to its claims."

§ 44. From the very limited means of investigation within my reach, I am inclined to think that there

The small number who are in the way of salvation. is not more than one in ten of our adult population who make a public profession of Christianity, by a regular observance of the stated ordinances required by the denominations to which they may severally belong. In this estimate I include all denominations, of whatever name or kind; I include all who *call themselves* Christians, and not merely those who would be included by the rule or standard of any one denomination. For myself, I am unwilling to lay down any standard or test by which to decide at present, who will obtain everlasting salvation. If one asks what he shall do to be saved, I, of course, as my duty requires, have a ready answer. And if he does not do it, I can tell him that he has not complied with the conditions of salvation, and therefore has *no right to expect it*. But that he will not obtain it, is more than I consider myself authorized to affirm.

Reasons for hoping for a merciful construction of the Divine Law. § 45. Though it be undoubtedly true, as *Tertullian* has said, that "the Faith is fixed in a rule, it hath a law, and in the keeping of that law salvation," and though God has no where told us that in the final judgment He will deal with us more mercifully than the terms of His law require, yet we may perhaps be permitted to hope that such will be the case. In judging of the outward acts, He will estimate them, doubtless, by the motives and intentions of the heart. These motives and intentions are in all cases, to a considerable extent, and in many cases almost entirely, the result of previous information, education, and experience. To a certain extent, however—an extent which will probably vary with each individual—we are responsible for the state of our thoughts and feelings ourselves.

If, now, the prevalence of sectarianism—the presenting such a variety of doctrines and precepts by the preachers of the different denominations—has so confused the subject, in the apprehension of the common mind, as that for the most part people do not know what to believe or do, and from not having the right way presented clearly before them, without any of the obscurations of controversy, denial or substitution, a general indifference to the subject of religion supervenes, and the common sentiment and feeling of community is moulded thereby, we cannot doubt that this will form an excuse for much that would otherwise be inexcusable in favor of many who are not strictly within the terms of the Covenant.

On the ground of considerations like these, we may entertain hopes that the final condition of many of our fellow-citizens will be better than we should otherwise venture to hope. The cause of their omission of a required duty is not any perverseness of their own will, but the result of the faults of those who call themselves Christians. Their ungodly lives, their contradictions, their contentions and rivalries, their sectarian zeal—often showing more anxiety to gain a proselyte to their Sect than to convert a soul to Christ—is a stumbling-block over which multitudes will fall. And shall not the consequences of the fall be visited upon him who placed the stumbling-block in the way of his brother, rather than upon him who fell over it?

Among those who are left in the darkness of

heathenism, we not unfrequently see a sincerity, a zeal and a single-hearted devotion—bestowed indeed upon a mistaken object—which, if the object were the true God, would place these persons among the brightest ornaments of the Christian name. Among the children who, by the act of Providence, are placed in their tender years under the care of those who sustain no natural relations to them, we often see illustrations of filial duty and affection towards these foster-parents that constitute an example worthy of the imitation of those whose real parents are left, by the Providence of God, to be the objects of these sentiments. So, too, there is doubtless much in the world, that does not now appear under the Christian name, which would be in a condition to be considered the fulfillment of the terms and requirements of the Covenant, if the misfortunes of our age and nation had not exerted their influence upon it.

These, and many other considerations, make us hopeful, even against the strictness of the letter of the law.

§ 46. While the Word of God abounds in plain and awful warnings against departures from the Rule of Faith and the Communion of the Saints, as though the full and entire responsibility for each soul rested with itself, there can be no doubt that a large share of the responsibility is placed upon those who are sent to be Preachers of the Gospel—or set in places of influence and authority—so as to be looked up to by others. St. Paul, in writing to the Hebrews, says, that the Ministry watch for

The responsibility for Sins often rests with those who do not appear to be the immediate agents of their commission.

souls as they that must give account. He says to Timothy, that by taking heed to himself, and to his teaching, he should save both his own soul and the souls of them that hear him. The condemnation, therefore, which it seems at first thought must overwhelm multitudes of our fellow men at the last day, may, as it appears on further consideration, be visited on those who have been the chief cause of the prevalence of such a bewildering variety of religious teaching.

§ 47. It can be proved from general reasoning, and the conclusion is confirmed by abundant experience, that the comparatively small number of adults in our country who are living within the terms and conditions of the covenant of salvation, is the result of sectarianism.

Sectarianism the Chief Cause of so few being within the covenanted conditions of Mercy.

It operates in various ways. By presenting so many systems as true, an impression is made on the mind of the unconverted that none of them are true, and perhaps that the truth itself cannot be of any great importance, even if it can be ascertained. It presents occasions for contentions and jealous feelings among the different Sects, which beget a disgust for the whole subject of religion—a belief that it is all hypocrisy and imposture, among those on whom the influence of religion is most needed. It presents so many different forms and doctrines, that many, who are convinced of the importance of the subject in general, and are anxious to make a profession of religion somewhere, often delay year after year, in hopes that they will find time and an opportunity to look into and comprehend the whole subject before they finally make up their minds. During this interval multitudes are called away to their final account.

Now, if I may be permitted to judge of the experience of others by my own, and by what I have known of theirs, there is no apology or excuse so often given for the non-attendance upon the religious duties required by God in His Gospel, as the fact that there are so many different denominations that no one can tell which is right—that they do not yet sufficiently understand the subject to take a decided stand any where.

Without stopping to consider who is to be blamed for it, the fact, I suppose, cannot be denied, therefore, that sectarianism is the principal cause of the infidelity—practical or speculative—which abounds in our land. And because of the prevalence of this evil, we are compelled to see the multitudes going on in the "broad road that leads to death," notwithstanding that Blood has flowed from the Redeemer's broken Body and pierced side, in abundance sufficient for the sins of the whole world.

The state of things different wherever only one Denomination prevails.

§ 48. I have not now within my reach any statistics, of a very dignified or reliable character, to which I can appeal, but I refer in general terms to what is known of those countries in which there is but one denomination, or church, generally prevalent. Without referring, now, to countries in which the Roman Obedience prevails, or where the Oriental Communion is in possession of the jurisdiction—as in Russia, for instance—we shall see in Sweden, a Protestant country, an example that strongly confirms our conclusion. In these countries the children are all baptized in infancy; they are taught the fundamental Articles of the Christian Faith, as they are received by those Churches, more carefully, in fact, than we teach our children the common branches of an English education; and there is but little, if any, more disposition to deny them, or to neglect the duties growing out of them, as those Churches inculcate those duties, than we see among us to deny the principles of science which are taught in our most approved books of instruction. The children are regarded, from the moment of their Baptism, as Christians, and members of the Church. In its communion they grow up; by it their opinions, their habits, their feelings, and their characters, are moulded, to a very great extent; and an irreligious man, according to their standard of religion, is a phenomenon scarcely to be met with.

An approximation to this state of things, sufficient for the purposes of the present argument, is often seen in portions even of our own country. In those neighborhoods where one denomination only exists, the people are to a very much greater extent, professors of religion, than where several sects present their rival claims and contradictory views of the way of salvation.

This is the direct and natural result of unity of instruction. There is no reason why there should not be as universal a reception of the fundamental articles of the Christian Faith, if there were the same unity of instruction and testimony in regard to it, as there is in the principles of English Grammer, Arithmetic or Geography; for the vast majority of people always believe and act as they are taught. But, as it is, the people are bewildered by the multitude of varying and contradictory theories.

§ 49. But this is not all. The standard of religious character and attainment is lowered down so far, that even many of those who profess to be Christians, and who stand well as such in the general estimation, can hardly be considered as coming much more within the conditions and terms of the Covenant than those who make no pretensions to Christianity.

<small>The standard of Christian attainment reduced by the prevalence of Sectarianism.</small>

It will be quite impossible, within the limits to which we are now confined, to give any adequate idea of the coldness and indifference of our own age in comparison with the earlier centuries. The bare mention of the facts that the Christians then met *daily*, morning and evening, for public worship; that they gave at least one tenth of their income to the Church for religious purposes—so that not only the Clergy were well supported, but the poor also, and converts, who by the change in their religion were obliged to abandon their former mode of life—(a thing which was by no means unusual)—were supplied with all the necessaries of life, and persons in slavery were redeemed from their bondage; and all this from the proceeds of the devout offerings of the worshippers; and that the Holy Communion was administered at least every Lord's Day, and other Holy Days, and sometimes even daily, is, in this age, enough to lead many to think that we are speaking of ages of fanaticism and folly, which ought to be regarded rather as a warning than as a pattern for imitation, or an example for our rebuke. But such were the usages of the Church in the earliest ages of which we can obtain any account.

And these were *real* acts of self-denial, and piety, and renunciation of the world. They took time and money from the service of Mammon and devoted them to the Lord. What a death-blow to the ambition, the avarice, the luxury, and all the extravagant and sinful follies of our age, would be given by the return of that spirit of devotion which would make these usages characteristic of the Christians of our day!

§ 50. That Christianity requires of men a renunciation of the world, a practice of self-denial to which, by the instincts of their nature, or the circumstances of their situation in life, they are not inclined, is held by all persons. *This reduction is chiefly in the Doctrines and Duties which are peculiar to Christianity.* Hence, in the strife among the Sects to gain numbers and outvie each other, there is always a strong temptation to lower down the standard, and underbid, as it were, one another, while they hold out equally confident assurances of salvation to all who will adopt their views and follow their guidance.

Reasons will readily occur why this state of things should be less likely to lower the standard of morals than that of religion. Any open and avowed reduction of the moral standard would defeat the object. "*The world*" will be likely, as it always has done, to test a man's piety by what it calls his goodness—that is, his morality. Hence the prevalence of sectarianism will lead to the nominal elevation of the moral standard, while doubtless many delinquencies that can easily be concealed will be permitted to go unchecked, and the opinion may prevail, as the result, that good morality is the best thing that there is in religion, if not its only valuable element.

But the reduction of the standard is in other particulars. Some of the doctrines of the Gospel do not flatter the human understanding. These may, one after another, be pretermitted as unessential and open to dispute, and finally denied as erroneous; and thus an advance towards Deism, if not Infidelity, will show what is the influence that is carrying them on.

Again, some of the requirements of the Gospel come into collision with our plans of ease, pleasure or aggrandisement. An omission of these is at first winked at, then becomes the general rule, and finally their observance is reviled as superstition and formality—a relying upon works to the disparagement of the corner-stone of Christian Theology—justification by faith. Hence, instead of a Daily Worship, consisting of reading the Scriptures and a sacrifice of praise and thanksgiving, performed as both a duty to God and a pleasure to man, people will scarcely come out once in a week even, except when some excitement or pleasing novelty offers its gratification.

Hence we have, by the confession of all persons, an exceedingly undevout age. And many doubtless, who consider themselves in "the enjoyment of religion," are carried on by something of a far different character, and (as, alas! we cannot doubt) many will not come to see their mistake until it is too late to amend it.

Let any denomination in our land insist upon the primitive standard, and the piety of earlier days—

when the fires of martyrdom and persecution consumed the dross and kept at a distance all that were not prepared to deny themselves and take up the cross daily, as that piety was tested—not by mere feelings and emotions that are easily excited and cost nothing, but by those outward works and duties which break the power of worldliness and avarice, and take large portions of time and money for the service of the Lord—and they would find but very few of their members comparatively, remaining to fulfil their conditions of church-membership.

§ 51. I am limited to a few of the most common topics, and my space is nearly exhausted. I cannot, however, forbear to allude to one other point, and that is, the expulsion of the Bible and of religious instruction from our common schools. It is true that each denomination may have schools of its own, in which children can be trained in the religious opinions and usages which they prefer. But for the most part the people must depend upon our public schools. And these schools, in consequence of sectarian jealousy and rivalry, must be without religion. They are open to all Sects and classes of persons, and no one of them will consent that his children shall be taught the religious views of the others, and therefore none can be inculcated. *The influence of Sectarianism on education.*

Hence our children are taught all the principles of secular education, all the facts of history, all the precepts that are expected to guide them to usefulness and respectability in the world—as things about which all men are agreed, and the importance of which is denied by no one. But religion is omitted, as either a thing not of sufficient importance to occupy any portion of the precious hours of childhood and youth, or as a matter so uncertain and debateable as that the safest way is to let it alone. And thus the most susceptible age, the season in which the impressions that sink the deepest and last the longest are made, is permitted to pass in infidelity and irreligion, as though God had never said, "they that seek Me *early* shall find Me." Soon the engrossing cares of manhood succeed, and reach over into the infirmities of age, and thus multitudes go down to the grave as unprepared as though no Saviour had died, and no Holy Ghost had been sent to sanctify them.

The Faith of Believers not so firm and active as it would be if there were no Sectarianism. § 52. And among those who are led to a faith in the Saviour, the truths of Christianity do not enter into their souls and become a part of their very life and consciousness, as do the things which they learn in early years, and which they have not been accustomed to hear doubted, contradicted or denied. Their faith is at best sickly and limping. It yields and bends before the fierce onset of the temptations and strifes of the world, or the continuous pressure of appetite and passion. Alas! alas! how often does the Ambassador of Christ hear, as a reply to his entreaties, made for His Master's sake, that men would be reconciled to God, that they dare not undertake the solemn vows of the Covenant until they are differently situated in regard to their worldly concerns.

If, now, all who profess and call themselves Christians were united in faith and in righteousness of life, and Christianity could enter into every system and enterprise of education together with the useful sciences—as a thing not less important, and equally as certain, as themselves—what a harvest of souls would be gathered into the Redeemer's Kingdom!

But now our public means for training the mind and forming the character, by neglecting and omitting Christianity, tend to infidelity—practical at least, if not speculative. The Faith for the most part retains its hold upon the mind only by the influence of the instructions which are received at home: and the irregular and spasmodic efforts to awaken an interest in the subject of religion, which are made from time to time, under the great disadvantages of a world of opinion, and the force of education against them, fail altogether, to produce the desired effect.

§ 53. We cannot, therefore, but regard the development of Sectarianism as the great modern manifestation of the spirit of Anti-Christ, which, as St. John says, was even in his day evident in the world. It leads, as we have seen, in various ways, to irreligion and infidelity, and thus to the ruin of the souls for which Christ died. *Sectarianism the great Modern Artifice of the Adversary of Souls.*

§ 54. Now there is no remedy for these evils but a suspension of their cause. This implies that we seek out and identify the Church which our Blessed Redeemer founded in His own blood, and which must, at last, triumph over all rivalry and opposition. Such is the unchangeable decree of Him who worketh all things after the councils of His own will. *No remedy for these evils but a return to the Communion of the Church.*

In this country the return from Sectarianism to the

19

Church is neither difficult nor uncommon. It is not attended with the acquiescence in anything that is repugnant to right feelings, or contrary to a sound interpretation of the Word of God. It is nothing unusual to see congregations of very good size made up entirely of persons who have been gathered in from the surrounding denominations. A comparison of statistics shows that in our oldest and most established congregations even, about one-fourth of the annual admissions to our Communion are persons who have belonged to some of the Protestant Sects. And besides all the clergy that we raise among ourselves—and the proportion of our young men who incline to the Ministry is very great—probably not less than two-thirds of all we have—were brought up in some of the surrounding sects; and about one-third had been trained for, and actually entered, the ministry among them before they sought it among us. It is stated that "out of every two hundred and eighty-five persons, ordained by the late Bishop GRISWOLD of the eastern Diocese, *two hundred and seven* had come from other denominations." The number which we have lost to go to any of the Protestant denominations, is inconsiderable. And the few who have become Papists—some ten or fifteen in the whole, from first to last—were, I believe, without an exception, persons who had been brought up among the Sects—had never fully understood the Church—and in most cases did not stay with us long enough to get into the spirit of our system.

I speak not of these things by way of boasting—God forbid!—but as significant facts, which show very conclusively that the course of reasoning which I have endeavored to present to the reader, has not failed to impress others—and those, too, who are the best capable of judging of it—with the same sense of its force as it has myself.

§ 55. The abandonment of Sectarianism—and it must be abandoned, for a kingdom divided against itself cannot stand—may require much self-denial; in many cases a severe and protracted struggle. But the reader certainly needs not be told that such a struggle may be required by His Saviour. I have the utmost confidence in the good intentions of the vast majority of those whom I believe to be in error. I entertain not the slightest doubt that their salvation may be confidently hoped for through the mercy of the Atoning Redeemer. But I do believe that the subject of this Book has not yet been presented to their minds and consciences as it admits of being presented, and as it ought to have been. Whether I have done anything towards so desirable an object, is a question which I must leave to others to decide. *The Effort which this return will require may be only a part of the Repentance and self-denial which are necessary to gain God's Favor.*

§ 56. Yet undoubtedly the state of heart from which a measure that results in so much evil proceeds, cannot be right.

I speak not now of the external causes which have acted upon many of the founders of the modern sects, and which, as we confidently hope, will be regarded as their excuse in the day of judgment. But after making due allowance for all such causes, there is no doubt that the chief moral causes of Sectarianism are *pride* and *self-will*. *The Moral Cause of Sectarianism inconsistent with a right state of the Heart.*

Men naturally have preferences, and the *natural* preferences, as we must admit—unless we will deny human depravity—are not likely to be in accordance with Christianity. If, therefore, men are too proud to learn of Him, who was " meek and lowly of heart," or too wilful to deny themselves and yield their preferences for the sake of unity, harmony and peace, the consequence is likely to be the foundation of a new Sect.

The cases in which the Church is in the error, and the recusant separates from her communion for the sake of a truth more valuable than the bonds of peace which are sundered by his secession, are so very rare and unlikely to occur as that they hardly need to be taken into the account at present. For one such case, there are doubtless a hundred in which the opinionated individual himself is in the wrong.

Yet, as I fully believe, the chief responsibility for the evils of Sectarianism must rest on those who are its leaders and chief promoters. In every society or party, the majority are always well-meaning persons, even though sadly misled and deluded. Still, however, none of those involved in Sectarianism, can altogether escape its evils.

There may be much Sectarianism in the Church. § 57. But, after all, it is not chiefly on account of those out of the Church that I have written. Among ourselves the custom has been far too prevalent of resting the whole subject of the claims of the Church on one or more of the peculiarities of its constitution; thus, in appearance at least, making the difference between the Church and the Sects to depend upon mere form or circumstantials. This method can prove, at best, only similarity, but not identity, between any Church now existing and that which our Lord and His Apostles instituted; and labors, moreover, under the disadvantage of appearing to attach more importance to matters of outward form and organization than is consistent with the spirit of Christianity.

But further, this method exerts an unfavorable influence upon the minds and characters of our members. It is one reason, as I have no doubt, why we have so many among us who seem to think that the Church belongs to them instead of their belonging to the Church; and therefore they claim to guide, control, and modify its doctrines and usages, rather than submit to be guided by it. Thus the spirit of Sectarianism—which is a great blight upon genuine piety—is fostered in the Church, and by maintaining its peculiarities, no less than if the object of our zeal were merely a device of our own. The difference between a sectarian spirit and genuine piety is of the most fundamental character. The former is a zeal for that which we have chosen to adopt: the latter is the humble submission to what we have seen to be the will of God. I hope that the mode of presenting the subject, which I have pursued in the foregoing pages will have some tendency to promote this last named state of mind in the Church. For without it, outward forms are of no avail, and it can be of but little consequence whether one is in the Church or not.

§ 58. The leading design of the merciful dispensations of God to man appears to be, to bring back as many as possible to holiness and submission to his

Unity and Harmony in the Church conducive to the grand design for which our Saviour came into the World. will. In the accomplishment of this work, the Church is the chief visible means and agency. It is the economy of second causes through which He works. In this, so far as we are permitted to judge, depends its whole value. Doubtless it is intrinsically better adapted to that end than any one differently constituted could be. But how well soever it may be adapted to the end, the whole tenor of the Scriptures, no less than many explicit declarations, teach us that membership in it—unless one submits to it, as to the Messenger and Ambassador of Christ, in meekness, humility and love—will be of no avail. "Christ formed within us," is the grand result at which all its principles, functions and powers are directed. For this an outward organization was given it, and incorporated into the very "foundation that was laid" by Jesus Christ Himself, "that there might be no schism in the body;" for this the elements of its constitution were made channels of divine grace; for this the Holy Ghost was sent to abide with it forever, and for this, CHARITY—which suffereth long and is kind, which envieth not, vaunteth not itself; is not puffed up, which doth not behave itself unseemly, seeketh not its own, is not easily provoked, and thinketh no evil, rejoiceth not in iniquity, beareth all things, believeth all things, hopeth all things, endureth all things, and never fails—is declared to be "the more excellent way," and greater than even "faith and hope."

Seen in this light, the Church is no mere matter of outward form, or combination of forms. It is the living witness and testimony of God—the sheet anchor of religion. And we enter its communion, not because one or more of the peculiarities of its constitution commend themselves to our judgment, or please our fancy, but because we see, as St. Paul says of the Ministry, that unto it, God has committed the work of reconciliation, and by it, as an Ambassador, Christ comes to us, beseeching us that we be reconciled to God. In its communion we may be trained for the Church and communion above, where schisms and divisions can never prevail, and where we shall see, not as now, through a glass darkly, but face to face, and know even as we are known. Such a view of the subject produces a softening and humilitating effect upon the native hardness of the human heart, and teaches us to renounce our own will, that the will of God may be done; to become nothing in ourselves, that Christ may the more fully dwell within us, and occupy all the faculties of our mind and soul. And if I shall be found to have done anything towards the accomplishment of such a result, I shall feel myself most amply rewarded for the hours of assiduous toil and prayerful thought which I have taken from other labors to bestow on this. That such may be the result, is my prayer to Him who overruleth all events, and uses all things as the agents of His Blessed Will.

THE END.